Inside
the Circle

A UNION GUIDE TO QWL

by Mike Parker

A LABOR NOTES BOOK

SOUTH END PRESS
Boston • 1985

A Labor Notes Book
Copyright © 1985 by the Labor Education & Research Project
First printing July 1985

The illustrations on pages 68, 69, 71, 73, 102, 108, 131, 132 and 136 are courtesy of the Lansing Area Joint Labor-Management Committee. Thanks to Mike Konopacki, Fred Wright, Carol★Simpson, P.S. Mueller, Cathy Guisewite, Gary Huck, Richard Chadwick, John Z. Gelsavage, and David McCullough for other cartoons, and to Jim West for photographs.

Designed by David McCullough

Library of Congress Cataloging in Publication Data

Parker, Mike, 1940-
    Inside the circle.

    Bibliography: p. 153.
    1. Quality of work life. 2. Trade-unions.
3. Industrial relations. I. Title.
HD6955.P37 1985   85-50600
ISBN 0-89608-303-9
ISBN 0-89608-302-0 (pbk.)

CONTENTS

Part II

__ACKNOWLEDGMENTS__

A central theme of Quality of Work Life is that workers have heads and brains as well as hands, muscles and backs. The main sources of information and ideas for this book were other workers who shared their experiences. Some wrote articles for their local union newspapers, or leaflets, or articles and letters for *Labor Notes*. But the vast majority of ideas were developed and exchanged in person. I learned much through conferences, workshops, and especially informal discussions.

Much of my four years spent researching QWL has been as an active participant in the programs and as a union activist. Most of my workmates and the unionists I talked to in workshops or at union meetings knew that I was working on this book. But we all say things in conversation which do not really express what we mean, or which express an opinion to be changed moments later. I have no desire to embarrass my union brothers or sisters even where I disagree with them. Normally, where I have had a choice of several quotations or incidents to illustrate a point, I have chosen ones that were published or made in presentations at public conferences. Where I do use direct observation or conversation I have checked with the people involved to insure accuracy and to ask if they minded being identified.

The existence of this book demonstrates how important it is that organizations like Labor Notes exist within the labor movement. Discussion by union activists within its pages and at Labor Notes conferences revealed the need for a serious attempt to understand and respond to the QWL phenomenon. The Labor Notes network of union activists and supporters provided much of the raw material and ideas which are recounted here. Finally, Labor Notes provided the organizational and editorial assistance which made it possible to attempt a book-length treatment.

B esides those whose writings, photographs, or cartoons are explicitly credited, the ideas of dozens of people have added to this book. Many have supplied me with hard-to-get materials or descriptions. Some do not agree with my main ideas about QWL, let alone the details. I owe thanks to all these people as well as many others:

Buzz Alexander, Ronnie Allen, Brenda Anderson, Bill Apple, Jane Armstrong, Paul Baicich, David Bensman, Barb Boylan, Rusty Brown, Bruce Burek, Elissa Clarke, Pat Colella, Nick Contri, Bill Denney, Steve Early, Charlotte Eatmon, Enid Eckstein, Kay Eisenhower, Dave Finkel, Steve Fraser, Vern Gagner, Al Gardner, Jeremy Genovese, Jerry Gillespie, Frank Hammer, Al Hart, Bill Horner, Linda Kaboolian, Pete Kelly, Bob King, Carole Kirby, Hy Kornbluh, Dan La Botz, Joanne Landy, Tom Laney, Les Lawrence, Mark Levitan, Nelson Lichtenstein, Ken Lisiecki, Dan Luria,

Rick Martin, Gersh Mayer, Rob McKenzie, Jack Metzgar, Joe Montuori, Kim Moody, Louie Nikolaidis, Barney Oursler, Ken Paff, Bill Parker, Bob Parker, Jerry Parker, Marilyn Penttinen, Laverne Pon, John Porter, Judy Rhinestine, Jim Rinehart, Selwyn Rogers, Paul Roose, Lee Schore, Gay Semel, Harley Shaiken, Phil Shapira, Mike Slott, Todd Smith, John Snow, Jane Stinson, Sun Press Collective, Bob Thomas, Wendy Thompson, Jon Traunfeld, Peter Unterweger, Mike Urquhart, Gary Von Minden, Bob Weissman, Al Welker, Saul Wellman, Don Wells, Von White, Jim Williams, Grover Woodruff, Jim Woodward, Craig Zaballa.

Without certain people this book would not have been possible at all:

My parents, Mary Milgram Parker and Ben Parker, helped me develop the values and commitment to the labor movement that are the basis of this book.

Johanna Jordan Parker, my five-year-old daughter, found numerous ways to be cooperative as well as provide pleasant diversion. She was also a reminder that whether we and our children have a just future depends on how we respond to the present.

Margaret Jordan played a critical role in what started out as a project and turned into an engulfing monster. She provided inspiration, criticism, ideas, research, proofreading, draft editing, and layout as well as support and encouragement during difficult periods.

Much of the early material gathering and research was done with Dwight Hansen. We wrote several articles together, including "The Circle Game" (*The Progressive*, January 1983), which I believe is still a good summary of the problems QWL poses for unions.

Hal Stack, Director of the Labor Studies Center at Wayne State University in Detroit, guided me through the academic and theoretical literature on QWL as well as teaching me much about methods of worker education. His knowledge of labor issues, as well as his willingness to give serious thought and discussion to ideas with which he disagrees, forced me to examine and revise my arguments on a number of points.

David McCullough, a former UAW local vice-president, a Teamster and a graphic artist, volunteered his skill and his time after work to design and lay out this book.

Jane Slaughter, *Labor Notes* staff writer, served as my main editor—and organizer. She combines ability as a writer with an extensive knowledge of the labor movement and QWL. Frequently her editing went beyond style or organization and added important information. She has sufficient patience to work with non-writers like me who think that every garbled sentence is really a brilliant formulation, as well as the organizational ability to pull together the countless loose ends. Her dedication to the labor movement is a constant source of encouragement. ☐

FOREWORD

On the day that I read Mike Parker's discussion of the QWL program at Wheeling-Pittsburgh Steel, the *New York Times* reported that Wheeling-Pittsburgh had petitioned a federal bankruptcy judge to dissolve its contract with the United Steelworkers. The event epitomizes the central theme of Parker's insightful analysis of the latest fashion in American industrial relations.

Amid reams of adulation of Quality of Work Life programs by employers, unionists, consultants and analysts, this book stands out in sharp relief. It combines careful scholarly research with a strong hands-on empiricism rare in most discussions of QWL. It names the names of those whose work and experience are being analyzed, in sufficient detail that the reader can make his or her own judgment about the author's conclusions; I for one found them persuasive.

Union officials and rank and file workers will find here indispensable information and ammunition as they weigh the pros and cons of QWL. Whether it is proposed as a defensive measure to save jobs, departments or whole plants, or as a next step away from an adversary relationship toward more peaceful and productive cooperation, QWL's potential impact on American unions is serious enough to require the most careful weighing before unions embrace it. For this Mike Parker's book is indispensable.

The merits of this book are related to how it came to be written. Parker, a long-time union activist and skilled worker, found in the labor and academic networks linked to *Labor Notes* a rich source of experience and insight on which to draw, and strong evidence that a book like this one is badly needed by union members and officials. He used his academic connections to deepen his understanding of the labor movement, the corporate economy and business' strategic planning.

Labor studies programs in academic institutions which are committed to understanding, serving, and where necessary criticizing the decisions or strategic choices of the labor movement serve an important role which merits greater recognition and support than it receives. Too many labor leaders equate constructive criticism with anti-labor views. One source of labor's difficulties has been its isolation from its true friends in academic life, a mistake which its business adversaries do not make.

The dream of transcending the Taylorized world of maximum control by management is an old one, particularly in the United States, where workers have never fully internalized their class identity and where our national experience and rhetoric continues to foster a sense of individual worth and aspiration. Mike Parker understands the appeal and the power of this dream.

He also understands how readily it can be appropriated by employers who use QWL as the newest and most attractive tool in their search for a more controlled and compliant workforce. His detailed descriptions show in case after case how the hard-won knowledge of workers has been skillfully solicited under the guise of participation, only to be put to use in support of the employer's goals of lower costs, greater efficiency, and higher productivity.

The tragedy portrayed in this book is that of workers who seek respect for their ideas and know-how, who are ready to share what they know with employers who promise to give them that respect, and who find themselves betrayed by skilled, plausible, ultimately cynical scenarios carefully developed by industrial psychologists and other "experts." These scenarios are then put forward as solutions to the threat of job loss or earnings loss, or both.

QWL pits group against group, plant against plant, firm against firm, and workers against workers. In pursuit of the illusory goal of job and wage protection, workers are led, step by step, to turn away from the principles of unity and solidarity. They are like the people in Plato's cave, mistaking the shadow of cooperation for the reality of employer exploitation and control.

That so many advocates and promoters of QWL fail to recognize and warn against these illusions speaks eloquently of the quality of most American thinking and writing in the field of labor relations. One is doubly grateful that Mike Parker has seen that in fact the emperor has no clothes on, and has given us the written evidence.

We need to understand more fully why so many union leaders, particularly in major unions like the Auto Workers, the Steelworkers, and the Communications Workers—the principal unions discussed in this book—have embraced the QWL gospel so uncritically and enthusiastically. A generation of corporate managers, amplified by national political, academic and media spokesmen, have preached the story of American labor's obstructiveness, narrowness, rigidity, and irrelevance to the challenges of modern economic life.

Some union leaders, to their credit, have rejected these pronouncements as simply new versions of the old, self-serving message which American business has always sought to communicate. But others, including some at the top, have bought the message and have hastened to adapt in order to keep from losing touch with a membership who reads and hears the same message.

A generation of union members, largely taken for granted in their unions and taking their unions for granted, has lost sight of the historic vision of the labor movement as the sole instrument for the defense of workers' needs and rights. It is this missing consciousness which opens workers' minds to the message of QWL and which brings some of their leaders in haste to embrace it. While Mike Parker does not explore this process in detail, he demonstrates the painful consequences which QWL has produced in much of the traditional heartland of American unionism.

QWL works worst in large multi-plant corporations which hold the power to locate or relocate plants, to shift production among plants, regions, and areas of the globe which are ultimately beyond the reach of today's unions, even the largest, to counter or control. In these settings, as Mike Parker shows, QWL has become the employer's instrument of choice for achieving or restoring workplace control.

In other settings, the prospects may be better. The record is still not in on QWL's potential in state and local government, where union security and employer immobility combine to change considerably the stakes and motivations at work. Some QWL activities in place, and other still on the drawing board, may well promote authentic shared goals and improved services to clients in mental hospitals, prisons, schools and other settings in which workers' skills are not readily automated, Taylorized or co-opted out of existence. These settings are found more often in small and medium-sized manufacturing, and in the public and non-profit sectors where QWL may well have a useful role to play in the future. Where QWL has been linked to authentic—not ESOP—worker ownership and control, the record may prove constructive.

Readers with long memories will remember the series of studies published in the 1950's by the National Planning Association under the rubric of "Causes of Industrial Peace under Collective Bargaining," and its predecessor, *The Dynamics of Industrial Democracy*.[1]

Both were associated with the name of Clinton S. Golden of the Steelworkers, who later directed the trade union program at Harvard University.

Golden's most illustrious disciple was Joseph Scanlon, who taught a generation of academic industrial relations specialists at M.I.T. in the first postwar decade. The Scanlon Plan for "gains-sharing" has survived and flourished in many workplaces until the present day.

Joe Scanlon fully understood that no plan to enlist the cooperation of workers could succeed unless it was rooted in a strong union, one able to negotiate on equal terms with the employer and with the power to enforce adherence to the terms of the contract. This limited the plan's applicability to those settings where employer and union were able to ensure that commitments made by each side were honored. The Scanlon Plan probably represents the best available realization of the concept that workers seek more than a job, that they have brains and insight which merit respect and which can make work more than a routine, alienating, demeaning and exploitative experience.

But even in the best of settings, as experience with Scanlon Plans has demonstrated, it requires a rare combination of qualities to succeed. In no case can QWL make obsolete or irrelevant the need for a strong, effective union to unite workers, protect and enhance their rights, and embody and articulate their basic solidarity with all those who must work in order to live.

Mike Parker has made this lesson clear and convincing; he deserves a wide and serious reading. We are all in his debt.

—*Sumner M. Rosen*
Columbia University

[1]Clinton S. Golden and Harold J. Ruttenberg, *The Dyamics of Industrial Democracy*, Harper & Brothers, New York, 1942.

__INTRODUCTION_____

After all the accomplishment that I saw today, I felt like going in the corner and crying. This union is in the process of reform. And to stay alive we can't be adversaries any more.

— **Frank Locricchio, chairman, UAW Local 15, at a management-union retreat**[1]

Employee Involvement has reduced production costs and absenteeism and played a major role in what one outside expert calls "an industrial miracle" in improving product quality.

— **Business Week**[2]

The rolls at one rolling mill were being damaged while in storage. The Labor-Management Participation Team recommended a method to protect the rolls saving $21,000 each year. The company engineering department then designed a solution based on the LMPT recommendation costing nearly $34,000. The LMPT came up with a better design costing only $1,200.

— **Sam Camens, assistant to the president, United Steelworkers of America**[3]

At the level of public discussion, it is harder to find a person with misgivings about "employee participation" than to find an opponent of apple pie. Yet despite such public testimonials to Quality of Work Life programs, many unionists are uncomfortable with them. Often their discomfort takes the shape of under-the-surface grumbling, sometimes in hoping the whole thing will go away. Even in unions where top leaders have wholeheartedly embraced QWL, such as the Auto Workers or the Communications Workers, significant sections of the unions remain opposed.

There are plenty of reasons for unionists to be suspicious of QWL: Participation programs have been a favorite tactic of union busters. The business press and business leadership have embraced them. The Reagan administration is pushing them too.

The use of QWL represents an enormous change in employers' strategies, in daily conditions on the shop floor, and in the institutions and procedures of collective bargaining. Yet there is almost no material available to guide the trade unionist who is trying to come to grips with these new programs from a union point of view. The business community has flooded the market with both analyses of QWL and "how-to's." Most of the supposedly objective studies are by people who themselves act as QWL consultants. These consultants typically charge $500 to $3,000 per day, so they are not likely to bite the programs or the companies that feed them. Academic publications are behind the times and frequently miss the significance of issues to workers.

Trade unionists who turn to their own unions for information find that virtually everything available has been prepared jointly with the employer—and frequent-

ly this means that the employer prepared it and an over-worked union official stamped it okay.

This handbook is an attempt to help fill that void. It is for union leaders and union activists who are trying to figure out how to respond to QWL, and it is written from a union point of view. Thus this book takes as its starting point two assumptions:

1. Unionism is the central means by which workers achieve dignity, self-respect, influence, protection, advancement and job security. No program which claims to offer these benefits is to be believed if at the same time it undermines the union.

2. The primary job of the union is to protect and advance the conditions of its members and those of other workers—not to protect and increase company profits, market share, or reputation.

HOW THE BOOK IS ORGANIZED

The book is divided into two sections. The first section is a systematic assessment of QWL programs—their methods and their goals. It appraises unions' responses to QWL and ends with practical suggestions for the concerned unionist. It includes examples, descriptions of exercises, a questionnaire, lists of possibilities, and resources.

The chapters in the second section go into depth on a number of topics. "QWL and the Law," written for this book by attorney Ellis Boal, demonstrates the shaky legal basis of QWL, particularly unilateral company programs. This information may provide unionists with important leverage. Chapter 17 is a reprint of John

Junkerman's powerful description of working life under the Japanese system.

Public relations and industry politics have created a hype around QWL. But little about the effectiveness of QWL has been firmly established as fact. In Chapter 18 we examine the few substantial academic studies that have been conducted and see that the research does not support the public image.

Chapter 19 contains a number of statements by unions critical of QWL, as well as one of the best thought-out statements by a union which supports QWL. Those who have not seen the many pro-QWL statements from unions or from business can check chapter 20 to find out how to get them.

While I have drawn on the experiences of a range of U.S. and Canadian unions, a good number of the book's examples come from the auto industry. This is partly because the size of the auto industry and its massive commitment to QWL means that its programs are the pace-setters for other industries. But it also reflects the fact that my own first-hand observations of QWL are in the auto industry, as are many of the unionists I have worked with in QWL workshops. I believe this immediate shop floor perspective is crucial to understanding what QWL is about. I am sure that unionists in other industries will be able to draw the parallels.

Finally, to be sure my own position is clear from the start: I firmly support efforts to improve the quality of working life, increase workers' control over their jobs, and democratize the workplace and the entire economy.

I believe that is what unions are all about. I also believe that most of the QWL-type programs currently in place, despite their titles and promises, are not about improving the quality of our working lives and may in fact be destroying what little we already have. Instead of providing us with more control or influence over our jobs as they sometimes claim, they are taking away our only real power by undermining our unions.

This is not to say there is nothing positive in QWL. A program like QWL could not be as effective or have as many adherents unless it had some genuinely positive features. Throughout this book I have tried to identify these positive features, separate them out, point out where they may reflect union failings, and indicate how unions might put some QWL techniques to good use.

Nor am I trying to convince local unions to withdraw from QWL. In some cases unions may be able to make these programs work for them. Indeed, I have tried to go into detail (in chapter 10) to consider under what conditions a union might use QWL to its own advantage. But in QWL or out, unions must pay attention to the challenges of QWL and meet them as a union, in solidarity.

—*Mike Parker*
May 1, 1985

Notes

1. *Detroit Free Press*, October 11, 1982.
2. *Business Week*, July 30, 1984.
3. *The Work Life Review*, September 1983.

UNION ABBREVIATIONS

Following are union abbreviations used in this book:

ACTWU	Amalgamated Clothing and Textile Workers Union
AFGE	American Federation of Government Employees
AFL-CIO	American Federation of Labor-Congress of Industrial Organizations
AFSCME	American Federation of State, County, Municipal Employees
APWU	American Postal Workers Union
ATU	Amalgamated Transit Union
CALEA	Canadian Air Lines Employee Association
CUPE	Canadian Union of Public Employees
CWA	Communications Workers of America
GAIU	Graphic Arts International Union
IAM	International Association of Machinists
IBEW	International Brotherhood of Electrical Workers
IBT	International Brotherhood of Teamsters
ITU	International Typographical Union
IUE	International Union of Electronic Workers
IWA	International Woodworkers of America
LIUNA	Laborers International Union of North America
NALC	National Association of Letter Carriers
OCAW	Oil, Chemical, and Atomic Workers
OEA	Ohio Education Association
OPEIU	Office and Professional Employees International Union
SEIU	Service Employees International Union
TNG	The Newspaper Guild
UAW	United Auto Workers
UBC	United Brotherhood of Carpenters
UE	United Electrical Workers
UPIU	United Paperworkers International Union
USWA	United Steelworkers of America

THE RISE OF THE NEW INDUSTRIAL RELATIONS

I would hope that those of you who have not yet put your foot in the water will do so very shortly. Try it, you'll like it. It pays off for management, it pays off for the union, it pays off for the workers.
—**United Auto Workers Vice-President (retired) Irving Bluestone.**[1]

Now, more than ever, and more than anyone else, we know we all share in this together: management and labor, working together for a stronger Wheeling-Pittsburgh [Steel Corporation]. The result: the new Wheeling-Pittsburgh, through equipment modernization and enlightened labor-management relations, is becoming one of the leanest, lowest cost, and most efficient producers of quality steels in the United States.
—**Advertisement (joint statement by a Wheeling-Pittsburgh vice-president & the president of Local 1190, United Steelworkers of America)**[2]

Before [QWL] was initiated, there were problems, and you knew it but couldn't do anything about them. Now you can. You feel like somebody. You can go to the superintendent and he'll listen.
—**Audrey Neal, steel worker**[3]

Detroit Free Press photo by Mary Schroeder

At a union-management retreat, Ernie Gomez, an officer of United Auto Workers Local 15, takes a sunrise walk with Roger Elle, a General Motors official, to iron out problems.

The enthusiasm for Quality of Work Life programs displayed in the quotes above has been widespread for only a few years. The well known *Business Week* article proclaiming "The New Industrial Relations" appeared May 11, 1981. Yet labor-management cooperation arrangements are not new. There were a number of important union-management experiments during the 1920's and again during World War II.[4] The river of QWL, now at flood stage, contains contributions of four distinct tributaries from the 1950's, 60's, and 70's.

The Origins of QWL

1. Small sections of business became interested in a more "human relations" approach to management. Along with allies in academic fields like organizational psychology, some managers concluded that the stick was not always the most efficient means of moving the donkey, much less a human being, and that management should be using more carrots. In fact, some theorists said, management might not even need the carrot at all. If workers were given a chance, they might want to do a good job on their own.

Psychologist Douglas McGregor's influential book, *The Human Side of Enterprise*, published in 1960, defined two opposite management styles. "Theory X" managers believe that most workers avoid work, avoid responsibility, and have to be directed and threatened with loss of security to get them to do what the organization needs done. "Theory Y" managers assume that most workers actually seek responsibility, want to be and are creative, and can exercise self-direction when committed to the organization's goal.[5]

In the same period psychologist Frederick Herzberg developed the notion of "job enrichment" to make work more interesting and less alienating.

In most industries, particularly the major unionized

ones, these ideas were scarcely given notice until the early 1970's. It was the 22-day strike against speed-up at General Motors' Lordstown assembly plant in February 1972 which drew attention to worker alienation, the blue collar blues and the white collar woes.

Theorists declared that there was a "new breed" of workers. Many of the Lordstown workers were young Vietnam vets and had some college education. The ideas of the civil rights, anti-war and student movements of the 1960's were reflected in the factories. At the same time, decent paying jobs were easy enough to find that the traditional means of disciplining workers—the threat of firing—was not much of a threat after all.

The job enrichment theories were dusted off. General Motors decided to allow its obscure Organizational Development (OD) department to conduct some experiments in several plants, especially its southern, nonunion ones. In 1973 GM and the United Auto Workers signed a letter of understanding, on a proposal initiated by the union, which vaguely recognized "the

---

GETTING SOME TERMS STRAIGHT

Worker participation programs go under a bewildering array of names and include a wide range of activities. They include:

Suggestion boxes.

Quality circles. In their narrowest definition, ongoing voluntary groups of workers and management which meet to discuss specific problems of production or quality of the product, following a defined set of steps.

Participation groups. Ongoing voluntary groups of workers and management which operate with a wide range of procedures and discuss a wide range of topics including production problems, quality problems, and working conditions.

Task forces. Groups organized to deal with a single question such as the launch of a new product.

Work teams. Teams usually consist of a supervisor and all of his or her workers. The team may have certain management functions such as job assignments, performance evaluation, work organization and absentee control. The supervisor is sometimes called an "advisor." Until recently, work teams were found mainly in nonunion companies.

Worker representation on the board of directors.

Worker ownership or Employee Stock Ownership Plans (ESOPS). Worker buyouts usually take place to prevent a company from closing down. The degree of actual worker participation in day-to-day or overall management varies considerably.

Worker representation in top management and worker ownership are not necessarily related to the shop floor participation plans, and will not be examined in this book.

Consultants and other specialists in the QWL field will argue long and loud over the differences in purposes, philosophies and procedures of the various types of groups. Many consultants maintain their roles (and incomes) by stressing the uniqueness of their own programs. But the fact is that despite different origins, over the past few years the various programs have evolved in the same direction. A "quality circle" will be involved in pretty much the same problems, using the same procedures, as an "employee participation group." What is common to all the variants is:

1) They are designed to increase worker involvement with and commitment to the employer.

2) They claim to provide the worker with more respect, dignity and influence.

3) They involve specific organizational forms—that is, the circles or groups—as well as a change in management (and worker) philosophy.

We will use the term Quality of Work Life, or QWL, to refer to all participation plans, although in fact they come under many different labels.

TYPICAL QWL ORGANIZATION CHART

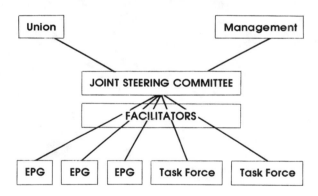

THE CIRCLE

The main vehicle for employee participation in most Quality of Work Life programs is the *circle*, also called participation group, team or task force. Typically, the circle consists of six to twelve workers and one to three members of management who meet once a week for one hour. If the work process allows, it will be during regular working time, otherwise meetings will take place after hours, and employees will usually be paid overtime rates. In most cases participation is voluntary. A program facilitator or facilitator pair (management and union) may regularly attend circle meetings and a union steward may also attend.

Until recently, members of management usually

desirability of mutual effort to improve the quality of work life for the employees.'' The letter provided for a joint committee to oversee possible projects, but for more than two years the committee did nothing.

2. Union leaders were looking for ways to extend democracy to the shop floor. In the 1960's and early 1970's both economists and popular writers were celebrating the successes of the American free enterprise system. Economic crisis, we were told, was a thing of

the past; we had achieved a society of permanent and ever increasing prosperity; the working class had become middle class. If you worked in a factory that job was your floor, not your ceiling. If you were young you would only work there until you were ready for your big move—a college degree or your own business. If you were older, your son (and possibly daughter) could at least get a sure job in the plant, but probably they would do better.

The mood of permanent prosperity and optimism was

---

chaired circle meetings and set agendas. Now it is common for groups to select their own leaders.

Circles are usually supposed to use a series of procedures defined in QWL training (see chapter 2) although frequently the procedure breaks down or is not applied. Circles usually select the problem they wish to work on.

INITIALS AND NAMES

The following list of names and initials used in QWL-type programs is not exhaustive. Many corporations have adopted their own names (Tektronix, for example, calls its program "TEK Circles'').

BT	Business Team
EI	Employee Involvement
EIC	Employee Involvement Circle
EIG	Employee Involvement Group
EIT	Employee Involvement Team
EPC	Employee Participation Circle
EPG	Employee Participation Group
EPT	Employee Participation Team
LMPP	Labor-Management Participation Program
LMPT	Labor-Management Participation Team
PEP	Program for Employee Participation
PPS	Participative Problem Solving
PM	Participative Management (usually refers to the management side of the program)
QWL	Quality of Work Life
QC	Quality Circle
QCC	Quality Control Circle
SAWG	Semi-Autonomous Work Group
SPC	Statistical Process Control
SQC	Statistical Quality Control
TF	Task Force
TM	Team Management
WPC	Worker Participation Committee

(Note: Both "employee" and "employe" and "work life" and "worklife" are commonly used. Where referring to a specific program we will use its spelling.)

THE ROLES

We will use the following standard terms to define certain roles throughout this book:

Consultant. An outside expert who helps set up and maintain the QWL program.

Facilitator. A coordinator who organizes groups and trains participants. Often a full-time job. Many programs have both management and union facilitators working together. This job may also be called the coordinator, trainer, advisor or internal consultant. To make matters more confusing, sometimes the group leader (see below) is called the facilitator.

Group Leader. Leader of one of the groups or circles within the program. May be a rotating position, designated by management, or selected by the group. May be either a supervisor or a worker. Responsibilities range from leading group discussions, to representing the group externally, to being mainly concerned with procedural matters and staying out of substantive issues (facilitation).

Practitioner. Any person who considers him or herself a specialist in installing, working with, or advising about QWL programs. Includes industrial relations professionals and organizational psychologists as well as facilitators and consultants.

Steward. The official shop floor representative of the union. Also called committeeperson or griever.

Shop Chairperson. The union officer in charge of shop floor issues, including grievances and contract bargaining. In many locals the president has these responsibilities.

Plant Manager. The highest management official in a particular location.

Steering Committee. The committee designated to oversee QWL activities at a particular location. Usually a joint union-management body, at least on paper.

so pervasive that the starkly different reality for minorities and for families headed by women, if noted at all, was seen as a temporary problem.

Unions had won substantial wage improvements for their members. A number of more far-sighted labor leaders believed that unions also had to join the social movements of the time and to deal with the issue symbolized by Lordstown—the actual content of work. However, most union leaders rejected the theories about the "new breed of workers." They pointed out that an older workforce at the GM Norwood plant had struck for 172 days over nearly the same issues as at Lordstown. As the former Director of Special Projects for the UAW, Nat Weinberg, put it in 1974:

> The recent discovery of the job satisfaction problem is, in one sense, much like Columbus' discovery of America. The people most directly concerned—the Indians in one case and the workers in the other—knew all along that it was there.[6]

Union leaders were also cold to "job enrichment." After all, management was still making the decisions and workers were still carrying out orders on the "enriched" job—which turned out to be three boring operations instead of one.

While rejecting the employers' proposals as a manipulation to increase productivity, some labor leaders cast about for the next steps for unions. They adopted as models developments in European social democratic countries. These included "codetermination" in Germany, where labor is represented on top management boards, and job design and worker participation programs in Sweden.

UAW Vice-President Irving Bluestone, then in charge of the union's dealings with General Motors, was one of the key labor leaders who pushed QWL programs as the logical continuation of unionism. In 1978 Bluestone wrote:

> A persistent and historical goal of unionism is to bring democracy into the work place....
> The thrust of a true quality-of-worklife program includes a process in which workers, armed with ample information, exercise the democratic right to participate in workplace decisions including job structure and design, job layout, material flow, tools to be used, methods and processes of production, plant layout, work environment, etc. In its broadest sense it means decision-making as to how the work place will be managed and how the worker will effectively have a voice in being master of the job rather than being subservient to it....
> Over time, the structure of work organization will... move inevitably to a recognition that work should be designed to achieve human fulfillment as well as the production of goods and services.[7]

Bluestone was emphatic. The purposes of QWL were democracy and dignity, not productivity. If productivity should improve as a byproduct, that was fine, but that was not what the programs were about. Bluestone is credited with choosing the name "Quality of Work Life" for the UAW-GM program precisely to make clear that its purpose was a more humane

workplace rather than a speed-up or productivity trick. As Bluestone's successor, Donald Ephlin, points out, the QWL proposal of 1973 assumed full employment and job security were already taken care of.[8]

3. Sections of industry looked to Japan for quality control methods. By the mid-1970's Japan had shed the image of shoddy goods. Japanese imports had captured the consumer electronics industry, and companies such as Sony had established themselves as the leaders in quality and innovation. U.S. corporations began experimenting with quality circles modeled after those used in Japan and began teaching elementary statistical concepts. (Most of these quality concepts had actually been introduced to Japan by two Americans, W.E. Deming and J.M. Juran, who decades earlier had found U.S. management unresponsive.)

A few large corporations such as Honeywell and Lockheed and many smaller ones set up full scale quality circle programs. The circles usually followed strict rules and focused narrowly on production issues. Their goals were to solve quality problems and increase productivity; improved morale and harmony were expected only as by-products. They made no pretense of sharing decision making power. They were organized in the management structure and the circle leaders were almost always supervisors.

During the 1970's quality circles were concentrated mainly in high technology industries, for three reasons. First, these were the industries that required a maximum of precision. A car might still run with leaky oil seals or poor valves, but a printed circuit board containing hundreds of parts for a computer is usually junk if one part fails. Second, these were often new industries, so new methods of management or production could be designed in rather than added on. Third, most of them were nonunion, so management had a free hand.

UE News Service

" Do you think it gives me that ' I can't afford a union' look? "

4. "Humanized labor relations" was a strategy to avoid or beat union organizing drives. IBM, for example, was famous for its combination of paternalism with a ruthless willingness to purge dissenters, not to mention people with union sympathies.

One of the most famous "worker participation" programs of the 1970's was part of General Foods' plan to run away from unions. The company sought an alternative to its unionized Kankakee, Illinois dog food plant and built a new one in Topeka, Kansas where, according to the company's planning document, "no power groups will exist within the organization that create an anti-management posture."

In consultation with Harvard business professor Richard Walton, General Foods carefully designed the new plant as a "sociotechnical system" including work teams, job rotation, and "pay for knowledge." The plant, which opened in 1971, was highly publicized as a "humanized" factory of the future until the experiment degenerated after a few years (largely because of corporate-wide management politics).[9]

There was some overlap between these four different strands: corporate paternalism to maintain morale, union strategy for industrial democracy, quality control, and union busting. But in the main, none of them succeeded, on their own, in gaining support outside the relatively narrow sectors in which they were spawned. Throughout most of the 1970's the approach of GM's Organizational Development department was shunned by most of the GM organization. The Irving Bluestones were a minority in the UAW and even more so in the broader labor movement. The quality circle approach, for reasons described earlier, didn't find fertile ground outside the high tech area, and even in high tech circles seemed to have a fairly short life span. Finally, corporate union busting, though on the rise in the 1970's, did not sweep traditionally unionized areas.

The cause of the big leap to QWL and the "new industrial relations" was the economic crisis of the late 1970's. Competition from foreign producers and the realization that they had seen the end of U.S. unilateral rule in the world economy led corporations to turn to QWL. Massive unemployment caused the labor unions to accept it.

This had been true on a smaller scale even earlier in the 1970's. GM Vice-President Alfred Warren explained that when the company wanted to conduct cooperation experiments, GM "always looked for plants that were in trouble because they were willing to do anything, so our greatest successes have always been with plants that were on the brink of failure."[12]

What had been true for these individual plants now became true for entire industries. In GM QWL appeared everywhere. Ford Motor Co. had had its Employe Involvement program on the books for six years but did nothing until 1979 when the company began pouring in resources. The Labor-Management Participation Program in the steel industry and the Communications Workers-AT&T Quality of Work Life program were both signed in 1980. In 1981 *Fortune* magazine observed that the interest in QWL "has come

on so suddenly that it has caught many longtime partisans off guard."[11]

Shotgun Wedding

The new programs resembled shotgun weddings, with the companies holding the shotgun. They were put into place hurriedly. Structures, guidelines, and training were not worked out and agreed upon in advance. At the same time that they were implementing QWL, the companies were demanding and getting contract concessions. Union staffs and financial bases were shrinking, reflecting the decline in union membership. Thus weakened, the unions were in no position to shape these new programs or to make inroads into managerial prerogatives.

General Motors, which has the most extensive QWL programs of any corporation, also had the freest hand, and installed many with only token union involvement. As UAW Vice-President Ephlin delicately puts it, "In the period 1979 to 1982, QWL was not a priority of the union in GM because of other problems."[12] The brief GM-UAW joint guidelines for QWL were not distributed until 1984.

The economic crisis also helped to shape the programs' stated goals. In the 1970's management QWL advocates had to pay lip service to the notion that these programs were aimed not at productivity but at job satisfaction, in order to get any union endorsement or cooperation. But today management and unions alike openly declare productivity and increasing competitiveness as central aims of QWL. Most unions now defensively insist that QWL goals must "include both human satisfaction and economic efficiency."[13]

For the same reason there is now considerable pressure to move away from the name "quality of work life" because it raises expectations that the programs should be directed toward improving just that. "Employee involvement" raises fewer expectations about the programs' goals.

On one point, however, the companies have never given even lip service. They made it clear from the beginning that these programs were not a sharing of power and were not a step toward industrial democracy. Workers were allowed to "participate" to the extent that they could *give* information or ideas, but participation did not extend to making the serious decisions. The 1982 Manual for the UAW-Ford EI program provides the following definitions:

> Managerial prerogatives: The ultimate decision authority and responsibility is retained by management.
> Supervisor role: Supervisory management still directs the task, however their role is changed to a participative-catalyst role.

By the mid 1980's only Irving Bluestone and a few others continued to talk about QWL as a step toward industrial democracy.

Except for this one point, both employers and consultants have found it useful to avoid pinning down exactly what QWL is supposed to be about. As long as they basically control the program, keeping the definition vague and slippery allows employers the maximum flexibility. Thus QWL is purposely mystified with cliches such as "It is a process, not a program." In the next chapter we look at some of the appealing aspects of "the process." ☐

HOW BIG IS QWL?

How many employers use QWL? How many circles are functioning? How many workers are involved?

Most major corporations in the U.S. now have some program which falls under the QWL umbrella. In the auto, communications, electrical and electronic industries the programs are extensive. In the postal service, steel, military employment of civilians, hospitals and the public sector, QWL activities are growing rapidly. In trucking they are just beginning. While there are relatively few QWL circles in the construction industry, many construction unions have long been active in area joint labor-management committees. Most unionized companies conduct QWL activities jointly with the unions, although a few (such as Roadway Express and Kroger's) have tried to bypass the union completely.

But figures are mainly guesswork. There are no agreed upon definitions and accurate information is almost impossible to get. Some companies, such as IBM, reveal nothing. Most only reveal what they consider good public relations. Many programs have a short burst of activity and then die, leaving only a program on paper. Many "independent" observations are self-serving.

With this in mind, here are some indicators: A 1982 New York Stock Exchange Survey found that 44% of firms with over 500 employees reported quality circles, 35% reported task forces, and 25% reported labor-management committees. In the previous two years 74% of firms with more than 100 employees had added quality circles, 36% had added job redesign, and 29% had added production teams.[14]

In 1983, the Secretary of the International Association of Quality Circles estimated that over 135,000 circles operated at 8,000 locations in the United States, involving more than one million participants.[15]

Here are some representative figures for 1984. Westinghouse claimed 20,000 of its 140,000 employees were active in more than 2,000 circles.[16]. General Motors claimed to have approximately 3,000 groups nationwide.[17] The United Steelworkers said there were 500 teams functioning in the steel industry.[18] The Communications Workers estimated that in the previous two years the number of its teams went from 150 to over 1,200.[19]

Notes

1. Speech, October 1981. In *Cutting Edge*, publication of the Lansing Area Joint Labor-Management Committee.
2. *Detroit Free Press*, May 1982.
3. *Update*, U.S. Steel Irvin Works, Summer 1982.
4. See, for example, Sanford M. Jacoby, "Union-Management Cooperation in the United States: Lessons from the 1920's," *Industrial and Labor Relations Review*, October 1983.
5. Douglas McGregor, *The Human Side of Enterprise*, McGraw Hill, 1960.
6. Speech at the 27th Annual Conference on Labor, New York, June 14, 1974.
7. "Human Dignity Is What It's All About," *Viewpoint*, AFL-CIO Industrial Union Department, Vol. 8, No. 3, 1978.
8. Speech, Michigan Quality of Work Life Council, November 10, 1983.
9. Daniel Zwerdling, *Workplace Democracy*, Harper and Row, 1980.
10. Quoted in John Simmons and William Mares, *Working Together*, Alfred A. Knopf, 1983.
11. *Fortune*, June 15, 1981.
12. Speech, Michigan Quality of Work Life Council, March 11, 1983.
13. *Workplace Democracy*, Summer 1982.
14. New York Stock Exchange Office of Economic Research, *People and Productivity: A Challenge to Corporate America*, 1982.
15. Philip Thompson, *Quality Circles in the U.S.—Growth and Trends*, paper at National Convention on Quality Circles, October 5-8, 1983.
16. Ralph Barra, speech to the Society of Automotive Engineers Conference, February 29, 1984.
17. Warren Hydra-matic *Conveyor*, July 1984.
18. *Steelabor*, November-December 1984.
19. "The Quality of Work Life Process at AT&T and the Communications Workers of America," draft, January 1984, sponsored by the U.S. Dept. of Labor.

__Inside the Circle: A UNION GUIDE TO QWL____
Labor Education and Research Project, P.O. Box 20001, Detroit, MI 48220. (313) 883-5580.

WHAT HAPPENS IN QWL TRAINING

Why QWL Feels Good

Some of the most ardent defenders of QWL are the rank and file workers who participate in the programs. As attractive as an hour a week off the job can be, it's something more that generates the excitement and fervor that some workers feel about their QWL experiences.

Some workers support QWL in the hope that they can make industry more rational and more competitive. Others believe that through QWL they can improve their job security or make changes in working conditions. But the surveys indicate that for most workers, the strongest reasons for participating come from the activity of participation itself. Workers become committed to QWL because, as one put it, "it just makes me feel good."

Feeling good is not an accident. The explicit aim of QWL is to have the participant identify with QWL because the "process" itself fulfills a number of worker desires. With this kind of motivation, the ends are not as important as the means; the outcome is not as important as the group process.

This is different from the kind of motivation that usually gets us to do things. Most union members, for example, go on strike to improve their contract, not because they enjoy standing on a picket line. But for most QWL "practitioners," as QWL facilitators, coordinators and consultants call themselves, it matters less whether the group works on placement of fans or work rule changes or quality improvements than whether everyone in the group participates and takes pride in what the group is doing. Thus QWL training draws heavily from sociology and psychology, particularly from the subfields of industrial psychology, management training, and human relations.

QWL draws on a number of important needs for both process and outcome:

1) QWL builds on workers' natural desire to identify with the product they produce. While there may be some satisfaction in going to work to make money, there is much more in being able to say with pride, "I made this, I created this."

2) QWL identifies with the desire to do a good job. Remember that for years "being a good worker" had nothing to do with producing a good product or service. Management philosophy was unambiguous—good workers were those who did exactly what they were told. The quality of the product or service was management's problem, not the workers'. QWL promises a 180 degree turnaround. Now workers are not only asked to think about the quality of "their" product, they are invited to take responsibility for it.

3) QWL expands workers' opportunity to make a contribution. They can deal not only with their own jobs but also with those around them. In circle meetings members are encouraged and rewarded for observations and proposals covering the entire operation.

4) QWL provides new skills. The organizational,

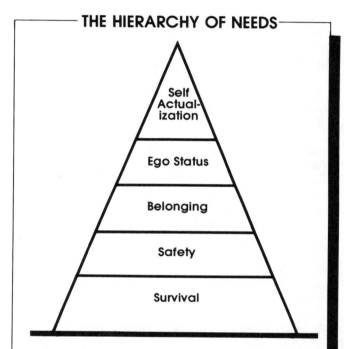

THE HIERARCHY OF NEEDS

- Self Actualization
- Ego Status
- Belonging
- Safety
- Survival

A good part of the assumptions behind QWL comes from a theory of psychologist Abraham Maslow.[1]

Maslow ranks human needs. The first level involves immediate physical survival—food, clothing and shelter. In the workplace context, the first need would be the wage itself. The next level, safety, might include such things as insurance and pensions. The third level, belonging, is being accepted by a group. The desire to excel in some area is an example of the ego-status level. At the top is the need for personal fulfillment.

The idea is that once human beings' basic survival needs are satisfied, they can move on to meeting higher ones. Applied to the workplace, the argument translates: Unions (or prosperity or management's generosity) have pretty much satisfied the "survival" and "safety" needs. Now workers can focus on higher objectives, such as individual recognition and a sense of satisfaction with work. Happily, this corresponds with what the employers say they need too.

management, statistical, problem solving and even personal skills give people a sense of being more in control of their lives. Entire areas such as statistics or accounting are demystified. Most workers have not previously received training in chairing a meeting or making a brief presentation. Now, for the first time, they learn these skills and begin to envision themselves in a leadership role.

5) QWL promises to end needless conflict with supervision. The program is supposed to end harassment and change the supervisor into someone who actually helps in dealing with problems on the job.

6) QWL offers respect to the individual. The entire process is built on the idea that each person's ideas are important. In "brainstorming" everyone gives ideas and no one's ideas are rejected out of hand or even criticized directly. Around the QWL table, everyone from top management to the lowest production worker is equal and on a first name basis.

7) QWL provides a group identity. Meeting together regularly to solve problems naturally builds cohesiveness. QWL's own special procedures and jargon further build that identity. And the QWL program consciously nurtures it. Often the first thing a QWL circle does is to decide on a special name, often one with an in-joke. (At Eastern Airlines: In the Chips, Solutions 84. At Ford Motor Co.: Autobiotics, Sweatshop.) Groups often develop their own symbols or slogans and order circle jackets, shirts, buttons, or caps. They may hold circle parties or picnics.

QWL fills needs that are legitimate. There is more than enough in everyday experience to make people feel bad—bad about themselves and bad about the world. Work is one of the major contributors. Anything that promises to make people feel better about their work and better about themselves in relation to work is bound to win avid supporters.

This is where outside consultants and training come in. The consultants, more than anyone else, understand that the process—the sum of the nitty-gritty step by step procedures—has a lot to do with whether QWL is accepted or rejected, whether or not it "feels good," and whether or not the program is judged a success.

QWL Training: What Goes On

QWL training is expensive: consultants charge hundreds of dollars per hour, not to mention the cost of "lost time" from production during the classes. In many programs only the facilitators or group leaders receive the training. In others, all QWL participants are trained.

Most QWL consultants do not claim to understand industrial processes or technology, collective bargaining issues, or the labor relations history of the particular workplace. Rather, they are there to teach a process.

Following are some samples of the topics covered, materials used, and training methods. The examples here are taken from a number of different training programs from different industries. Certain techniques, such as the extensive use of flipcharts, brainstorming, fishboning, and problem solving examples, are common to all programs. Most of the basic techniques and ideas have been around for a long time in industrial psychology or management fields.

SEVEN STEPS TO PROBLEM SOLVING

One of the most useful tools taught in QWL training is a methodical approach to problem solving. Group members learn the advantage of this approach over a scatter-shot attack. Here is one version:

1. Identify the problem. Get the group to agree on just which problem it is trying to solve. Be explicit, write it down.

2. List all possible causes. Try to make the list include all possibilities.

3. Choose the most likely causes.

4. Consider all possible solutions. Get as many as possible. Encourage creative, seemingly wild solutions. There are no limitations at this point.

5. Choose the best possible solution.

6. Implement the solution.

7. Evaluate results.

The most important part is to take the process of problem solving one step at a time. Simply defining the problem explicitly often puts you on the right track. By taking the steps in order, your mind is freer in each step to consider all possibilities. Be aware of conditions, but don't impose your own additional conditions unconsciously (see the "Nine Dot Problem" for an example).

THE NINE DOT PROBLEM

Connect the nine dots with four connected straight lines without lifting the pencil from the paper or retracing any of the lines.

    O   O   O

    O   O   O

    O   O   O

(Hint: Most people fail to solve this problem because they impose a condition on themselves which isn't stated: namely, that they can draw the lines only within the square created by the dots, or that lines must begin and end on dots. Once people understand that this is not a condition, the problem is much easier to solve. The answer is on page 13.)

BRAINSTORMING

Brainstorming is not just "hard thinking." It is universally taught as a specific method in QWL training.

The group leader goes around the circle taking ideas one at a time; all ideas are accepted, and far-out ideas are encouraged. All suggestions are written down so that everyone knows that his or her idea was heard.

Ideas are not criticized or even discussed at this time. This is the time to go for quantity and a broad scope. The ideas are usually written on "flip-charts," big pads of paper mounted on an easel stand. A good brainstorm usually results in many of these sheets taped to the walls for everyone to examine.

THE FISHBONE

Another common technique for finding and organizing possible causes of problems is the Fishbone or Ishikawa Diagram (developed by Professor Kaoru Ishikawa of the University of Tokyo in 1950). The idea is first to list the general causes of the problem. These

are usually categorized as "the 4 M's" (manpower, materials, methods, and machines). The general causes are then subdivided, and further subdivided, until all possible causes are listed and their position in the flow is stated.

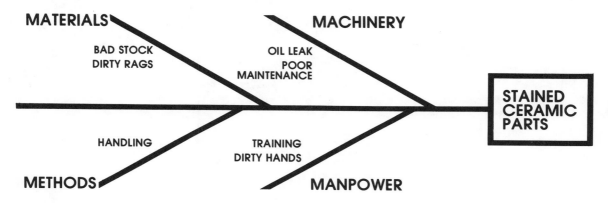

STATISTICAL TRAINING

After all possible causes are identified, the next logical step is to determine which one actually causes the most problems. Here is where statistical training is useful. Most start by teaching graphing in order to visualize trends and distributions. Particularly popular is Pareto analysis (named after an Italian mathematician), which uses bar graphs with the data shown in

order by size. This shows the most likely problem-causers to be worked on first.

Here is an example used in one training group. The group was trying to reduce keypunch errors. To identify the possible causes, they drew Pareto diagrams showing keypunch errors according to two different factors—by operator and by type of keypunch machine.

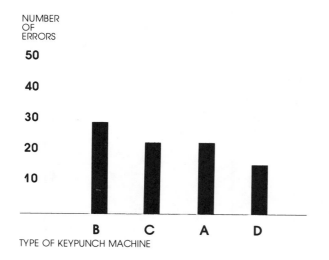

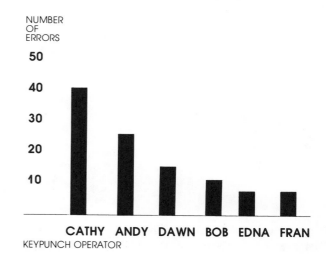

The first Pareto diagram indicated that the errors seemed to come pretty evenly from all the different types of machines. The second Pareto diagram indicated that most of the errors were made by one or two people. This led the group to look at possible reasons that Cathy and Andy were making errors. Happily, the problem turned out to be insufficient lighting in their work areas. When the lighting was improved, Cathy's and Andy's errors decreased.

In some programs more advanced statistical concepts of probability and normal distribution are taught.

Here are some sample pages from a GM training pamphlet.[2]

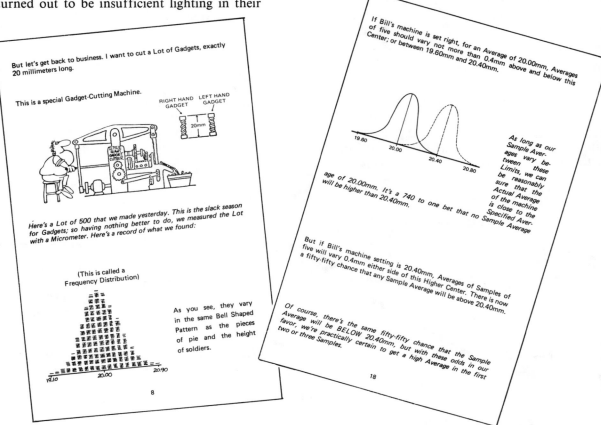

Once the causes of problems and their possible solutions are identified, the next step is to determine which, if any, of the proposed solutions should be pursued.

COST/BENEFIT ANALYSIS

The idea behind cost/benefit analysis is to add up all the ways in which a proposed solution will provide benefits and all its possible costs. The ratio of costs to benefits can then be calculated. The lower the cost/benefit ratio, the more desirable a proposal is.

For example, the General Motors QWL training manual[3] gives this hypothetical case: "A group is considering one solution which involves the installation of an additional machine. The machine itself would cost $1,000." The problem gives the costs and benefits for the first year as follows:

NEW MACHINE COST/BENEFIT ANALYSIS

COSTS		BENEFITS	
Machine	$1000	Reduce rejects by 10%	$ 750
Rewiring and installation	500	Reduce production time	500
Lost production during change	500	Reduce shipping delays	250
Retraining operators	250		
	$2250		$1500

Clearly from this analysis the costs would exceed the benefits for the first year. But by the second year, total benefits would more than pay for the new machine.

ORGANIZATIONAL AND SOCIAL SKILLS

Most groups are given some training in organizational, leadership and social skills, although these are usually done more intensively for facilitators and group leaders. They include such topics as:

How to organize a meeting
How to prepare an oral presentation
How to improve your memory
How to listen
How to draw out others
How to encourage participation
How to deal with conflict

Try It Yourself

You can best understand the power and impact of these training techniques by trying them yourself. If possible, get a number of people together to actually try out the exercises in this section. This is an excellent first step for a union group beginning to investigate QWL. The instructions that follow are shortened versions of the regular exercises. If you can spend longer on each exercise, then do so.

1) Ask everyone to pair off with someone they do not know well. For five minutes one person should interview the other to prepare a one-minute introduction of that person. Then the roles should reverse for five minutes. When the group reassembles, everyone introduces his or her partner to the whole group.

2) Divide the group into small groups of 6 to 10. Use a method, such as counting off, which will put people with people they don't know. The following activities take place within these small groups.

Have each group member introduce him or herself. They should tell where they were born, how many brothers and sisters they have, and whether they are older or younger.

Then have each person take a minute to describe his or her first paying job and how he or she felt about it. Start this exercise with the person born farthest away and continue around the group clockwise. (If time permits do some additional questions in the same way, but start with a different person for each one. Ask each member to describe the worst problem they have had with government bureaucracy. Have them tell which was their most difficult subject in high school and how they got through it. Have each member tell the name of their favorite TV show and what they like best about it. Ask them to name their favorite spectator sport and participant sport.)

3) First ask group members to consider this problem individually and write down their answers:

--------- **LOST AT SEA**[4] ---------
You are adrift on a private yacht in the South Pacific. After a fire the yacht is now sinking. Your location is unclear, but your best estimate is that you are approximately 1,000 miles from the nearest land. You have a rubber life raft large enough for everyone in the group, and oars, pocket items, and the 15 items listed below. Your task is to rank the 5 most important items below in terms of their importance to your survival.

_____sextant	_____shaving mirror
_____5 gallon can of water	_____mosquito netting
_____1 case C rations	_____maps of Pacific Ocean
_____flotation cushion	_____2 gal can gas oil mix
_____transistor radio	_____shark repellent
_____20 sq ft opaque plastic	_____1 qt 160 proof rum
_____15 ft nylon rope	_____2 boxes chocolate bars
_____fishing kit	

Now each group discusses the problem. After 10 minutes they report their recommendations. Spend some time discussing the different answers. Finally, the leader should present the "experts'" answers.

It should become clear that some answers are better than others. For example, if you are a thousand miles from the nearest land, you are not likely to save the group by rowing. Therefore items like the sextant or maps should be low on the list. Starvation is not an immediate problem, but dehydration is. Hence materials that can help prevent dehydration, including water and the opaque plastic, are a high priority. Food, particularly protein and alcohol, causes extra water usage so the fishing kit, rum, and other food items go low on the list.

Making sure that you can be seen by a search party should be the top priority. The shaving mirror would reflect sunlight, and the flotation cushion soaked with the oil-gas mixture, set on fire, and towed with the rope would serve as a signaling device.

While the Seven Problem Solving Steps discussed earlier may have appeared self-evident, most groups don't use them naturally. Groups which do use that procedure will start by trying to agree what the problem is (is the main task to row to safety or to survive while waiting to be rescued?). They will usually come to better and quicker answers.

4) Have the group discuss what it learned about the process of group problem solving from this exercise. What roles did individual group members play? Look for roles like the "dominator," the "facilitator," the "cynic." How did the original individual answers compare with the group answers? A group process can generally improve thinking. This is called "synergy."

SOLUTION TO THE NINE DOT PROBLEM

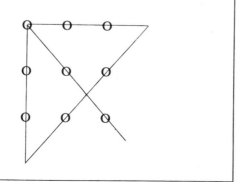

*   *   *

Even these abbreviated QWL exercises should demonstrate how attractive these training techniques are. You learn some useful skills. You learn about the other people. You get to talk about yourself. It is clear why many people believe that QWL has opened up a new world to them and why they enjoy it.

If QWL increases workers' self-confidence and provides a little fun at work, that is a big plus. But is there a trade-off involved? Is there a price to pay for this pleasurable experience at work?

In QWL training "involvement" is discussed and encouraged. But:

WHAT we are to be involved in is left vague.

WHAT we are to accomplish is left vague.

WHO benefits from what we accomplish is rarely mentioned.

In the next chapter we will take another look at QWL techniques and see that they are used to teach much more than they claim.   □

Notes

1. A.H. Maslow, editor, *New Knowledge in Human Values*, Harper & Row, 1959.
2. *Statistical Control Made Easy*, General Motors Hydra-matic Division, no date.
3. *Leader Manual*, GM Education and Training, Publication SIF-334, 1984.
4. Abridged version of exercise used in PPG Industries, Circleville, Ohio training program, based on 1975 Annual Handbook for Group Facilitators.

HIDDEN MESSAGES OF QWL TRAINING

If you have not read the previous chapter which describes in some detail what goes on in QWL training, please do so before reading this chapter. Here we will look again at that same training, and find some concealed messages.

QWL is sold to unions as a program that will benefit both labor and management. The neutral image of QWL training is carefully nurtured. This is one of the reasons that outside consultants are used. The presence of the outside consultant, acceptable to both management and the union, in and of itself suggests impartiality. Most consultants recognize that maintaining the QWL program is possible only if the union believes the program is not benefiting management at the union's expense.

Yet despite this carefully cultivated image, QWL training is far from neutral. The training that we looked at in the last chapter is thoroughly biased in favor of managment. The language of neutrality serves only to make it go down more easily.

Precisely because of its "neutral" image, QWL can more easily penetrate natural defenses and is therefore a powerful tool for challenging and shifting our traditional assumptions about the way the world works. Because of its apparent simplicity, most participants do not recognize that QWL is a highly sophisticated form of attitude and behavior modification. Most QWL training programs are developed either by the corporations that use them or by outside consultants who draw their materials and experience from established management fields such as industrial psychology. This is not surprising. After all, the companies butter the bread and consultants are smart enough to recognize the butter side.

I'VE FOUND A WAY OF GETTING WORKERS...

...TO INCREASE PRODUCTION... TAKE LESS PAY .... SPY ON....

OUTPUT

...THEIR FELLOW WORKERS AND THINK IT'S FOR THEIR OWN GOOD...

HOW DO YOU DO IT?

I GET THEM TO FORM A QUALITY CIRCLE!

Learning to Think the Company Way

QWL training goes beyond instruction in problem-solving techniques. The training is also designed to change the way group members think—about their work, about themselves, about their relationship to management and their union. QWL training uses a number of strategies to get these different ways of thinking accepted. Consider the example we looked at in the last chapter, cost/benefit analysis:

NEW MACHINE COST/BENEFIT ANALYSIS

COSTS		BENEFITS	
Machine	$1000	Reduce rejects by 10%	$ 750
Rewiring and Installation	500	Reduce production time	500
Lost production during change	500	Reduce shipping delays	250
Retraining operators	250		
	$2250		$1500

Notice that "reduce production time" is listed as a $500 benefit. To whom? Where does the savings come from? The company saves $500 because it is paying the workers for fewer hours.

"Retraining operators" is considered a "cost." Why should retraining be considered a cost rather than a benefit to the workers who will increase their skills? The new machine is listed as "costing" $1,000. But what if it is built in another department in the same plant, and therefore means more jobs for workers in that department? "Rewiring and installation" may be a cost to management, but it is certainly a benefit, in the form of more jobs, to the plant's maintenance workers.

Cost/benefit analysis can be a valuable tool—if it is clear by whose standards the costs and benefits are being measured. In the example used here, the unstated assumption is that costs and benefits are measured in terms of company profits, and not in terms of workers' needs like job security or learning new skills.

In fact, almost every item in this example involves a conflict of interest. Sometimes it is a conflict between workers in one department and those in another. Sometimes high seniority workers ("our jobs are more secure if we do it cheaper") are pitted against low seniority workers ("doing it cheaper means laying us off"). And sometimes it is the more basic conflict between the interests of workers and the interests of the company.[1]

But one of the assumptions of QWL training is that there is only one set of interests. So when a QWL trainer teaches cost/beneft analysis, he or she can do so only by ignoring any possible conflicts.

QWL training depends heavily on the psychological theory of "behavior modification": If you can get people to *act* on the basis of certain assumptions, even if they do not initially agree with the ideas, over a period of time they will move closer to accepting those assumptions. It is part of a process psychologists call "cognitive dissonance reduction." QWL training is designed to get people to act on the idea that "we and management are all in the same boat." This notion is in conflict with many union members' previous experiences and thinking: "management is only out for itself." The purpose of QWL training is to get group members committed to the new idea and to alter or drop their previous opinion.

Much of QWL training seems elementary and trivial. This is not because the designers of QWL programs think that this is the only way workers can understand it. QWL is like the illusions of the best magicians: the audience is led to believe that it has seen every step along the way.

The training is purposely designed *not* to directly challenge the fundamental beliefs of unionism such as solidarity, or that management's bottom line is profits and not people. Instead, the training tries to tip-toe past or outflank these ideas and establish new outposts in the mind. These new sentiments are then constantly reinforced with the good feelings, the sense of accomplishment, and the new group identity, as well as the physical perks of QWL (the hour off the job, the conferences).

Poor Lighting Is Usually the Answer

In QWL training manuals the solutions to the problems presented are never disadvantageous to workers. No jobs are eliminated, no one has to work harder. In the previous chapter, for example, recall that the group discovered by using Pareto bar graphs that most of the keypunch mistakes could be traced to one or two workers. The group then investigated and found out that the problem was poor lighting.

A similar exercise, used in General Motors' QWL training manual and elsewhere, is called "The Assembly Problem."[2] Team A is not quite meeting the company-set targets for production or quality. The QWL group is given a floor plan and some data showing better quality figures during the summer months and for teams nearer windows. Again, the solution turns out to be higher wattage. Everybody wins and everybody is happy. Meanwhile, the QWL group members have gone along with the notion that they should measure and compare the productivity of their fellow workers.

This example illuminates another problem with QWL training: the real questions are kept in the dark. Who set the production targets in the first place? Are they fair? Is this the kind of issue the QWL group wants to work on, or is the issue work satisfaction? The facilitator guides the group toward certain answers. In this case, the leaders' manual suggests that the proper way of defining the problem is "how to achieve 93% production and 4.5% rejects for Team A."

But the exercise is cleverly constructed so that it usually isn't necessary for the trainer to intervene. Even in all-union workshops where the group has defined

The Assembly Problem

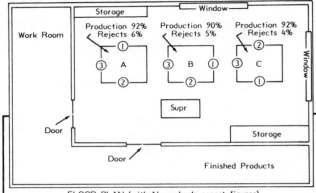

FLOOR PLAN (with November's report figures)

Jim, Bob and Susan work together on Assembly, Team A. In their area are two other assembly teams doing exactly the same detailed work. Each team can choose its own method of operation. Jim, Bob and Susan rotate positions every hour or so. They began this procedure in May. Team C rotates, too. Team B doesn't.

Jean Smith became the new supervisor of all three teams in November. She reviewed the records of past production and rejects. She also timed all operations and made check lists for November. She feels there is a problem with Team A, but can't put her finger on it. There is no pattern to their rejects. And an inspection of their materials and tools failed to show a problem. Yet they fail to meet the targets of 93% production and 4.5% rejects.

You have been asked to identify and solve the problem. You talked to Jim, Bob and Susan and they gave you the information on the next page.

QWL as "people, not productivity oriented," most members will define the problem in this example as productivity and quality.

In the real world of work, of course, the problem isn't always poor lighting. In fact it usually isn't. Suppose that in the keypunch error case, Cathy was just not quite as accurate as the others. Family problems prevented her from getting sleep, she had arthritis, she was having trouble with the supervisor, or she just was not as coordinated as the others. What would the group do then? Again, the psychological process comes into play. If the group has gone this far in trying to solve the problem of the keypunch errors, then it is committed. It will try to solve the problem, perhaps by peer pressure on Cathy to improve. Even if the group does nothing, it is more likely to passively accept management's attempts to deal with "the Cathy problem."

QWL training uses examples with neutral solutions to legitimize an approach which is, in fact, thoroughly pro-company—that some workers should cooperate with management to determine which workers are not measuring up to company standards. How long will unionism survive among the keypunch operators with workers fingering each other or using peer pressure to enforce management's arbitrary rules?

QWL's emphasis on statistics and gathering data tends to encourage workers to delve into areas traditionally carefully watched by unions. For example, unions have long understood the danger of company time-studies—that they mean speedup, not easier work. Most union contracts include limitations on the company's right to (or method of) time-study. Yet one of the results of QWL is that workers end up doing a time-study on themselves.

At Ford's Dearborn, Michigan assembly plant, a group of electricians was justifiably proud of an electronics repair facility it had initiated. In order to demonstrate how much money they saved the company, the electricians kept extremely accurate records showing exactly how much time was spent on each repair—the very kind of recordkeeping the union had successfully fought in the past. (After this was pointed out, the electricians kept their records in more general terms.)

No More We/They

T he "we-they" concept is really the fundamental idea in trade unionism. Solidarity means *we* stick together against *them*. QWL training doesn't attack the notion of union solidarity head on. But one of the main purposes of QWL is to establish new group identities to replace old ones.

One of the eleven "foundations" of quality circles, as described by Sud Ingle, a leading consultant, is:

> Reduction of the "we" and "they" mentality...Since everyone (labor and management) is encouraged to participate in problem solving, the feeling develops that the employees are all in it together...[3]

The Lost at Sea exercise described in chapter 2 builds this group identity. Virtually every training program uses a "survival" problem of this type: plane crash on the desert, survival after an accident on the moon, Antarctic exploration, lost in the woods. In their imagery, these survival problems contain the hidden assumption of QWL: "We are all in the same boat. We will sink or be saved together. We all share a mutual interest in this process." When the group members act on those assumptions to solve the exercise—and this can be fun—the assumptions are reinforced.

Again, the exercise leads naturally toward certain conclusions. Rarely does a group come up with the idea of throwing part of their numbers overboard so the remainder will have a better chance of survival.

If a QWL program simply wanted to teach problem solving skills, it wouldn't necessarily have to use exercises with a "we're all in this together" philosophy. Suppose that the Lost at Sea problem were stated differently:

> There are two kinds of people in the boat, Blue people and Green people. Only the Greens can row. The Blues have guns. The only search helicopter is controlled by Blues. It only has room for the Blues plus a few Greens. It will rescue the people in the boat if the boat can be quickly rowed a considerable distance to a calm area and if the number of people in the boat is reduced to the number the helicopter can hold. There are 15 items....

Imagine how different the group process would be with this story. And these assumptions are a far closer parallel to the situation in most industries than the Lost at Sea story in the last chapter. This revised exercise could also be fun and interesting and teach problem

UE News Service

" Give him our loyalty test... See if he'll take a 10% rate cut..."

solving skills. But it would require a different set of assumptions. It would bring up for discussion a point that QWL training would prefer to leave untouched.

Another assumption of QWL training is the acceptance of the QWL group and its limitations. When the group discusses possible problems to solve, one of the first questions is whether a particular problem is appropriate for the group. The facilitator encourages the group to deal with problems whose solutions are within easy reach so the group can experience success. That is why QWL training concentrates so heavily on group identity. If group identity is strong enough and someone suggests a solution that "isn't appropriate" for the group, the pressure will be to drop the solution, not the group.

QWL MEANS COMPANY LOYALTY

General Motors has a questionnaire to measure improvements in the quality of work life. The survey mentions 16 "areas, or dimensions, of the quality of work life." The first one is "employee commitment: feelings of loyalty to GM." The interpretation guide explains that if an employee believes the union and the company have different goals, or that the union and management are opposed to each other, this is evidence of a low quality of work life.

QWL is a joint union-management program at GM, presumably built on a foundation of mutual respect. But apparently GM management wants it both ways. As part of the questionnaire, GM workers who aren't union members are asked how much they agree with the statement, "I feel that employees like me should be represented by a union." An employee who says that he or she doesn't need a union scores high.

Blame the Victim Psychology

The psychological theories presented as part of QWL training also play a part in promoting pro-management thinking and undermining unionism. Maslow's "hierarchy of needs" (the pyramid described in chapter 2) can be used to put unions in their place—low on the hierarchy. And since the supposed aim of QWL is to get "members of the organization" to operate in the higher levels of the hierarchy, the message is that unions are not very relevant.

The contemptuous view toward unions, union goals, and strong union members comes through clearly in a taped lecture used as part of Ford's Employe Involvement training in 1982. Jay Hall, a well known consultant, explains the meaning of each level in the needs hierachy. Note also how the term "organizational objectives" is used as a synonym for company goals.

> This second, or safety security need, level pertains to the individual's desire to protect and preserve those satisfactions of basic creature comfort needs which he has been able to achieve.
>
> To the extent that one is primarily motivated by the safety and security need system, he will attach a great deal of importance to such goal objects as seniority protections, tightly defined job descriptions which minimize the number of decisions he must make, strong retirement programs along with a whole fringe benefit package, clear cut rules and regulations so that he will know what is expected of him and can avoid surprises or unwitting risks. And finally, he may value union membership as a protective mechanism against management practices which threaten his security.
>
> Again it should be apparent that such goal objects have little to do with organizational objectives and... it can be expected that the behaviors... will be cautious, compliant, and uncreative drone-like behaviors.[4]

"Unions were perhaps necessary in the old days," goes the theory, "when the issue was survival. When people were hungry they were not concerned about group identity, excelling, or self-actualization. Now that the basic needs have been met through wages and benefits, workers can turn to their higher needs, which can best be met not by their unions but by identifying with the company."

This theory "blames the victim." Workers are supposed to think that the reason companies didn't concern themselves with providing fulfilling jobs in the past was that *workers* didn't care about them. Workers couldn't be capable of wanting wages *and* self-respect, could they?

In fact, union history is filled with struggles for dignity in the workplace and for real quality of work life. Little can match the sense of dignity and self-respect of workers who have just won a hard-fought strike.

The reason these psychological theories are dropped into the QWL training is that their seeming scientific neutrality is an easy way to separate workers from their unions. It is the familiar message of QWL: We leave it to unions to bargain about wages and benefits. Your new needs, like respect and dignity, you get from thinking like your boss.

* * *

QWL works. It gets workers to act like management. Joe Torres belongs to a QWL team called the "Hi-Liners" at the San Diego Gas and Electric Company. He describes the Hi-Liners' activities:

> Since most of our projects involve work efficiency, we make on-the-job time studies to show just how much time can be saved. As part of each project, we prepare a cost-benefit analysis. The analysis helps us identify potential savings compared to the one-time cost the company might have for any changes that may have to be made. In the last project alone, we identified total savings of $100,000.[5]

It is not hard to show the inherent anti-union assumptions of QWL training. But unionists can do more than point out the problems or object to the training. The reason that QWL succeeds in shifting loyalties and breaking down the ideas of union solidarity is that it does fulfill some needs. It fills a vacuum. When a union challenges QWL but has no alternative of its own, it risks reinforcing the very message of QWL—that satisfaction comes from the new group identity and that the union stands in the way of satisfying work.

The void that QWL fills is real. But there is no reason that unions cannot fill it. □

FRED WRIGHT

Joining the Family

As part of their QWL program most of the 22,000 employees of General Motors' Hydra-matic Division will attend week-long "Family Awareness Training" sessions over a three-year period. Hydra-matic Division and the UAW-GM Training Fund will spend close to $40 million on the training, including full wages and salaries for those attending and luxurious facilities like the Four Winds Resort in Bloomington, Indiana and the UAW's resort-like education center at Black Lake in northern Michigan. Presumably, GM thinks it's getting its money's worth.

The "family" in the conference title does not refer to spouses or children, who are not invited. As the information packet says, the conference is about "establishing a family atmosphere within the division."

The notion of family is central to the week of emotionally intense activities designed to change union members' perceptions of their identity. The props include hats, jackets, stickers, notebooks, and diplomas with the large "family" logo. The specific exercises in "family training" change regularly. What follows is a summary of the fall 1984 version:

The process starts with an orientation before participants leave for the conference site. The first ground rule is that no one tells whether they are hourly or salary (union or management). Stripping away these identities is an explicit purpose of the training. Hopefully everyone will arrive at the conclusion of one enthusiastic facilitator of "the Black Lake experience": "Union or Management. Does it really matter? People are people first."[7]

On the first day at the conference there is much discussion about the benefits of a family, including the security it provides; conference participants can become a family too. After this begins the process of building the new family. Participants start by pairing off as learning partners. The family grows as pairs join together.

The week is spent participating in exercises. Some are related to the factory, such as one in which participants develop lists for the best and worst characteristics in a supervisor. But most focus on developing interpersonal skills and relationships. The exercises are designed to develop a feeling of personal trust and intimacy, and thus to create a new family relationship to replace the old "we-they," union-company relationship left back home. The delegates from each plant are drawn from the same department so that they will be able to continue as a group after the training.

Over the past two years, GM has refined its program. The company has trained a crew of union and management QWL staff so that the program is executed with professional polish. Most of the participants find it an enjoyable as well as a highly emotional experience. The bottom line is that people want more.

Here are some of the exercises used at Hydra-matic's Family Awareness Training:

Developing Trust

One person in each pair is blindfolded and must depend on his or her partner for help in accomplishing several assigned tasks without mishap.

Personal Feedback[8]

Each participant writes the name of every other group member on separate cards. On the opposite side they write a characteristic or impression of each person. For example:

> This person is a good leader because...
> I think this person should...
> I would like to know if this person...
> My impression of this person was...

The cards are then shuffled. Without looking at the name, the facilitator reads the description on each card and the group members decide which person they think is being described. The card is placed in front of this person. Then the cards are turned over, one by one, and

OTHER APPROACHES

Many QWL programs do not use intensive preliminary training as GM does. The philosophy at most Ford plants, for example, is that group process training is best done as the groups are actually dealing with problems rather than ahead of time.[6] But the kinds of exercises and the content of the training remain substantially the same.

the group discusses whether they accurately decribe the intended person or why they were assigned to the wrong person.

Johari Window: An Experience in Self-Disclosure and Feedback[9]

Each person in a small group writes a list of his or her own personal assets and liabilities as well as those of every other person in the group. The feedback is read and each person compares his or her own list of assets and liabilities to others' descriptions of them. This process leads to developing a model of oneself with four "windows":

	Known To Self	Not Known To Self
Known To Others	I. Area of Free Activity (Public Self)	II. Blind Area (Bad Breath)
Not Known To Others	III. Avoided or Hidden Area (Private Self)	IV. Area of Unknown Activity (Unconscious)

The object is to enlarge Window I, so that as much of one's "self" is known to others as possible. The group does exercises to help increase the proportion of Window I. According to the theory, learning to take feedback (hear criticism or praise) will shift the vertical line to the right. Giving information shifts the horizontal line down. Opening oneself up means being willing to share more of one's joys, fears and needs with other members of the group.

COG's Ladder[10]

This is an exercise within an exercise. One group participates in a problem solving activity, while a second observes it to follow the different stages in group development. The final stage of healthy group development, according to the facilitators' handbook, "is one of unity, high spirits, mutual acceptance, and high cohesiveness. It is the *esprit* stage."

At Hydra-matic Family Awareness the group being observed discusses the following story and then ranks the characters in the order in which they appeal to the group.

> A ship sank in a storm. A girl, a sailor and an old man reached an island. The girl was certain that her fiance and his best friend were on another island within sight. She begged the sailor to repair the boat and take her to the other island. The sailor agreed on condition that she sleep with him.
>
> The girl agonized and asked the old man for advice. He told her to look into her own heart. She finally agreed to sleep with the sailor, after which he repaired the boat and took her to the other island.

> The girl found her fiance and ran into his arms. After a while she told him what had happened. In a rage he pushed her away, saying he did not want to see her again.
>
> The best friend put his arm around the girl and said, "I'll try to patch it up, but in the meantime I'll take care of you." (abridged version)

The Hot Seat

This exercise takes place on the last evening of Family Awareness week. One by one each person sits on the "hot seat" and listens to group members say positive things about him or her. It is hard to say which is the more moving experience—sitting in the "hot seat" or seeing those in the seat moved to tears.

LABOR RELATIONS IN A HOT TUB

A primary goal of most of these sophisticated exercises is to break down a person's psychological defenses and develop openness. For example, the COG's Ladder exercise is designed to develop intimacy by opening discussions of morality, women's liberation, and sex.

But defenses serve a purpose. In the unreal atmosphere of Family Awareness Week, it may be easy to let them down. But back home, some "family members" have the power to assign jobs, grant exceptions, and even destroy the livelihoods of others. Does naive openness in the work situation always make sense?

Technically, Family Awareness training is conducted jointly by Hydra-matic Division and the UAW. The sessions are "co-facilitated" by one union and one management person, both of whom have been trained by management trainers. But many union facilitators have little training in the union itself. The program is tightly planned by Hydra-matic's Organizational Development and Planning staff. Any chance that the workers might identify themselves as union members is minimized by instructing them to leave their union identity behind. While management has a strong presence at the training, there are only a couple of union officers present.

There is no reason to talk about the union during Family Awareness Week. So if the union has a role at all in this "family" model, it is to be the lawyer—unnecessary as long as things are going well, but available in case one side threatens divorce. Acknowledgement of any independent, active role for the union would mean that training had failed.

IS IT BRAINWASHING?

"Brainwashing" is one of those terms that depends mainly on your vantage point:

I changed my mind.
You were convinced.
She was swayed.
They were brainwashed.

Like the cults of the 1960s and 1970s, which also talked about creating "new families," QWL training uses powerful psychological techniques to bring about major attitude changes in a short time. The training takes people out of their normal environment. In the context of a very comfortable, controlled situation, feelings of insecurity and needs for belonging and intimacy are manipulated in an attempt to redefine workers' identity.

Notes

1. James Rinehart of the Department of Sociology at the University of Western Ontario uses this example in "Appropriating Workers' Knowledge," an excellent study of QWL at the GM Diesel Plant in London, Ontario.
2. *Leader Manual*, GM Education and Training, Publication SIF-334, 1984.
3. Sud Ingle, *Quality Circle Master Guide*, Prentice Hall, 1982, p. 5.
4. Jay Hall, *Models for Management*, instructional tape provided as part of Teleometrics Int'l training materials.
5. *Annual Report*, San Diego Gas and Electric Company, 1983.
6. Robert H. Guest, "The Sharonsville Story," in Robert Zager and Michael Rosow, *The Innovative Organization*, Pergamom Press, 1982.
7. *QWL Quarterly*, October 1983.
8. *The 1978 Annual Handbook for Group Facilitators*.
9. *The 1973 Annual Handbook for Group Facilitators*.
10. *The 1974 Annual Handbook for Group Facilitators*.

MANAGEMENT'S GOALS

The closest thing to a theory underlying Quality of Work Life programs is the idea of mutual interests. At first it seems quite simple and even obvious: Management and labor have an adversarial relationship when bargaining over certain issues such as wages, but they also have much in common. On these common issues they should work together to find solutions which benefit both.

Certainly even the most militant worker, or the nastiest boss, could think of interests which fit in the shaded area. Both normally have an interest in the workplace not burning down. Or, given the high costs of hiring and training, it is to both sides' advantage to help workers overcome alcohol problems rather than simply firing them.

In the language of QWL these mutual interests are the basis of "win-win" solutions—both sides gain and neither loses. Such solutions are different (and presumably better) than the "win-lose" solutions which come out of an adversarial situation, where if one side wins the other must lose. There do seem to be some workplace situations where both parties could gain. This is the starting point for the logic of QWL.

However, QWL reasoning leaps from this beginning to the conclusion that the *central* issues facing labor and management today are ones of mutual interest.

In order to assess this proposition we need to take a closer look at how employers' define *their* interests. Employers do long term planning to assure that their short run actions contribute to long term goals. We need to look at the strategies employers are using in the 1980's to pursue those interests, and especially how those strategies relate to QWL.

Company Goals

QWL has become popular in management circles since 1979, when it became clear that U.S industry was no longer the undisputed world leader. The recession and underlying economic crisis forced companies to find ways to improve their profitability. These included some changes in labor relations: contract concessions, forcing strikes, the use of scabs,

ONENESS ON SATURN

The theory of mutual interests reached a new high in General Motors' Saturn Project. In 1984 the United Auto Workers and General Motors set up the UAW-GM Joint Saturn Study Center to work out methods of production, reward systems, and the overall relationship of worker, machine, and management. One decision the study center made was to change its name to remove the word "joint." In a "joint" presentation roadshow, GM and UAW representatives explained why the name was changed:

"Joint" implies two parts coming together. *We are one!*[1]

The study project did not give workers input into the design of the car, plant location, marketing, or price structure. They were given some input into plant layout and certain production techniques, but mainly concentrated on employee-management relations.

Although there is not yet a formal agreement, many of the concepts developed for Saturn have been presented to other local UAW leaders as accomplished fact, including the use of work teams, no automatic carryover of the current UAW-GM national contract, few job classifications or lines of demarcation between skilled trades, and a minimal local contract if any at all. The lines between management and union will be further blurred; instead of stewards, there will be union "advisors."

Saturn, along with the GM-Toyota joint venture in Fremont, California, will provide the leverage for GM to spread the new techniques and work rules to other plants. According to a Federal Trade Commission report this could save the company about $4.8 billion annually.[2] Since most of the savings are realized from reduced labor, this would translate into a loss of more than 150,000 jobs.

union decertifications, phony bankruptcies—and QWL.

In the last five years the roll call of employer aggression against unions runs from PATCO to Greyhound to Phelps Dodge to Wilson Foods to AP Parts to US Steel, as well as thousands of smaller employers. It is no coincidence that QWL is on the rise at the same time that employers are playing hardball with labor.

Public relations handouts suggest that the employers' principal strategy for regaining their competitive edge is to tap the ingenuity and creativity of American workers—to "work smarter." But in their own internal memos, in the business press, and in their actions, corporations reveal another strategy—to reduce labor costs by shipping production abroad or to low-wage areas, and to slash hours and pay for the work that's left. What employers want from QWL fits neatly into this strategy.

1) Management wants access to workers' knowledge about the work process. This is the grain of truth in management's expressed desire to "work smarter." Those who do the work every day know the problems and also many of the solutions.

Former UAW Vice-President Irving Bluestone likes to tell about the time when he was a union official and came upon a group of management officials and engineers huddled around a machine. For hours they had been trying to figure out why the machine would not grind accurately. Bluestone noticed the machine operator standing quietly off to one side and asked him what was going on. The operator casually mentioned that they could solve the problem by changing the grit of the grind wheel. "Why didn't you tell them?" asked Bluestone. "No one asked me," was the reply.

QWL advocates such as Bluestone believe the chance to share knowledge with management is one of the best things about QWL. Here, they say, is truly a "mutual interest"—management gets to improve the work process and the worker gets to make a contribution. QWL literature is filled with the notion that such contributions add to worker feelings of self-respect and autonomy.

Clearly, obtaining worker knowledge is in management's interest. But sharing that knowledge through QWL does not add to workers' autonomy because

management maintains complete decision making authority. Even in so-called "semi-autonomous work groups," workers are allowed to divide up a given amount of work, but do not decide on the tasks themselves or set the work pace.

QWL suggestions can even result in less worker control over the work process. One of the most famous QWL stories is the solution to windshield leaks discovered through QWL at General Motors' Tarrytown plant. Workers had been free to start applying sealant around the windshield at any point they wished. At a worker's suggestion, management required workers to start and finish applying the sealant at a particular point in order to build up sealant there.

As tiny as it may seem, the bit of freedom that allows a worker to decide how to move his or her arms, and to occasionally change that decision, makes an enormous difference in a repetitive assembly line job. Perhaps this erosion of autonomy was the best possible solution to the leak problem. But perhaps an entirely different design or different material could have been used. The point is that *management* made the determination. The QWL process collects worker knowledge for management's use in making decisions which workers are then required to carry out.

QWL theory says that it wants to change Frederick Taylor's famous "scientific management" dictum that "all possible brain work should be separated from the shop" and kept by management. As practiced, QWL only slightly modifies the theory to more effectively achieve the spirit. The improved Taylorism accepts the fact that workers have eyes, ears, and brains—and makes use of them—while striving instead to remove all possible decision making from the shop floor.

Many unionists believe that expropriation of worker knowledge is management's primary interest in QWL. In some cases unions can use this knowledge as a bargaining chip to win concessions from management, but there are two important limitations to this tactic.

Workers' knowledge is developed over years of experience (that is why it is so difficult for management to ferret it out in any other way). But once shared with management the leverage is gone. The union can agree to cooperate in QWL by sharing worker knowledge, on management's promise to be cooperative and nonadversarial too. But if management changes its mind and decides to start acting nasty, demanding concessions, or threatening to close the plant, the union can't then take back the information.

Further, once the knowledge about windshield leaks, for example, is shared in one location, management can transfer that knowledge to its other operations without

conceding anything to the union there.

Management is usually most interested in such knowledge during the initial phases of a QWL program when worker enthusiasm produces an outpouring of suggestions. But after the initial enthusiasm, management's interest in the circles' suggestions tends to fall off considerably. Groups often complain that they get slow action on their proposals even when they promise the company a savings, and no action at all when there is no savings involved. Management generally comes to regard the productivity gains it can make from worker suggestions as the icing on the cake, compared to its other goals for QWL.

2) Management wants cooperation in introducing new technology. New technology is a central management strategy in virtually all industries, including the service sector. The Canadian Air Line Employees Association, for example, is facing the introduction of machines which dispense tickets and information, collect payment, and route baggage. According to an Upjohn study, in the auto industry robots alone could replace 50,000 jobs in the next six years. Another study concludes that up to 80% of all material handlers (fork lift drivers and warehouse workers) could be replaced by automation.[3]

Technology is quickly becoming cheaper and more available. The speed with which this technology will be installed and operational is limited only by worker resistance and the inevitable "debugging" process.

Historically, workers have resisted automation, sometimes in an organized way, but often individually, recognizing it as a threat to job security. One of the chief aims of QWL, from the company point of view, is to neutralize worker resistance and even enlist cooperation in installing, debugging, and putting this new technology "on-line" with a minimum disruption of production schedules. (See chapter 13 for more on QWL and new technology.)

3) Management wants more flexibility in the workplace. Renault's Vice-President and Director of Quality, Gerald Toth, comments on restrictions on management's ability to fire employees:

> Industry nowadays needs flexibility more than ever, if it wants to survive. Without labor flexibility this is impossible. The ability to fire employees at whim might seem totally unfair to well intentioned people with more goodness than good sense in their brains, but the [threat] of making all of an industry less competitive vastly outweighs the possible injustice....[4]

A main component of the desired flexibility is the right to expand each worker's tasks and to assign workers interchangeably. William J. Abernathy, a Harvard Business School professor and auto industry expert, suggests that each worker should have to set up, operate and maintain his own machine, instead of having the job functions assigned to different workers. Such reorganization would require changing long standing job classifications and lines of demarcation between

GETTING IN ON MANAGEMENT'S RIGHTS

One of the frequent claims for QWL is that it gives workers and unions some power in areas that were previously "management rights." The reality is that QWL does not share any significant power. At most it shares the power of the lowest level supervisor, who has little power to begin with. Every major QWL program is clear: Decision making power is not democratized. It remains solely with management. A QWL group proposes, but the employer, like God, disposes. The employer picks and chooses the proposals that best fit *its* purposes. General Motors' policy is typical and emphatic:

> The participative problem solving system is a two-part process:
> 1. Development of alternatives to current practices can originate from the involved worker.
> 2. Decision to act and commit resources resides with management.
> The system makes it possible for employes at all levels of the organization to develop alternatives to current practice. However, the decision to select among the alternatives and to commit resources to implement changes, is solely that of management at appropriate levels.[6]

skilled trades. Its main effect would be lost jobs. Aber-nathy comments:

> The implication that all the labor reduction is going to come from robots is probably mistaken. The main source of labor loss will be work-force reorganization with increased worker involvement.[5]

One of management's chief aims in QWL is to gain acceptance from workers and their unions for replacing classification systems with "flexibility." The campaign to do away with classifications conceals an attack on a number of union protections. We will examine what increased flexibility means in more detail at the end of this chapter.

4) Management wants contract concessions. Employers expect that QWL activities and the very idea of the cooperative approach will make it easier to get workers to identify with employer goals and thus pave the way for inroads into the contract.

General Motors showed a film called "The Road to Survival" under QWL auspices as part of its campaign to win contract concessions. A top Ford negotiator details a number of ways Employe Involvement led to the 1982 concessions contract and points out that in the ratification vote "membership support for the new Agreement was consistently higher where EI was strong."[7] A publication of the Work In America Institute explains:

> The Ford-UAW and the GM-UAW landmark agreements would have been improbable, maybe impossible, without Employe Involvement at Ford and QWL at GM.... those familiar with labor-management relations agree that the new programs on the shop floor—on a day-to-day basis—opened a window for concession-type bargaining.[8]

5) Management wants to undermine unionism. The "ideological" offensive of QWL, as described in the next chapter, is perhaps its most important function for the employers. They will not necessarily try to break the unions, since the struggle to do so could be costly and dangerous. But their long range goals require both massive change and a docile and cooperative work force. This, in turn, requires unions which have no sense of independent purpose or power and indeed help the companies to direct and discipline their employees.

Corporations believe they have found in QWL the formula to neutralize labor resistance to management goals. They want cooperative unions to provide legitimacy to their plan to undo most of what labor has won in the past thirty years. It is much easier for the employers if the unions believe in "mutual interests," and therefore they are willing to spend a great deal of money on QWL to promote that theory.

Carrot and Stick

How corporate goals and QWL fit together was neatly summed up in a secret document intended for General Motors' top management. The document, which was obtained by the UAW, detailed GM's bargaining goals for the 1984 contract. The company was aiming to introduce changes which would cut approximately 80,000 people (or 20% of its payroll) over the next five years. The excerpts from the document (see below) show how QWL and "jointness" were to be an integral part of the strategy.

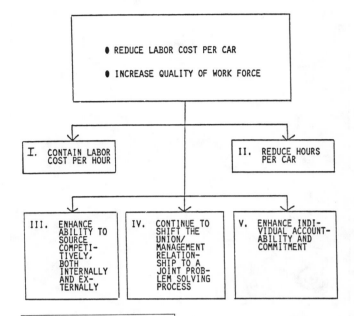

Slide "visuals" from GM management strategy document.

In the documents GM discussed frankly the difficulty of getting union members to okay sweeping concessions when GM had just made its largest profits ever and had distributed huge executive bonuses. Nonetheless, company strategists felt they had a good chance of winning these objectives "through developing a cooperative atmosphere" and increasing "joint involvement activities with the International."

Two other examples graphically demonstrate the link between QWL and the employers' other, less refined strategies.

An internal memo from Jack A. Gollan, president of Refiners Transport (a division of the giant Leaseway Transportation), to all his terminal managers describes a plan to reduce labor costs to meet the new "gypsy" competition caused by deregulation of the trucking industry. Gollan encloses a number of clippings he thinks the managers "might find interesting." They describe the decline of the Teamsters union, the union busting tactics of Toledo's AP Parts Co. against the UAW, the downward slide of airline wages, and the general trend toward wage cuts. Gollan then ends his memo:

> You should also keep in mind the forthcoming "In-House Management Development" meetings...What we are talking about is an attempt to create a team atmosphere in each terminal to eliminate, to the greatest

possible degree, the adversary relationship that has existed between driver/mechanics on one hand and on the other, terminal management.[9]

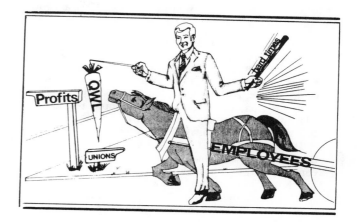

This cartoon appeared on the cover of a 1983 report on QWL from the Centre for Labour Studies at Humber College in Ontario. The study was financed in part by a grant from the Ministry of Labour of the Canadian federal government, which then refused to pay the money until the cartoon was removed. A book by Don M. Wells based on the study has since been published (see chapter 20).

THE ULTIMATE COOPERATION

In November 1982, Ford Motor Co. gave six months' notice that it would permanently close its Milpitas, California assembly plant. Up to 2,400 hourly and salary employees with seniority up to 37 years would lose their jobs. There were no auto plants remaining in the area and few comparable manufacturing jobs.

One might think that the workers would have felt betrayed. They had voted heavily for contract concessions and had an extensive Employe Involvement (EI) program. One might have predicted resistance, or at least that there would be some difficulties in maintaining production during those last six months. But not at Milpitas, according to Stan Jones, Chairman of the Bargaining Committee of UAW Local 560, and Hal Axtel, Labor Relations Manager. They frequently make joint appearances to tell the story, and they give most of the credit to the EI program.

Jones admits that when the closing decision was announced a few union committeemen wanted to find a way to fight the closing. But thanks to EI, he and other union leaders had "developed some kind of trust" and understood that the best course would be to work with the company. Axtel suggests that through the on-going process of management information sharing, employees were

able to see the reasonableness of management's decision to close the plant.

The EI program at Milpitas had been extensive. The entire plant shut down for a half hour every week for circle meetings, so there was almost 100% participation in the 107 circles. These meetings, according to plant management, generated thousands of useful suggestions. Management also credited EI with reducing costs. Absenteeism declined by 50%, says Axtel, "as a result of peer pressure."

During the final six months before shutdown, the EI success story continued. Cost performance, absenteeism and quality continued to improve. In fact, the plant achieved its highest quality rating in the last two weeks before the plant closed.

The cooperative atmosphere also saved the company money on the costs of closing down. A joint retraining program cost only $650,000 and, according to Axtel, helped avoid the bitterness that was a part of other plant closings.

> If we had a closure [like other auto plants in the area] with mass Workers' Comp cases filed, we would have lost four to five million dollars additional in Workers' Comp.... So really, [the retraining program] was cost effective. We saved money.[10]

In 1983 U.S. Steel threatened to close its Fairfield Works in Fairfield, Alabama. The company would keep the mill open only if the Steelworkers union agreed to contract changes. The new contract included the following provisions:

> All Local Working Conditions as heretofore reflected in past practices or local agreement at Fairfield Works which concern such matters as manning, crew-sizes, job assignments, hours of work, late starts, early quits, wash-up time, coffee breaks, lunch breaks, off days or shift selection, or which otherwise would restrict or eliminate the Company's competitive operation at Fairfield works [are] eliminated.
>
> The company at all times shall have full discretion to determine the manning ...of all operations.... the company may install the job of maintenance utilityman [combining skilled trades into a supercraft].
>
> [The] union agrees that the Company shall have the right to contract out work...[including engineering functions, instrument repair work, janitorial work, and hauling work].
>
> All presently installed incentives shall be discontinued, except for existing direct incentives...
>
> All pending complaints, grievances and arbitration cases... will be withdrawn.

The final article in the agreement states:

> The parties agree to the installation of Labor-Management Participation Teams at Fairfield Works....

* * *

It is a truism in the labor movement that the corporate bottom line is profits. This isn't just a vague goal for top managers but their reason for being, which determines their fundamental decisions.

Union members have frequently bought into QWL because their employer said it would help save their plant, save their jobs, or save the industry. But corporate behavior proves that none of these are significant corporate goals. Indeed, they are the first to be discarded in the pursuit of profit maximization.

U.S. Steel, long the country's largest steel manufacturer, symbolizes corporate arrogance in pursuit of its bottom line. For years steelworkers made profits for the corporation. But the corporation chose not to modernize its steel mills. It chose not to invest in ways that would provide new jobs for its loyal workers. It chose, instead, to speculate in other companies, as with its six billon dollar purchase of Marathon Oil, and to lay waste the steel communities of the Mahoning Valley in Ohio and the Monongahela Valley in Pennsylvania.

Large corporations are not just bigger versions of a family enterprise or a small business. The corporation has no loyalty to any particular product or to any particular country, let alone to any community, to the lower levels of its own management, or to the "families" it pretends to create through QWL. □

Flexibility and Job Classifications

Management insists that it needs to minimize job classifications to achieve the flexibility that modern production demands. The media has accepted this view and restates it as obvious fact. After all, who could be against flexibility? Attacking classifications is popular sport among industrial analysts and economists, especially those who promote QWL programs.[11]

The drive to reduce classifications is well advanced in the auto, airline, oil, and steel industries. Steel companies have pressured local unions to create "supercrafts" where several skilled classifications are combined. At one mill, U.S. Steel's South Works, the company wanted enough overlap so that skilled and production workers would do each other's jobs. In auto, every plant opened in the last few years has cut the number of classifications drastically. Reduction of classifications is clearly at the top of management's agenda.

Management loves to portray worker defense of classifications as irrational, inefficient and petty. How else to account for a worker refusing to pick up a part from the floor because "it's not my job"? But the underlying issues turn out to be not so petty ones: shop floor power, job loss, safety, favoritism, and seniority.

The classification issue can be confusing because there is such great variation in the systems. In the auto industry, each corporation uses a different set-up. At General Motors classifications are determined locally while at Chrysler, the corporation establishes new classifications with the concurrence of the international union. Procedures vary even between plants in the same corporation.

Here is how a typical classification system works in an auto assembly plant for what are called "non-skilled" classifications, currently about 80% of hourly employment. (We look at additional considerations for skilled trades classifications such as electrician and toolmaker in chapter 13.)

The union and the company have negotiated the number and the scope of classifications. A large assembly plant may have 50 to 100 non-skilled job titles, which sounds like a lot until you think about the complexity of a modern plant. Examples include assembler, assembler-trim, assembler-cleaner, welder, spray painter, fork lift operator, metal finisher, utility-relief, machine operator-lathe, inspector, stock chaser, and crib attendant.

Some of these classifications, such as metal finisher or paint sprayer, require considerable skill; they may be paid ten to thirty cents an hour more than the assembler, the largest classification. Some classifications make less than the assembler rate, including material handler and cleaner (janitor).

The higher-paying classifications are not necessarily the most popular. Indeed, workers often bid out of the assembler classification to the lower-paying ones of sub-assembler (making sub-assemblies off the main line), cleaner, and material handler—jobs where the worker has a greater degree of control over the work pace. Under the current system an opening in a classification is filled by the applicant with the most seniority, provided he or she can do the work. If there are no applicants for an opening, management can require low seniority workers to take the job or assign new-hires.

What management proposes to replace this system is reminiscent of the "shape-up." Only a very few broad classifications would exist, and within those classifications workers could be assigned at management's discretion. Workers would no longer have some rights to a specific job every day, but could be used like interchangeable parts.

WHAT IS NOT AT STAKE

1) A classification system does not prevent management from increasing or decreasing the number of people in a classification. It only requires that management abide by seniority among qualified applicants for voluntary changes or when forcing changes.

2) A classification system does not restrict management's ability to change job assignments within classifications (although other provisions of the contract may restrict this right).

3) A classification system does not prevent management from temporarily assigning employees out of their usual classifications. Normally, the company is required to pay the higher rate of pay when it does this. Some contracts limit management's ability to get around bidding requirements by abusing "temporary" exceptions.

4) A classification system does not prevent adapting to new technology. All the contracts require for adding or altering classifications is the consent of the union.

5) A classification system does not force unreasoning adherence to rules. Assemblers pick up parts that have fallen off a rack without waiting for a material handler. Many assemblers will make a repair on the spot rather than leave it for the repair station down the line. Lines between "rigid" classifications are regularly blurred *voluntarily*.

In addition, workers do not have a right to refuse a direct order from management (except under certain conditions involving safety). They are required to follow the order and then write a grievance later if they wish.

WHAT IS AT STAKE

The current classification system does not prevent a flexible approach to manufacturing, or the use of new methods. But it does provide workers individually and their union with a small amount of power. The attack on classifications is an attack on that power.

Overwhelmed by the employers' and media's assault on unions as both outmoded "special interest groups" and "too powerful," union leaders have not fought back against this attack wholeheartedly. Yet beneath the rhetoric of "flexibility" a number of crucial trade union issues are at stake:

1) Shop floor power. The only way a plant can function at all is if there is already a great deal of cooperation between workers and management. A willingness to bend the rules is necessary for the smooth functioning of the plant, as described above. Because it is so necessary, individual workers or organized groups can withhold cooperation when they're trying to get something from management or in response to harassment. One of the most important sources of influence workers have on the shop floor is the "work-to-rule"—that is, following the letter of all management's rules and provisions of the contract. If these rules and contractual provisions no longer exist, neither does this kind of shop floor power.

2) Job protection. A detailed classification system places some limits on management's ability to combine two jobs into one. Managment cannot tell an assembler to do his or her regular job *and* inspect it *and* repair it *and* sweep the floor without either getting union agreement or facing a grievance. It is therefore a protection against both speed-up and job loss.

3) Worker safety. Factories are dangerous. Continually moving workers to unfamiliar jobs only increases the danger.

4) Fair treatment. The demand for broad classifications is a disguised attack on the seniority system. When supervisors have more power to assign workers at will, seniority counts for significantly less in determining who gets the more desirable jobs, and favoritism counts a lot more. While the seniority system has many flaws, it has proven vastly superior to a system of "merit" as judged by management in providing for fair treatment.

5) A bit of work life quality. The existence of classifications means that workers have some say in choosing the kind of job they want. Many workers prefer an entirely routine operation so they are free to think about other things or listen to the radio. Others prefer jobs that involve more thought. Some prefer a "stock chaser" job which entails considerable responsibility but also considerable stress. Others prefer more physical jobs and less responsibility. Some prefer jobs that provide greater ability to vary the pace of work and some prefer jobs that pay more.

Classifications also allow workers to look forward to getting off the harder jobs and doing a job which is more manageable when they are older. It says a lot about the nature of assembly line jobs that many workers would rather clean toilets at less pay.

In and of themselves, classifications or strict work rules are not principles of unionism. In fact, unions came to rely on shop rules and classifications in the 1940's and 50's in place of other forms of shop floor power, such as a strong line steward system. Adherence to defined job classifications could be replaced by returning to such a steward system.

Similarly, the other benefits for workers provided by the classification system could be achieved in other ways. Safety could be addressed by granting workers the right to refuse jobs for which they do not feel adequately trained. Finding the most suitable job would be possible if restrictions on transferring were eased.

But management is dead set against such flexibility—for workers. As it stands now a classification system, or "job control unionism," as economist Harry Katz calls it, is the main way that union members really do have influence over their conditions of work and therefore the quality of their work lives. And it is this "job control unionism" which Katz and others urge unions to give up as part of a QWL approach.

Notes

1. Presentation at Michigan QWL Council Conference, November 19, 1984.
2. *Detroit News*, February 8, 1984.
3. *Business Week*, May 23, 1983.
4. Gerald Toth, letter to *Business Week*, May 5, 1984.
5. *Business Week*, May 23, 1983.
6. GM EPG Reference Manual, Publication SIF 331.
7. Ernest J. Savoie, "The New Ford-UAW Agreement: Its Worklife Aspects," *Work Life Review*, Issue 1, 1982. Introduction by UAW Vice-President Donald Ephlin.
8. Quoted in *UE News*, Canada, January 31, 1983.
9. Letter dated May 15, 1984. Thanks to Teamsters for a Democratic Union.
10. Quotes from a seminar presentation on "Training, Economic Development and Employment," Sacramento, California, July 2, 1984.
11. See for example, Harry C. Katz, *Shifting Gears: Changing Labor Relations in the U.S. Auto Industry*, MIT Press, 1985.

__UNDERMINING THE UNION IDEA__

*When the Union's inspiration
   through the workers' blood
   shall run,
There can be no power
   greater anywhere beneath the
   sun.
Yet what force on Earth is
   weaker than the feeble
   strength of one,
But the Union makes us
   strong.
Solidarity forever
Solidarity forever
Solidarity forever
For the union makes us
   strong.*

　　　　　　　—Ralph Chaplin

When a football team "picks apart" its opponent's defense, it doesn't look for just a single hole and then repeat a frontal assault. Instead it concentrates on finding many weak spots for small gains, until the defense completely falls apart.

So it is with the corporate attack on unionism through Quality of Work Life programs. QWL programs include no frontal assaults on unions. Quite the contrary: within QWL, employers now praise their unions for responsibility and welcome them into partnership. Responding to a question about General Motors' opening of non-union plants in the South in the 1970's, Vice-President Alfred Warren told the Michigan QWL Council:

> It was a dreadful mistake—set back our relationship with the UAW ten years.... In the 1982 agreement I had the privilege of sitting down with Owen Bieber and working out how these plants would be unionized. We are a union company....[1]

But at the same time QWL programs welcome union participation, they "pick apart" the way of thinking that makes unions possible in the first place and gives them power. Unions, after all, are essentially voluntary organizations. They are not recognized unless a majority of the employees choose to be represented, and they can be decertified by membership choice. More importantly, the union's main power—the power of collective action—depends on the willingness of its members to identify with each other, with their union, and with other workers.

QWL picks apart the beliefs that make solidarity a way of life rather than just an old union tradition saluted on ceremonial occasions. What makes QWL particularly dangerous is that it gives this attack on solidarity a union label.

__Competition__

Unionism begins with the understanding that the individual worker has very little bargaining power in dealing with an employer. As long as a large pool of unemployed workers is attempting to find jobs, the competition between workers drives wages and working conditions to the lowest possible levels. The union idea, then, is to prevent workers from undercutting each other for jobs, by establishing uniform standards within a single company and even throughout an industry. From the understanding that we can't get anywhere by competing with each other comes the union alternative—let's find ways we can advance together.

QWL promotes competition. The strongest argument most unions make for participation in QWL is that through it jobs will be saved, as workers use American ingenuity to make American industry competitive with foreign producers (especially the Japanese).

Al Hendricks, one of the United Auto Workers' representatives in charge of Employe Involvement activities at Ford, can make this argument sound like a militant attack on the company. In a tone appropriate to leading an insurrection he told union members:

> Management has been driving this company into the ground. They don't know how to run it. *We* have the know-how.... *We* can make this company competitive.

Hendricks has told union groups that QWL programs

"No one said anything about life being fair."

are "the best thing to happen in the labor movement since the sitdown strike."

No matter how militant the rhetoric, once one accepts the idea that the union's key strategy for job security is to make the company competitive, the logic becomes inescapable. Let's look at the auto industry as a perfect example of the logic of competition in practice.

The U.S. auto industry is restructuring because of new technology, competition from imports, and the "downsizing" of cars. This reorganization gives the companies a sword to hold over each plant: the threat to chop "the least competitive." LeRoy Spencer, UAW chairman at Ford's Dearborn Stamping Plant, writes:

> The threat to close plants also helps these large corporations pressure different plants into a bid war against each other for their jobs. The corporations want to cut labor costs and the workers are giving without receiving any return value.[2]

UAW workers at Ford are told that they have to beat other UAW members, their competitors at GM, Chrysler and AMC, and now Volkswagen, Toyota, Honda and Nissan. Since individual plants bid on work from both the parent corporation and outside companies, UAW workers at each Ford stamping plant are competing against workers at other Ford stamping plants.

At one QWL conference, Al Christner, then president of a GM Buick local in Flint, Michigan, proudly explained how his plant had gotten more work thanks to QWL, because Buick could underbid GM's Pontiac division. At another conference, long time union activists at a GM Oldsmobile plant were pleased to report that savings resulting from QWL enabled them to win work away from Buick.

Particularly at the local level, the job security-competition-QWL argument is the same argument as that for contract concessions.[3] It is no accident therefore that the two get mixed together.

Management at Ford's Dearborn Assembly plant showed its skilled trades EI groups a set of "confidential" figures for costs per vehicle at all its assembly plants. Dearborn Assembly was much higher than the Edison, New Jersey plant in several categories, particularly "indirect labor costs." A well-liked management official explained that he and the whole plant "looked bad" with these figures and asked for the skilled maintenance workers' help in reducing the gap. Since management salaries were not included in "indirect labor costs," the only way to save was to find ways to reduce maintenance and cleaning jobs. The manager was certain that it was possible to make big cost cuts. The proof: the Edison workers had been told they had to cut costs or be closed down, and they had then become the model for other plants to match.

How did the Edison plant do so well? *Business Week* tells part of the story:

> The more cooperative relationships fostered by EI have enabled local unions to negotiate work-rule changes with a direct impact on efficiency. At Edison, Local 980 in 1983 agreed to eliminate 220 jobs, saving $8 million,

to keep the plant competitive.[4]

The competition game, pitting members of the same union against each other, is most intense in the auto and steel industries. The public focus on foreign competition and new technology makes workers in these industries particularly vulnerable. But the competitive fever is spreading. In the telephone industry, where the notion of competition used to be a joke, a QWL newsletter now exhorts:

> ...we really don't have a lot of time to be patient about participation. Our business has changed since divestiture, and the competitive alligators are all around us. We must move more rapidly towards a participative process to meet the competitive challenge.[5]

THE WORLD'S FASTEST BRAKES

Management at GM's gear and axle plant in Detroit complained to foreman John Wojtowicz that there had been no increase in output of brake assemblies. Wojtowicz is a QWL enthusiast. His QWL group discussed the problem and figured they could boost the line speed. Wojtowicz explains:

> Since nobody else in the world is running a brake line that fast, we have been getting a lot of criticism for doing [it]. But I tell them that it was the men and women on the line who set the rate. This experience has increased the pride of all of us in our work. We want to say that we are working on the fastest moving brake line in the world and we call it the Amtrak to Toronto....

The new line speed of 560 per hour represented a 12 percent increase in productivity—more than four times what management had hoped for.[6]

*Lose-Lose

Once a local has acquired the proper competitive spirit through QWL, it is less resistant to granting the company its requests for contract concessions. Thus QWL becomes a sort of ideological grease for what local union leaders call "whipsawing," or playing off one local union against another. As Al Gardner, chairman of UAW Local 600's Tool and Die Unit, points out,

> In the end, playing this game doesn't help. All the locals at stamping plants will give concessions and in the end Ford will still close one because it has too much capacity. We will lose the jobs in one plant and maybe even more, because we will also lose jobs in the plants where we agreed to work rule changes.

The kicker, of course, is that labor cooperation or low labor costs may not even be the determining factors in management decisions about which plants to close. For every success story where a plant is supposedly saved from extinction by a QWL program (GM's Tarrytown plant is an often-used example), there are instances where corporate headquarters gave the axe to plants with the most cooperative workforces. Ford's Milpitas, California assembly plant (discussed in the previous chapter), its Michigan Casting Center, and its Sheffield, Alabama aluminum casting plant all had model EI programs before the company closed them down because of marketing or outsourcing decisions.

What makes this competition game especially dangerous is that even if the local union understands that it is rigged and that every union player will come out the loser, there is not much a local can do about it *by itself*. As the "Prisoner's Dilemma" makes clear (see box), the only way a union can win the game is through systematic communication and coordination between locals. National union structure should prevent competition between locals and provide the organization for effective collective action. The UAW constitution, for example, specifically provides that:

> The International Executive Board shall protect all Local Unions who have succeeded in establishing higher wages and favorable conditions and have superior agreements, [from] infringement by Local Unions with inferior agreements...[7]

Unfortunately, the UAW International has mainly allowed locals to fend for themselves, thus leaving them open to the companies' competitive pressure tactic.

THE PRISONER'S DILEMMA

The theoreticians of QWL are fond of game theory. Game theory is an area of social science which attempts to discover the rules which explain why certain interactions turn out the way they do. A "zero-sum" game, for example, is one where in order for one person to win, someone else has to lose the same amount. A poker game or a Presidential election are examples. A "win-win" solution, on the other hand, occurs in a two-party game when both parties come out ahead. QWL logic assumes that "win-win" solutions are the best, and claims to produce them.

One of the most famous situations explored in game theory is the Prisoner's Dilemma:

You are one of two people arrested following a bank robbery and immediately held in separate cells. The prosecutor goes to each of you and says exactly the same thing:

"We can't pin the bank robbery on you unless one of you cooperates and gives us a full confession. But if neither of you confesses we certainly can get you both on the less serious charge of driving a stolen car.

"If you confess and Other does not, you will get off free and he will get 25 years in jail. Of course, if he confesses and you do not, he will get off free and you will get 25 years. If both of you confess you will each get a 20-year sentence. If neither of you confesses you will both get 2 years for the stolen car charge."

We assume that the prosecutor has described the situation honestly and accurately, and we also assume that each prisoner will have to decide alone. No communications or deals between the prisoners are possible.

If your only concern is to do the best for yourself, your decision becomes clear when you look at the alternatives.

Your Sentence If:	You Confess	You Do Not Confess
Other Confesses	20 years	25 years
Other Does Not Confess	0 years	2 years

You might reason this way:

"Either Other confesses or he does not. In the case where he confesses, I am better off by confessing myself (I get 20 years rather than 25). But supposing he does not confess. In that case I am still better off by confessing (0 years as compared to 2). So regardless of what Other does I am better off by confessing."

That certainly is the rational self-interest way of approaching this situation. But of course Other, your former partner in crime, is also presented with the same choices. If he acts rationally he too will confess. And you will both go to prison for 20 years.

Thus the curious result: If each of you acts as isolated individuals, you end up with a poor solution for each of you and the worst solution for both of you together (serving a total of 40 years in jail). If you had had a mechanism to communicate, work out a deal, develop trust, and enforce the deal—that is, organization—your rational choice would be to stick together, refuse to confess—and serve a total of only 4 years.

Notice that it does not matter whether or not you know that the same deal is being offered to the other prisoner. It does not even matter if you know all the theory about this game. Beyond a certain elementary point, knowledge makes no difference as long as there is no way you can arrange to make and enforce some kind of deal with your fellow prisoner.[8]

And what about the "win-win" situations to which QWL practitioners point with such pride? They can best be understood as "games within games." When management proposes a "win-win" solution to a local union, it's as if the prosecutor in our Prisoner's Dilemma approached each prisoner and said, "Have I got a deal for you! If you confess, we both win. My job is easier and you will serve less time." A "win-win" solution that undercuts other local unions is really the first move toward a "win-lose" result (company wins, union loses) in a much bigger game.

Shifting the Meaning of "We"

Solidarity in the labor movement hinges on the concept of "we." QWL confuses and shifts the meaning of "we" in two ways. First, as we have just described, it encourages competition within the labor movement so that each local union sees another as "they" rather than "we." Secondly, QWL works openly to include the employer as part of the worker's definition of "we." Once this shift is made, the employer has won the game, because almost everything else flows naturally from identifying with the employer. Management understands this well.

Behavioral psychologist Charles Hughes is a promi-

nent union busting consultant. *Mother Jones* writer Ron Chernow describes one of Hughes' seminars:

> The first day's topic is how to prevent the union germ from ever entering our business. Hughes puffs gravely on a cigarette. "I would suggest that the term 'labor' be forbidden in the company." His voice chugs like a locomotive: "Management-labor, management-labor. It's teaching them the classic 'We-They' mentality of the 1930s." At IBM, Hughes tells us, you can't talk about "labor" or "employees" but only "people." "This is not word games, gang," says Hughes. "The more We-They, the more probability of a union."[9]

Howard Carlson, QWL director at GM Fisher Body, likes to tell the story of how a group of skeptical industrial engineers was convinced of the value of QWL. He introduced an hourly worker from a plant that was experimenting with "autonomous work teams."

> [The engineers] asked, "Who sets your standards? Do you know what a standard is?" She told them. "So what happens when you reach it during the day and the workday isn't over?" they asked. "Well, we keep working," she said. Somewhat surprised, they asked, "Why?" With a look of even greater surprise at the question, she responded, "We're in business to make money, aren't we?"

The sophistication of QWL lies in the fact that the company does not directly ask the worker to cross the traditional company/union line. Instead, QWL pro-

vides a convenient middle group as a new focus for group identity. In chapter 2 we saw how much of the training is devoted to establishing a new group identity as a first step to replacing identification with the union. QWL programs devote considerable resources to building group identity including distinctive names, emblems, special newsletters, friendly competitions, and social events, and their own special language, **rituals, and rules.**

For example, consultant D.L. Landen explains that in programs he installs, management or union officials who are not regular group members have to get the group's permission to attend meetings. It sounds equal. All the group members, management and union alike, develop a new sense of independent collective identity, reinforced by putting up a fence to keep out other possible identities. But the management participants continue to be directly tied in to the management structure. They report to and carry out the instructions of a superior. They do not lose their management identity. The only ties workers have to the union are voluntary, and therefore only as strong as their conscious identification with the union. Anything that breaks down that voluntary identity weakens the connection between a member and his or her union.

An Injury To 5%

One of the necessary ingredients in union solidarity is expressed by the old labor slogan, "An injury to one is an injury to all." We will not allow one member to be injured while the others stand by. Not only does division weaken us; what the boss can do to one member, he can do to any of us one by one, if we allow it.

A different idea is beginning to be heard more frequently in the labor movement, and it is associated with QWL programs. Communications Workers President Glenn Watts puts it this way:

> The QWL process then gives officers time and a mechanism to approach the concerns of the "hidden 90%" of the workforce: the members who rarely file grievances, but who are troubled by job pressures all the same.[12]

David Gromes, a local UAW financial secretary and EI facilitator, has a similar view:

> As I see it, EI is to help support those 95% of our employees in the plant who have good work records, good ideas as to how our plant and their jobs can be improved, and are looking to make our plant viable in future years.[13]

Or as UAW International Representative Al Hendricks explains:

> Before it was always the problem individual who was habitually filing grievances, the individuals who were accusing us of selling out and doing all of these bad things.... But there was 95% of our membership that we forgot about.... Now we can sit down as equals and start dealing with and representing all the membership.[14]

UE News Service

However intended, the message comes across: Our company could do well if it were not for those 5% of the workers who have bad attendance, bad attitudes, or bad ideas and are dragging us down.

Now that the companies are teaching statistics, the fallacy of the 5% solution should be much clearer. Absenteeism, "bad attitudes," or anything management defines as a problem will not occur evenly throughout the workforce. Something approximating a *normal distribution* (the "bell shaped curve" in chapter 2) is likely to exist. The stewards will always spend more time dealing with the most difficult 5% of the cases. If the union allows the company to chop these members off, then the stewards will spend their time dealing with the "worst" 5% of those remaining—until these get chopped off. And so on.

Note also that for any of these issues, there is no independently determined acceptable standard. What is "bad" is simply defined as whatever the lowest 5% do. If everyone were to improve, 5% could still be considered problems. Absenteeism (a "problem" tackled by many QWL programs) is a good example. Over the past several years, absenteeism in the auto plants has declined considerably. Yet the Big Three continue to push for still harsher absentee control programs.

Fighting for the 5% of union members who are squeaky wheels is an essential way that unions defend *every* member's conditions in the same way that *everyone's* civil liberties or democratic rights depend on protecting the rights of minorities. The conditions for the vast majority are set by the conditions that the union establishes for a minority. Conversely, management wins most of its flexibility in the same way. It continually tests its limits by pushing at the edges first. It pushes in lots of places and counts on the union not being able to defend all of them, which is why unions have to spend so much time defending the 5%.

By endorsing the notion that 5% of the work force are the problem, union leaders open the door for company attempts to pit worker against worker in QWL. As with the training exercises described in chapter 3, attempts at solving production problems often lead to pointing the finger at individuals. QWL creates an atmosphere where workers are in effect encouraged to snitch on others not in the group. Skilled trades workers may blame production workers for mistreating or even sabotaging machines. Production workers blame lazy maintenance workers for machine breakdowns.[15]

QWL and Scabbing

If QWL suggests that 5% of union members should be edged out of the definition of "we," it also tries to keep in a few who should be pushed out. In union tradition there is nothing worse than a scab—a union member who crosses the picket line. Unions usually attempt to isolate and pay back scabs to establish sanctions against further scabbing. The way QWL programs deal with scabbing says a lot about the relationship of QWL to unionism.

In August 1983, the Communications Workers struck the AT&T/Bell system nationwide for three weeks. Since this was just prior to the breakup of the Bell system, the contract and strike were exceptionally important, to establish the terms telephone workers would carry with them to the new companies.

After the strike, the QWL program continued. One study looked at two QWL groups which contained CWA members who had crossed the picket lines during the strike. In both cases, the issue of scabbing caused considerable conflict within the groups, but each finally decided to continue functioning with the strikebreaker as a member.

> The team faced a major crisis early in its existence when a member who returned to work during the strike wanted to continue with the team. It took a considerable amount of time for the members to get over their personal hostilities and resolve this issue. This issue would have destroyed the team and the QWL in this office had it not been for the active and strong intervention of the resource person.[16]

Note that the issue of working in cooperation with a strikebreaker is reduced to the level of "personal hostilities." Note also that the role of the supposedly neutral resource person is to protect the QWL institution even where doing so undermines the union.   □

Notes

1. Speech, Michigan QWL Council, November 10, 1983.
2. *Ford Facts*, October 29, 1984.
3. See Jane Slaughter, *Concessions and How To Beat Them*, Labor Education and Research Project, 1983.
4. *Business Week*, July 30, 1984.
5. John Bruce, *QWL*, Newsletter of Area Code 216, Ohio Bell/CWA, June 1984.
6. John Simmons and William Mares, *Working Together*, Alfred A. Knopf, 1983, p. 71.
7. Article 19, Section 6, UAW Constitution.
8. There are many books and articles which examine the Prisoner's Dilemma. See, for example, Douglas R. Hofstadter, "Metamagical Themas," *Scientific American*, May 1983.
9. *Mother Jones*, May 1980.
10. *Personnel*, July-August 1978.
11. D.L. Landen, speech, February 15, 1985.
12. *Workplace Democracy*, Summer 1982.
13. *The Work Life Review*, March 1983.
14. *Labor Studies Journal*, Winter 1984.
15. See, for example, Robert J. Thomas, "Participation and Control," CRSO Working Paper #315, University of Michigan, 1984.
16. "The Quality of Work Life Process of AT&T and the Communications Workers of America," draft, January 1984, sponsored by U.S. Dept. of Labor.

LOSS OF UNION LEADERS

Rick Merrelli has a solid union background. His father, George, was a Regional Director of the United Auto Workers and a member of the union's International Executive Board. Merrelli worked at GM's Warren, Michigan transmission plant for 13 years, most of that time as an alternate union committeeman. He is knowledgeable, talented, and presents himself well. In 1983, the UAW appointed Merrelli to a fulltime job as facilitator for Employe Participation Groups. In October 1984 Rick Merrelli applied for a job in General Motors management.

Two Roads

Competent, dedicated leadership is part of the strength of a union. Unlike management, most local unions do not attract leadership by offering more money. In fact, the best union leaders have abilities that could get them far more money in management or in other jobs outside the union movement. They choose to work for the union because they believe in unionism.

Active QWL participants, group leaders and facilitators are frequently dedicated union members with initiative and drive. Unions must continually attract such potential leaders. The unions compete directly with management, which seeks to attract these same people to its own ranks. Here QWL is a gold mine for management and a disaster area for the union. Since QWL focuses on management problems using management tools, it provides a convenient way for the employer to encourage and observe management skills among workers.

In addition, QWL makes other union jobs less attractive and less important. QWL is "in." It gets the new meeting rooms, the conferences, the travel. Since the company channels "goodies" through QWL, its participants get the successes and the gratitude. The union is left with the dirty jobs and the company's hard side. Part of the QWL message is that the old way of doing things, and by extension, the old people doing them, are no longer relevant. To the extent that QWL gets its message across, it demoralizes current union leaders and makes it difficult to recruit new ones.

At the same time, the structure of most QWL programs tends to drive participants into management's arms. This is most apparent with those union members who are put in charge of organizing and implementing QWL programs, the facilitators. (Other frequently used titles are trainer, coordinator, adviser, leader, and internal consultant.) Usually union facilitators are paired with ones from management. In a typical QWL program, all the pressures and inducements line up to push the facilitator away from the union and down the management path.

LOSING UNION INFLUENCE

In theory the QWL facilitator, as the name suggests, is a neutral force who only helps the groups do what they want to do. But every facilitator knows that he or she is much more. The facilitator is a leader in the groups because he or she is an expert, an authority figure. Participants look to the facilitator for guidance about what is possible, where to get resources, who has power to change things, and what other QWL groups have done. The facilitator's guidance often determines the outcome of a project.

Even the simplest techniques can increase the facilitator's influence. Facilitators are trained that *how* they record ideas on a flip chart, for example, can give direction to a group. The facilitator can draw out, reinterpret, or emphasize ideas he or she believes to be important. Likewise, ideas deemed destructive can be downplayed by jotting them down quickly and leaving them confused.

The facilitator is the main (and often the only) union person who knows what all the QWL groups are doing. He or she is the one person who has the most individual contact with union members. Where QWL programs have gotten off the ground, the number of union members who attend weekly QWL meetings usually far exceeds the number of members who attend monthly union meetings. Except when a worker is in trouble, most of the contacts between union officers and members are brief, taking place on work or break time. The facilitator, on the other hand, spends at least an hour a week in sometimes intense discussion with fellow union members.

When the QWL facilitator is not part of the union leadership team, the union loses an important source of influence.

1) Facilitator training is management training. It is based on materials developed for business schools and is often conducted by management consultants who have simply added QWL to their shingle. The main modification they make for QWL purposes is to increase the number of group identification techniques so that everyone identifies more strongly with "the organization" (which turns out to be interchangeable with "the company").

Facilitators' training is an exaggerated version of that given rank and file QWL participants. The sessions are longer, the accommodations often more luxurious. GM's Hydra-matic Division, for example, held "Family

Facilitator Training'' at the Shanty Creek Hilton Resort in northern Michigan. According to one participant, some facilitators were housed in rooms with fully stocked bars, natural fireplaces and Jacuzzis. The rates posted on some suite doors were hundreds of dollars per day. The training was run by management from Hydra-matic Division; there was no one present from the UAW International.

During training, facilitators are immersed in a management view of the world. A training problem called the Bagel Hockey Case, for example, comes from business school management courses. Groups read a description of the background and operation of a cafeteria. In the problem the manager enters the kitchen and discovers several of her employees playing a game of hockey with a stale bagel. The training groups then discuss what she should do. The main alternatives discussed are ''reprimand them'' or ''fire them.'' Facilitator training does not include information on the union contract, union procedures, or union history—much less a union outlook.

As part of the supposedly joint UAW-GM QWL training program, union facilitators are given a one-and-a-half inch looseleaf notebook, *The Employee Participation Groups Reference Manual,* published by General Motors Education and Training.[1] Of the 250 pages in the manual, one page consists of ''Seven Points'' by retired UAW Vice-President Irving Bluestone. The rest is material prepared by GM itself, organizational development techniques from the *Annual Handbook for Group Facilitators*, and reprints from management journals including *Personnel Journal, Quality Progress, Industrial Engineering, Training and Development Journal, The Internal Auditor*, the American Management Association's *Organizational Dynamics, Human Resource Management*, and the *Wall Street Journal*. The Resources section of the manual refers the facilitator to 41 articles and 16 books. Of these, at most six articles are written from a union point of view.

The facilitator training programs in other industries are not as blatantly one-sided. The United Steelworkers and a few other unions have made limited attempts to provide separate union training for their facilitators. But the unions are far outgunned by the employers, who can draw on seemingly unlimited resources. On the whole, facilitator training is management training.

2) Formal union authority over facilitators is weak. Few QWL agreements specify that facilitators are directly chosen by or responsible to the union. In fact, the term *hourly* facilitator is generally used rather than *union* facilitator to diminish direct union authority.

In the General Motors program the practice had been for the local union leadership to appoint hourly QWL personnel. But new guidelines drawn up after the 1984 contract gave that authority to the local ''joint'' steering committee. In the Ford program, the official rules clearly state that the hourly facilitator works under and is responsible to the company EI Administrator. An hourly facilitator is not chosen until after the company EI administrator has made the program operational, severely limiting the influence that the union facilitator might have in shaping the program. Until the 1984 contract, the company had final authority over selection or removal of hourly facilitators.[2]

3) Management offers perks to facilitators. QWL functionaries attend many conferences—and those facilitators whom management considers successful can go to the better conferences and go more often. Shortly after Charlotte Eatmon was appointed QWL coordinator at a GM plant, a management person welcomed her. Now that she was a ''reflection'' on the company, he said, she should feel free to make use of a company Cadillac.

Moving from a production job to a facilitator's job can be a large improvement in the quality of one's own work life. *Business Week* describes EI facilitator Leon Bradford at Ford's Edison, New Jersey plant:

> He hated the boredom, the dictatorial foremen and—most of all—the "environment of hostility" between labor and management.... Bradford floundered on the line for 13 years, often missed work and got into trouble with foremen. But finally in 1982 he was appointed to represent UAW Local 980 in coordinating the EI program at Edison.... Now he is enthusiastic about his job.[3]

The facilitator job can be one of the best jobs an industrial worker can get: clean clothes, interesting work, self-pacing, human contact and expense-paid travel, as long as you don't rock the company's boat.

4) Whether the facilitator's job is hard or easy depends primarily on management. Facilitators do not have a staff. They depend on management cooperation for an office, a telephone, typing and photocopying. If facilitators take their job seriously and try to get resources for the groups, or to get group proposals implemented, they need management cooperation.

On the other hand, management can load facilitators down with red tape and details. One facilitator who had fallen from company grace had to spend hours hand-collating materials because no one would authorize use of the automatic collater. Another facilitator spent many days trying to find a management person who was both willing and able to authorize a trivial payment necessary for one group's project.

5) The facilitator has few union resources to draw on. If he or she runs into a problem in QWL, it will be difficult to find an expert higher up in the union. The UAW's GM department, for example, has only three staffers assigned to QWL, and they often must work on other union tasks. The tendency is for the facilitator to turn to the source that does have expertise—management.

6) The facilitator often has little backing from the local union and may even face hostility. Under most arrangements, the facilitator is not part of the local union team. He or she is often in the position of choosing between past union practices and the desires of a QWL group. As the QWL program undercuts local union stewards and officers, the facilitator takes the heat, but the union provides no alternatives.

Thinking Like Management

All of these pressures are interrelated. The lack of strong union ties allows the company to play off the facilitator against the local union. Because the facilitator is not elected and does not have the union's backing, his or her authority can only come from "getting things done," which, in turn, requires developing good relations with people in management who have the power. The training encourages the facilitator to think and talk in management terms. The facilitator begins to act like a junior foreman. This

again widens the gap with union stewards and officers. And the facilitator may end up identifying with his or her management counterpart instead of with the union. One top Postal Service official is very proud of this: "After a couple of months of training you can not tell them apart."[4]

A Roosevelt University labor studies instructor, Jack Metzgar, describes a union-appointed facilitator from the International Brotherhood of Electrical Workers who came to speak to a class and brought along his company counterpart. When he arrived, the union facilitator asked the instructor not to tell the class who was union and who was company. One of the plusses of the program, according to this facilitator, was that the class would not be able to tell which was which. (The class did figure it out, however.)

"Won't keep you a minute, Schmidt — just like you to participate in the following decisions."

Dick Danjin, union coordinator of an extensive QWL program at GM's gear and axle plant in Detroit, describes how he views his role:

> [The company QWL coordinator's] job is to fight off management and mine is to fight the union politicians. We share everything and we have become literally one person.[5]

QWL's inducements and sanctions combine to exert a powerful pressure that can influence even workers with strong union backgrounds. Bob Roth had been a militant union committeeman, fired several times for leading wildcat strikes, before taking the job of union QWL coordinator at Buick Flint. Now he says:

> It is a new revelation of one's own personality when you are given a responsibility for something you are not sure you believe in, and suddenly you accept the change and strive to make it work. I know—I have had that experience—and I am quite a different person from the guy I was two years ago...[6]

A UAW local president thought he had the situation under control:

> I knew the dangers of the program. I appointed the strongest union person in the local. It was amazing. In six months he thinks like company. We're still friends but we can't talk about the union.

The company has an additional magnet: it offers a road for further advancement. Despite the short time that QWL programs have included significant numbers of union facilitators, there are already many examples of the position being a steppingstone directly to management.

Bill Lowry was vice-president of Steelworkers Local 2227 when he became the union facilitator for the Labor Management Participation Team program. When the union leadership and all but four members stopped participating in LMPT as a protest against job elimination, Lowry stayed on as facilitator. He later pressed internal union charges against the local president on some election technicalities, and then quit to go into industrial sales. Ken Alexander was a UAW committeeman who became a local union-appointed QWL coordinator. He resigned that job to become the company QWL coordinator for GM's entire Hydra-matic Division, at an estimated salary of $65,000 a year.

When facilitators have lost their union identity and are not a part of the union team, they frequently develop into a separate powerful political force within the union to protect their positions and interests. Facilitators are in an excellent position for union politics, since they usually have freedom to move around, get to know lots of members, and can dispense perks ranging from recogniton to trips. Even where facilitators are not allowed to run for office themselves, the possibility of playing "king-maker" may be too tempting to pass up.

The extensive QWL program at the GM gear and axle plant has gained the reputation for "empire building" and is a political force in the local at odds with the elected union shop committee. A member of the National Association of Letter Carriers points out how the QWL program is likely to change the nature of that union's politics. The NALC has been a relatively open and democratic union. But facilitators are being appointed by business agents and will soon outnumber full time union officers and be a substantial bloc at union conventions.

A Union Team Approach

Despite all the pressures, many QWL facilitators remain exceptionally dedicated union people. They became facilitators to improve conditions for workers and seek to stay involved in the union. They frequently "burn out" in the facilitator job rather than take the company path of least resistance.

In several instances local unions have taken steps to make the facilitator part of the union team. At Ford Local 600 facilitators meet regularly with the union leadership or participate in unit executive board meetings. The local president, Bob King, and union coordinator Rick Martin have firmly asserted the local's authority over the facilitators and have defined the job to include working for union interests in QWL. At the same time the local offers union training and support for facilitators.

Some union leaders expected resistance from facilitators to these measures. But most facilitators were pleased to be taken seriously by the union, given clear roles and clear expectations, and offered support. One described his view:

> We're left out there hanging. No one knows what we are supposed to do. No matter what it is I do, somebody damns me and nobody backs me up. I'm not company. But until now I didn't know what the union wanted.

In at least one case, the fulltime QWL facilitators themselves initiated a tighter relationship with the union. When UAW Local 909 appointed coordinators Charlotte Eatmon and Al Welker and some new facilitators in 1983, one of their first priorities was to schedule a conference for all the union officers, stewards, and union facilitators, to develop a common understanding and a collective approach to QWL.

Chapter 10 includes more examples of the union team approach to QWL. □

FACILITATOR: A UNION DEFINITION

Management may be unhappy when the union defines the union-appointed facilitator's job. GM management, for example, became upset when Wendy Thompson, a UAW Local 235 committeeperson (steward), put out a leaflet asking for nominees for plant Trainer (facilitator). In the leaflet Thompson included her view of the duties of the Trainer. Most are simply duties of every good union member:

- To represent the union within the Quality of Work Life Concept and work with the District committeeperson as a team.
- To attend all [QWL] meetings.... To help each [group leader] solve that group's problems in order to create a better working environment.
- To report regularly to the committeeperson about problems that continue without solution.
- To make the committeeperson aware when her presence is needed in Circle meetings.
- To organize weekly [group leader] meetings.
- To attend General Membership meetings....
- To represent the Union and Plant 3 members at any plant-wide QWL meeting or off-site QWL meeting.
- To have knowledge of employee rights under the contract so as to serve as a watchdog against management abuse of [QWL].

We need someone who is aggressive and dedicated to making sure work becomes a more satisfying experience.[7]

This sign decorates Ford's Ypsilanti, Michigan plant.

TRAINING FACILITATORS AT FORD:
A Course in Basketmaking

The "Annual Body and Assembly EI Coordinators' Conference" in December 1984 opened with the *Acme Basket* exercise. All coordinators and facilitators—both union and management—for Ford's B&A Division were set to work constructing baskets by stapling strips of paper together. Each basket-making department included several job classifications: supervisor, cutter, stapler operator, supplier, quality control, maintenance and clerk. According to the instructions:

> The basket department of Acme has a straightforward goal: to keep the rest of the organization well supplied with baskets which are used to transport material from one place to another. The demand for baskets within the organization is steady, so your department has been established to supply the baskets at lower costs than obtainable from outside vendors.

After producing baskets for a while, the participants realized that they could produce more if they deviated from the traditional organization of production. For example, the supervisor was generally unnecessary. The instructions provided that when a stapler ran out or jammed, the operator was to call the supervisor, who then called the maintenance person. Clearly, it was much faster if the operators fixed their own staplers. And production was increased if the operators also did quality control.

According to the session's instructor, William Passmore of Case Western Reserve University, the basket-making exercise demonstrates the virtues of "Socio-Technical Systems" (STS) in industry. Roughly translated this means organizing the work and workplace control around production teams, which may be self-managing.

For many industrial relations planners STS is the next step in employee participation programs. We will look at the substance of STS in chapter 11. Here we are concerned with how the company used the EI program, and specifically the facilitators, to try to introduce changes in working conditions established by the union.

Ford used a "neutral" consultant to introduce such major changes as abolishing classifications, having operators do their own repairs, and having teams set their own production goals and discipline each other. STS was presented as the logical continuation of the EI program. Facilitators were taught STS the same way they learned brainstorming or improved listening skills—as though it were just a technical issue.

It made sense for Ford to use the EI conference because, aside from the union facilitators themselves, there was no UAW presence. Management ran the conference—the appearance of UAW international reps for the opening and closing sessions just legitimized what went on in between. Where facilitators have little union experience and where the union is not vigilant, such innovations as STS can first be introduced as QWL-type experiments. If the company can win facilitators to the concept, management will have an important toehold when it presses for the changes in contract bargaining.

At the B&A Division conference many of the facilitators did buy in to STS. But some had strong union backgrounds and protested the presentation and its implications. Consultant Passmore apparently was used to giving his presentation only to management people. He was surprised at the response, and immediately began backpedaling:

> I don't say this is the way it has to be. If I did that we would be back to the traditional design system. Let the groups decide.

Of course, letting the groups decide is hardly a protection for union rights. A system where each individual or small group decides for itself undermines the solidarity and unity which is necessary for the union to protect everyone.

Notes

1. Publication SIF 331, revised June 1983.
2. ''Guidelines for Hourly Employes as EI Facilitators,'' January 16, 1984, Attachment to Letter 12 from UAW-Ford Joint National Committee on EI.
3. *Business Week*, July 2, 1984.
4. Eugene Hagburg, U.S. Postal Service Employee Involvement Process, Co-Chair, remarks at Federal Sector Conference, August 24, 1983.
5. John Simmons and William Mares, *Working Together*, Alfred A. Knopf, 1983, p. 72.
6. Speech at Buick-UAW QWL Seminar, October 2, 1981, quoted in Albert Verri, *The New Industrial Relations*, M.A. thesis, Roosevelt University, December 12, 1983.
7. Leaflet, November 1984.

HOPING FOR THE UNEXPECTED

Unions have responded to the challenge of QWL in a variety of ways. We look at these responses and their results in the next two chapters. In this chapter we take a brief look at the "strategy" which many unions have adopted by default because they are not sure what to do—that is, let the process unfold and see what will happen. What makes this strategy particularly interesting is that it is often attached to a militant-sounding theory.

Empowerment

A number of trade unionists and social scientists who favor more worker control in the workplace believe that QWL can be a step toward "full democratic participation" or even "workers' control." They urge unions to participate in QWL and let the process play itself out. Many recognize that whatever the claims about participation, management still controls the process. But the QWL experience is important, they say, because it "empowers" workers—it allows them to discover that they are, in fact, capable people who could manage themselves if only given a chance. Therefore, the argument goes, although management may have intended QWL to get workers to identify more closely with the company and its management, one of the most important effects of QWL is that workers, now feeling "empowered," will demand even more control and autonomy.

Although the argument is often smothered in jargon (see box), it contains two important ideas for the labor movement.

One is the idea that management's plans don't always work out the way they were originally intended—they have "unanticipated consequences." The example usually cited is the company unions of the 1930's, which often became the organizing centers for real unions.

The second is the idea that after a taste of power, people gain a new sense of what they want and what they can achieve. In the case of QWL-type programs, presumably the thinking works something like that of the British shop steward who explained:

> We are getting more out of our work. But it can't end here. You can't open men's minds and let them stagnate. The amount of work in this plant that can still be taken over by the men is tremendous. Control by the worker is inevitable. We are capable of running and controlling this plant. Obviously the next step for us is to have more involvement in the broader decision making.[2]

Unfortunately, QWL rarely works out this way in practice. When QWL programs come up against their built-in limitations, they usually just wither away and leave the participants feeling frustrated and weak, not strong and ready to demand more as the theory would suggest.

Why doesn't QWL work the way the sociologists predict?

First, the analogy with company unions misses a critical point. The company unions that management founded in the 1930's became real unions for a reason: the real unions continued to organize. On the outside,

---

IN THE LANGUAGE OF SOCIOLOGY

An article from *Sociological Inquiry* spells out the "empowerment" theory:

The theoretical perspective developed here suggests that the new RWA [Relative Worker Autonomy] labor process, like earlier systems, resolves some of the strains engendered by conventional structures, but in its very solution sets into motion other forces producing a new fundamental strain...

[Other analyses] suggest that RWA projects generate increased worker competencies, expectations, and desires for job challenge, autonomy, and—in our interpretation—self governance. These in the long run are inconsistent with the institutional boundaries of authority in the new RWA system. When these new desires are not fulfilled, their frustration gives rise to increased worker hostility toward, and alienation from, management.

Put most simply, the relative autonomy in the labor process required to reduce worker alienation and increase worker integration also "empowers" workers psychologically to seek wider autonomy in the workplace, thereby placing strains on the existing boundaries of authority. This ultimately gives rise to labor-management conflicts over workplace control and consequently to worker disintegration from the firm.

By *psychological empowerment* is meant a heightened sense of competence by workers, a sense that they are technically and socially capable of self management on the shop floor, a new desire for wider autonomy and self governance in the workplace, and the growth of the sense of entitlement to worker's control over production ....[1]

SELF-BREADING CHICKEN

WE TRY TO MAKE IT FUN FOR THEM.

P.S. Mueller © 1985

by their independence and activity, they showed what was possible. At the same time they developed a network of union supporters within the company unions who could "push the system" to show its contradictions.

Where is the equivalent today? Today there is as yet no organized attempt by unions to change QWL into something the employers didn't bargain for. The leaders of unions which participate in QWL show not the slightest interest in "pushing the system." Just the opposite, they appear to have the same goals for QWL that management does. When a QWL program turns sour in one workplace, international union leaders and management often try to sweep the whole affair under the rug. The more union leaders invest in QWL as a strategy and in QWL's organizational perks, the more they feel obligated to protect it from challenge and to isolate its critics.

The UAW-GM program is a case in point. Numerous problems bubbled to the surface in 1983 and several locals withdrew from the program. Although UAW publications covered QWL successes in glowing terms, they did not mention, let alone discuss, the problems so the membership could learn from the experience. Information about the pull-outs spread only through gossip and the media.[3]

Nor did the UAW organize leadership meetings to get a union handle on what was going on. The matter was handled through the joint GM/UAW National Committee on the Quality of Worklife, which was obviously committed to QWL as a starting point. The joint committee assigned a company-union team to make a study and recommendations. Not surprisingly, the main findings were that "wherever there was a problem... the underlying cause was a poor union/management relationship." The team suggested that more joint activities were the solution.[4] The answer to problems with QWL was—more QWL.

Second, it is by no means clear that the participants in QWL do feel "empowered." A study initiated by the AFL-CIO Industrial Union Department interviewed in depth 900 workers in five separate programs. Although the authors themselves were clearly favorable to QWL programs, the data they gathered throws serious doubt on the "empowerment" value of QWL.

The authors asked workers how much say they felt

they had in areas which are typical QWL concerns, such as "the way the work is done," "the quality of the work," and "how fast the work should be done." In the four blue collar operations, less than a majority felt they had even "some say" in these areas. In the fifth case (Newspaper Guild members) just over 50% felt they had at least "some say." Further, there were no significant differences in the sense of influence between QWL participants and non-participants.[5]

All Power To The Company

Sometimes QWL brings a new sense of personal power, as when a circle prepares and gives a presentation to senior management officials, and then chats informally with them in the executive conference room. The contact with and recognition by such powerful individuals can be a heady experience. More important, some changes may even take place as a result. QWL recognition systems are designed so that credit is given lavishly and the sense of accomplishment is magnified. Many such presentations are described in plant or QWL newsletters, complete with pictures.

But QWL is carefully designed so that any sense of power an individual gets from the experience is company power—not union power. The lesson is that QWL gets things done not because *workers* are capable by themselves or collectively, but because they have cooperated with management. Your influence comes from your friendly, first name, cooperative relationship with management. That is the message drummed in during the training sessions and the weekly QWL activities. If the cooperation breaks down, there is no power, no influence.

This can be seen when, for whatever reason, no management person is present at a circle meeting. Rarely does the circle carry on. It usually feels weak and frustrated; if it discusses anything at all as a group, it is how to get more management participation. The learned feeling is that without management there is no power.

At most workplaces QWL is organized by forming groups one at a time to deal with different issues. This

" Any more objections to my proposition?"

means that groups tend to come up against different limitations at different times. Each group ends up dealing with these institutional limitations as if they were the small group's problems or even personality difficulties, not union problems.

And if a group or an individual does try to challenge these limitations of QWL, as the "empowerment" model suggests? The attitude of QWL's backers, both union and managment, is usually, "QWL is voluntary. You don't have to participate if you don't like it." They may add, "The problem is not QWL—you just don't know how to get along." The message becomes: "QWL isn't the failure—you're the failure." Hardly a sense of empowerment.

There is, however, one way that workers have actually gotten some power through QWL. In many companies local managements are under orders to establish QWL-type programs. This provides the union some bargaining power: it can respond to a company action it doesn't like by threatening to pull out of QWL. The union at one GM Hydra-matic plant temporarily shut down its QWL program and other joint activities to force management to implement the new local contract.

Unfortunately, higher levels of the union may take away even this power. A policy letter to all UAW GM local unions states:

> Locals should not cancel a QWL Program as a means of punishing management when all they are doing is denying a contractual benefit that we demanded to be provided for our membership.[6]

In response to a number of major cases of anti-union activity by AT&T, the 1982 Communications Workers convention resolved "that CWA practice a policy of non-cooperation with AT&T and its affiliated companies so long as the company's anti-CWA policies continue." But CWA President Glenn Watts has stated that the resolution does not apply to QWL.[7]

Perhaps with aggressive union organizing, the QWL experience might result in a collective sense of "empowerment." But the more common result is summed up by Shirley Martin, a United Garment Workers Union member at a Levi Strauss plant near Knoxville, Tennessee:

> Ever since we got QWL, and the union backslapping with management, we feel like we lost the right to fight the company. □

Notes

1. Charles Derber and William Schwartz, "Toward a Theory of Worker Participation," *Sociological Inquiry*, Winter 1983.

2. Cited by Derber and Schwartz.

3. See Ann M. Job, *Detroit News*, January 8, 1984.

4. William Horner and Howard Carlson, *Report*, February 28, 1984.

5. Thomas A. Kochan, Harry C. Katz, and Nancy R. Mower, *Worker Participation and American Unions*, W.E. Upjohn Institute for Employment Research, 1984, p. 113.

6. Letter #746, November 11, 1983, from Vice-President Donald Ephlin.

7. Ronnie Straw and Charles Heckscher, "QWL: New Working Relationships in the Communications Industry," *Labor Studies Journal*, Winter 1984.

THE COLLECTIVE BARGAINING LINE

"Keep Quality of Work Life separate from collective bargaining!" This is the single most important, and in some cases the only, strategy that most unions have for dealing with the new participation programs. Yet a careful examination of this idea shows that it is almost never practiced, few QWL practitioners believe in it, and it has caused massive confusion. Far from being an important tool for unions, it works mainly against unions and for the employers. Since understanding the relationship between QWL and bargaining is central to developing any union strategy toward QWL programs, we will go into it in some detail.

The Collective Bargaining Declaration

Virtually all union-endorsed QWL programs contain contractual statements or guidelines which insist that these programs be kept strictly separate from the collective bargaining process. For example, the "Statement of Principles on Quality of Work Life" from the Joint CWA/AT&T National Committee declares:

QWL efforts must be viewed as a supplement to the collective bargaining process. The integrity of the collective bargaining process, the contractual rights of the parties and the working of the grievance procedure must be upheld and maintained.

The *EI Handbook II* issued by the UAW-Ford National Joint Committee on Employee Involvement states:

Right up front we should reaffirm that EI and collective bargaining matters are separate. If EI Teams raise issues that fall within collective bargaining, the Team leader can pass those on to the responsible supervisor or committee person.

These policy statements seem to mean that issues which can properly be taken up in the regular collective bargaining process should be left to that process. QWL should instead, as President Glenn Watts of the CWA put it, extend union "influence into the murky territory of 'management prerogatives,' helping to shape management practices and policies while they are being formed rather than after the fact."[1]

Both company and union representatives publicly affirm the separation. General Motors Vice-President Al Warren reminds us:

We have two different systems in relationship to our unions and our hourly people. One of those is certainly the quality of work life concept. The other is the collec-

---

OPEN AGENDA

The United Steelworkers is one of the few unions which did not start out by asserting that its QWL program was strictly separate from bargaining issues. The USW's formal policy is what almost all unions have come to in practice. The contract language establishing Labor-Management Participation Teams specifically encourages discussion of several collective bargaining issues:

Appropriate subjects among others, which a Team might consider include: use of production facilities; quality of products and quality of the work environment; safety and environmental health; scheduling and reporting arrangements; absenteeism and overtime; incentive coverage and yield; job alignments; contracting out; and energy conservation and transportation pools...

A Participation Team shall be free to consider a full range of responses to implemented performance improvements including, but not limited to, such items as bonus payments or changes in incentive performance pay.

"Anything can be put on an LMPT agenda, except a grievance or a change in the Basic Steel Labor Agreement," says Sam Camens, who directs the program for the Steelworkers.[3]

---

tive bargaining procedure.... The only time I have seen us come close to near failure is when some management and some union began to intermix those two to the degree where the attempt is made to replace the collective bargaining procedure by the QWL concept.[2]

The Collective Bargaining Line and the Law

Many unionists are under the mistaken impression that there are issues which can be tackled in QWL which cannot legally be taken up in collective bargaining. In fact, any issue which could come up in a QWL circle could also be discussed in bargaining. In either case it depends solely on whether the company and the union are willing to talk about the question.

The National Labor Relations Act (NLRA), which regulates bargaining, does makes a distinction between *mandatory* and *permissible* bargaining issues. (Note that this discussion applies to workers covered by the NLRA and not, for example, to government workers.) The NLRA requires management to negotiate about certain issues, specifically "wages, hours, and other terms and conditions of employment." These cover a lot of territory. But beyond these issues, the law *allows* unions and management to negotiate about any subject and to make any agreement as long as the agreement itself is not illegal.

For example, it would be possible for the union and

"VIEWPOINT"

THE EMPLOYER TRIES TO MAKE THE CONTRACT MEAN AS LITTLE AS POSSIBLE!

THE UNION TRIES TO MAKE IT MEAN AS MUCH AS POSSIBLE!

From the February 1949 issue of *Ammunition*, **the UAW magazine.**

the company to negotiate what products the company should produce, prices to be charged, quality standards for those products, or what colors the products should be. (However, since these are permissible, not mandatory, issues, if the company chooses not to negotiate about them, it would be considered an unfair labor practice for a union to "bargain to impasse" or strike over them.)

Even the distinction between mandatory and permissible issues is not firm. Although recent court decisions may be reversing the trend, over the years the tendency has been for the mandatory category to broaden considerably. For example, it is now considered mandatory for employers to bargain over contracting out.[4]

In practice unions can bargain effectively over permissible topics. Since bargaining is usually over package deals, it would be difficult for a company to prove that a strike was over a permissible issue. For example, one of the chief demands of the UAW in the 1979 auto negotiations was an increase in pensions for already-retired workers. Legally, this was clearly not a mandatory bargaining issue, but the UAW pressed and won its demand. QWL programs themselves probably fall in the permissible category, and yet they are now major contract items.

Sometimes management, or union officers, will cite a "management rights" clause in the contract as the reason certain issues cannot be addressed in bargaining. But such clauses do not confer divine rights or even legal rights. They are merely a statement that the company takes everything the union doesn't get in the contract. The Ford-UAW contract contains a typical clause:

> The Company retains the sole right to manage its business, including [a long list ranging from plant location to raw materials and machinery selection to assigning, transferring or promoting employes]; *subject only to such regulations and restrictions governing the exercise of these rights as are expressly provided in this Agreement.* [emphasis added]

Anything can be taken from management's rights simply by using the collective bargaining procedure. Anything the company can be convinced (or forced) to give away, it can give through union channels at contract time, or between contracts, just as legally as it can grant changes through QWL.

The Collective Bargaining Line in Practice

If we examine what QWL circles actually do, we see that many of the issues they deal with have traditionally been handled by unions in some form of collective bargaining. In fact most issues that would affect a worker's "quality of work life" come under the heading of "working conditions" and therefore could be bargaining issues. Virtually all of the items listed in the box are the kinds of issues handled by stewards, health and safety representatives, or union officers, either informally, through the grievance procedure, through letters of understanding, or through bargaining for the local contract.

A study of the QWL program descriptions in the U.S. Labor Department's *Resource Guide to Labor-Management Cooperation* found that about 50% explicitly dealt with mandatory bargaining subjects. Moreover, an additional 26% apparently dealt with such subjects even though they had guidelines stating they were excluded.[6]

Even limited quality circle programs which start out by focusing only on suggestions for improving product quality tend to try to maintain themselves by casting wider nets for issues. They end up talking about working conditions as well. Many observers have noted this shift. Michael Brower, author of the U.S. Department of Labor pamphlet "Starting Labor-Management Quality of Work Life Programs," remarks:

> ...early Circle organizers restricted attention to problems directly related to productivity and quality. This narrow focus does not maintain worker interest. Increasingly I find Circle facilitators drawing the lesson, and orienting to the broader concerns handled in QWL programs.[7]

And Kim Smith, former labor relations director for the National Association of Manufacturers, says:

> Companies using the concept will move slowly toward broader quality of worklife programs that include issues such as health and safety... If I were in the unions' shoes, I'd be concerned. Quality circles are trying to achieve a lot of things that are traditional union objectives.[8]

WHAT DO QWL CIRCLES DO?

A study of the joint Communications Workers of America/AT&T QWL program examined ten local QWL efforts in depth.[5] It is one of the few systematic studies of a major corporation's QWL program. Following is a list of the items worked on by the circles. Anyone with experience as a local union official or steward would recognize almost all these issues as mandatory bargaining subjects and indeed as topics often found in local union agreements.

Case 1

"a group of 'environmental concerns': break area facilities, improving air conditioning, reducing noise, etc. In addition the group was helpful in distributing information about the massive changes which were facing the workforce during [AT&T's] divestiture process. Managers met with the team on several occasions to explain pending changes, and the team then relayed this information to the work group."

Case 2

—clarification of standards for the handling of customer accounts
—building a break-time patio
—other projects which "pertain more to the work environment (including occupational health and safety concerns)..."

Case 3

—social issues (umbrella committee for bowling, picnics and Christmas Party)
—changes in vending machines
—heating and cooling
—summer dress code
—work station lighting
—non-glare VDT screens

Case 4

—health and safety
—comfort at the work station
—productivity
—work rules

—work schedules
—measurement and posting of Average Work Time figures
—procedures on third number calls

Case 5

"The issues addressed ranged from cosmetic concerns to health and safety issues to fundamental work structures and practices. The specific items include improved break areas and flextime scheduling options."

Case 6

—new procedure for operators to make requests for shifts
—refurbishing cafeteria and lounge
—better parking facilities
—redesign Average Work Time system
—information on divestiture

Case 7

"This team got off to a strong start by tackling...the problem of cross training...an issue that the union was prepared to grieve."
—a snow policy which alerts pay-phone collectors to hazardous driving and provides for stopping collections in the event of serious driving hazards
—phone in lounge
—replacement of toilet seat covers

Case 8

—parking spaces
—light dimmer for the lounge
—maintenance log for pool cars
—better organized supply cabinet

Case 9

—change information on work prints
—improve soap used for cleanup
—improve relations with the Motor Vehicles Department

Case 10

—cleanliness of operators' positions

Let QWL Do It All

The idea that QWL issues can be separated from collective bargaining has no basis in labor law, in the past practice or structure of collective bargaining, or in the day-to-day practice of QWL circles. As they have struggled to come up with a separation formula that works, many union leaders have dropped back to a position which tries to draw a line between the formal contract (which QWL must not touch) and everything else. Former UAW Representative Bill Horner, now a consultant, advises that it is all right for QWL groups to deal with any issue which is not currently in the grievance procedure or which does not directly violate the contract. The CWA's Glenn Watts writes:

I do not believe there need be any blurring of the *distinction* between collective bargaining and QWL. Our position is very simple: QWL groups can not bargain or alter the contract. They can, however, make recommendations; if their recommendations involve contractual changes, they must then pass through the normal collective bargaining process before being implemented.[9]

The problem with this approach is that the union is redefining its work as the narrowest possible conception of collective bargaining—the contract alone. This ignores the fact that a union also represents its members through letters of understanding between contracts, health and safety procedures, the grievance procedure, and stewards handling problems informally, as well as through work stoppages, work-to-rules, or other semi-organized methods of worker influence.

As the territory left to collective bargaining shrinks, there is significant support in the ''QWL community'' to go even further in reducing the scope of contracts.

There is discussion now in upper levels of the United Auto Workers about getting rid of local contracts altogether, or limiting them sharply, because they get in the way of flexibility. In their place would be joint union-management committees.

Where ''advanced'' QWL programs, like team production systems, have been instituted, major contractual items like many ''work rules'' simply disappear. One study reports that in a number of GM plants,

> ...the use of teams has accomplished the removal of any artificial separation between the work rule issues and participation processes. This has facilitated the creation of bargains that cut across the various issues, and thereby, allowed the kinds of compromises that are more difficult to achieve where collective bargaining and worker participation programs are kept separate.[10]

See the box for an example of such ''compromises'' at work.

THE SHRINKING CONTRACT

GM's Fiero plant in Pontiac, Michigan is a well-publicized QWL success story, work teams and all. A laudatory *Detroit Free Press* feature story on the plant included a picture captioned as follows:

> Above, supervisor William Schnapp works at welding at the shock absorber tower while subbing for a worker who is at a meeting. Supervisors regularly substitute for workers at the Fiero plant.[11]

Unions have long considered the prohibitions on foremen working to be a safeguard against erosion of the bargaining unit, particularly in times of heavy layoffs. When companies introduce new technology, they habitually try to assign new types of work, such as dealing with computers, to salaried rather than union personnel. With new technology on the upswing and union membership on the decline, union ''rigidity'' on keeping foremen from working should be even more important today.

In September 1983 the Department of Labor invited 25 prominent persons (representatives of business, labor, and QWL practitioners) to a conference to grapple with some of the difficult issues posed by QWL. The group discussed a paper which argues that the line between collective bargaining and QWL is fuzzy and the attempt at separation counterproductive, because most issues are better resolved through a QWL process. In fact, the paper argues, the traditional adversarial negotiations are appropriate only for division of the economic pie. All other issues (except perhaps the final step in the grievance procedure) should be handled through QWL.

The attempt to specify a dividing line between QWL and collective bargaining ends up turning unionism on its head. One facilitator from GM's gear and axle plant in Detroit explains that it is the union's job to handle individual problems—QWL covers issues that affect everyone.[12]

The Costs of Separation

Although separation of QWL from collective bargaining issues is not really possible in practice, *trying* to keep the two separate has a number of heavy costs.

1) The union stops trying to expand the territory of collective bargaining and establishing workers' rights. The areas turned over to QWL are the ones on the cutting edge of labor relations—introduction of technology, work rules, work methods, and even the product or service produced. By allowing the collective bargaining role to be narrowly defined as negotiations for a contract every few years and enforcing the hard rules in contracts which have fewer and fewer hard rules, unions make themselves irrelevant to the concerns of their members. They cut themselves off from precisely those areas they most need to address directly in the 1980's.

Usually the process of restricting the collective bargaining role is gradual and barely noticed. Sometimes it comes out in the open. Union representatives at the GM gear and axle plant asked facilitators for a list of issues which had come up in Employe Participation Groups, to see if any should be pursued in local contract negotiations. The facilitators refused on the grounds that QWL and collective bargaining had to be kept separate.

2) The union stewards are demoralized and confused. Most studies indicate that stewards and local union officers feel undercut by QWL programs. This perception is real, not imagined, as QWL proponents would have it. The number of grievances filed is often sharply reduced after QWL is introduced.

WE COULD ENJOY A CLOSER RELATIONSHIP IF YOU HAD A MORE PLEASANT DOG

SHOP STEWARD

MANAGEMENT

John Z. Gelsavage

Grievances may drop off because their causes have been removed. Or union leaders who control the higher steps in the grievance procedure may be so immersed in joint activities that they allow the procedure to become clogged, thus effectively discouraging members from filing. But the main reason grievances decrease is that members begin to bring their problems to the QWL circle instead of to the steward. While many QWL supporters deny it, an Administrative Law Judge, ruling in an important case involving federal employees and the Laborers Union, thinks it is obvious:

> It is evident that if employees can get a quick response from management on issues raised in quality circles, they will naturally channel their work-related concerns to the quality circles, rather than through the resources provided in the collective bargaining agreement.[13]

The usual answer from QWL advocates is that the steward should take on a new role, as part of the QWL process. When he was director of the UAW's General Motors department, Owen Bieber said:

> Quality circles, instead of ending the need for union representatives, merely frees up time to allow the union representative to work on more important issues, such as coordinating the approach taken in the various circles, participating in planning new additions to plants, and being more involved in the community political process.[14]

But it hasn't worked out that way. Regular union representatives have less and less contact with QWL circles as new union positions are created to do the "facilitating." In some GM plants, for example, there are now as many full-time union QWL appointees as there are union representatives.

There are several reasons that stewards are often isolated from the QWL process. First, the steward does not have the time to oversee QWL since he or she still has the hardest shop floor problems to deal with. The president of one local complains, "They let QWL shake all the low apples off the tree, and we're supposed to get the top ones without our ladder."

Second, because of the confusion over the QWL/collective bargaining relationship, the steward is expected to wear two hats. He or she is supposed to be adversarial when handling a grievance with a foreman, but walk into the QWL room and regard the same foreman as a "family" member. Third, it is management skills that are stressed in QWL training and activities, not steward-type skills. Fourth, when QWL discussions deal with technical issues involving production, the steward is not likely to be familiar with the topic; he or she becomes more irrelevant. Fifth, if the main role assigned the steward is the "watchdog," the steward is by definition an outsider.

Stewards are further undermined because management decides which procedure—QWL or bargaining—"works." A steward might fight for a new water fountain for years. When the company then installs one in response to a QWL circle's proposal, what conclusion do the members draw? They may well believe that if only the steward had presented the request as logically,

reasonably and non-adversarily as the circle did, then he or she might have gotten some results.

3) Circle suggestions can lead to job loss. Most proposals which save the company money do so because they translate into fewer jobs, or fewer labor hours, or the shifting of jobs to lower paid workers.

Even improving quality can cost jobs. As the President of the International Association of Quality Circles explains:

> Certainly, as you improve quality...you will eliminate scrapping of material; you will eliminate labor required to re-work or replace poor quality parts; you will eliminate the time required to rectify mistakes in records and other similar functions.[15]

The same is true for other kinds of cost savings. "Less machine downtime" means fewer paid labor

hours for the same production. "Saved maintenance costs" usually means fewer maintenance workers are required.

Improved training can cost jobs too. Training which broadens knowledge (creating "supercrafts" or a "jack-of-all-trades") might be the preparation for a management campaign to break down job classifications. "Enriching" jobs by teaching Statistical Process Control lays the basis for abolishing inspectors.

Job losses inherent in a proposal are sometimes hard to identify. For example, an electricians' group at GM Warren Hydra-matic developed a construction wagon so that they could have all the materials for a project right at hand. But the company used the system to prepare the cart on a weekday for weekend project work, thus cutting overtime for material crib attendants.

QWL's threat to job security should lead unions to *demand* that it be tied to collective bargaining so that QWL-generated improvements can be passed on either to the customer or to the workers. While most QWL programs have a general "no job loss" provision, it is difficult to trace through a suggestion's effect. Here union leaders can use their experience and knowledge of collective bargaining to recognize potential job loss from circle proposals and make collective bargaining adjustments to guarantee against job loss. This idea is discussed further in chapter 10.

HOW QUALITY CAN COST JOBS

Suppose a plant manufactures widgits. The perfect widgit has no gap between its two main parts. Under the plant's current quality control standards, a 2/100 inch gap is acceptable. Normally, out of every 125 widgits produced, 25 have too large a gap and are scrapped, and 100 get shipped out.

Now suppose that a QWL group makes an improvement to the process so that every single widgit produced has a gap of less than 2/100 of an inch.

The company can make a choice. It can set new, higher quality standards which do not allow the gap to exceed 1/100 of an inch, thus passing the quality improvement on to the customer. Or, more likely, the company will keep the quality standard the same and reap a 20% cost savings because it reduced scrap by 100%.

Where does this savings come from? Some of it is in the cost of raw materials, but in most operations, the main savings is in labor: workers now need to produce only 100 widgits instead of 125 in order to get 100 widgits out the door. Management gets the savings, some circle members get satisfaction from improving quality, and some workers lose their jobs.

4) Workers give up their specialized knowledge about their jobs. As discussed in chapter 4, QWL is designed to elicit workers' secrets about how to do their jobs faster, easier, and better. It may come as a surprise to many QWL practitioners that the reason management does not know these techniques is not that management doesn't listen. Rather workers often choose not to pass the knowledge on. This knowledge, plus readiness to offer extra effort in an emergency or to recognize and quickly report problems, are all part of a worker's ability to "bargain" with the supervisor for fair treatment and occasional special treatment, as well as protecting against speedup. UAW Regional Director Warren Davis describes the issue well:

> The workers know the short-cuts. *Would anyone propose that our members should report all short-cuts to the time study man?* Is it any different if a problem solving group is given the impression that they are involved in directing production, and proceed to break down the barriers to management's control through pooling and exposing the worker's hidden knowledge of the production process?[16]

This kind of information is developed over a long period of time. If workers are induced to turn it over to management because management momentarily turns on a friendly face, what do they have for defense if management decides it has nothing more to gain from being soft? At the very least shouldn't the union bargain for something real? Why give it away for free?

* * *

Unions have every reason to be wary of QWL. But they are not protected by insisting on some sharp distinction between collective bargaining issues and QWL. This doesn't work for the union, but it does for management. Whenever an issue arises in a circle that management doesn't want to talk about, it can cite the collective bargaining line and suggest the issue be taken to the union.

The union is caught in a trick bag. If the union insists on separation but allows QWL to handle "environmental issues," union leaders and established union procedures can be undercut. If it steps in and forbids a

QWL circle to work on a bargaining issue, then the union adopts the role of the bureaucratic outsider jealous that the membership might accomplish something and make the union officers look bad. If the union leaves the groups to work only on management problems, it is inviting the groups to turn into junior management, and possibly take actions which seriously harm central union objectives such as job security.

How to get out of the trick bag? Staying out of QWL is one way. But if a union is going to be in a program, the only strategy that has a chance is to tie the QWL program to union concerns instead of management concerns. Unions can try to tie QWL and the collective bargaining process tightly together, use the QWL structure to build an effective stewards system, and focus on all problems connected to job security and the quality of work life. We discuss some of the possibilities in chapter 10.

□

The Path of Least Resistance

Most people want to be constructive and certainly don't want to rain on someone else's parade. The QWL structure uses this tendency to gain a strong advantage for management.

You join a QWL circle to see what it's all about. Your group goes through training and you get to know something about everybody. Everybody, even management, is human and everyone wants to be friends.

At your first regular meeting, you brainstorm to determine the problem the circle will try to solve. You are impressed that everyone gets a say. The atmosphere is warm and relaxing. The coffee is free, the discussion interesting and, perhaps most important, you have some time off the job. Nobody attacks the union. On the contrary, the management participants have good things to say about the union. They even warn against taking up certain questions because the union might feel that they infringe on collective bargaining. Certainly no threat to the union here.

One of the circle's first tasks is to pick out a project. You suggest that the biggest problem your plant faces is management's decision to invest in Korea rather than to retool its U.S. production line. Everybody, management and worker alike, nods sympathetically. Then someone points out there is not really anything the circle can do about it. "Yeah, that's right. Let's try to pick something we can work on."

You suggest that it might improve your quality of work life to alter the company's attendance rules, or even institute a system of flextime. No one responds negatively. Management especially has been trained always to respond positively to the person, if not to the

idea. "That's really an interesting idea you have there." But then someone points out that it is a plantwide issue and asks whether there is anything we can do about it in this circle. "Maybe we should work on something we know more about."

You pursue your idea and suggest that your circle might do a survey of the entire plant workforce to see what alternative working hours people would like. But then somebody, possibly a supervisor, reminds the group that working hours are covered under collective bargaining and would probably be better left to the regular union-company discussions. "But it is a fine idea and this QWL group should call it to the attention of the union and the plantwide QWL steering committee."

You still want to be constructive, so you try to limit yourself to suggestions on which everyone agrees (your group operates by consensus). What makes most sense is to talk about things having to do with the operation of your department or section. So at first you talk about moving water fountains to make them more convenient, fans so they cool more effectively, and aisle markers to improve safety. Maybe you get some action on these, or maybe someone points out that these are also collective bargaining questions.

But how many water fountains can you move? You want to be constructive. You enjoy your weekly meetings and you want something positive to come out of them. Your group is "maturing." You have developed trust and a method through taking care of these "environmental" issues. You are looking for other issues so that your group can stay together, so you turn to issues of productivity and product quality.

This all happens naturally, but just in case it doesn't go this way, facilitators are trained...

Notes

1. *Workplace Democracy*, Summer 1982.
2. Speech, Michigan QWL Council Conference, November 10, 1983.
3. *Work Life Review*, September 1983.
4. Russell A. Smith, Leroy S. Merrifield, and Donald P. Rothschild, *Collective Bargaining and Labor Arbitration*, Bobbs-Merrill Co., 1970.
5. "The Quality of Work Life Process of AT&T and the Communications Workers of America," draft, January 1984, sponsored by U.S. Department of Labor.
6. Donna Sockell, "The Legality of Employee-Participation Programs in Unionized Firms," *Industrial and Labor Relations Review*, July 1984.
7. *QWL Focus*, Summer 1983, p. 20.
8. *Wall Street Journal*, September 22, 1981.
9. Thomas A. Kochan, Harry G. Katz, Nancy R. Mowrer, *Worker Participation and American Unionism*, W.E. Upjohn Institute for Employment Research, 1984, p. 198.
10. Kochan, Katz, Mowrer, p. 95.
11. *Detroit Free Press*, February 18, 1985.
12. Presentation to Michigan QWL Council Conference, November 19, 1984.
13. Federal Labor Relations Authority, Case No. 9-CA-20241, Decision, December 28, 1982.
14. *Quality Circles Journal*, August 1982.
15. *Industry Week*, June 28, 1982, p. 52.
16. Position paper, June 14, 1984.

JOINTNESS, WATCHDOGGING, & OTHER UNION RESPONSES

Over the last few years a short list of principles or guidelines has become more or less standard union advice for involvement in QWL projects. Glenn Watts, president of the Communications Workers, lists the key points from the Statement of Principles worked out between the CWA and AT&T:

1. The effort is *joint*; the union is involved as an equal partner from planning through implementation.
2. It is *voluntary* for the union, the company and each individual worker.
3. Collective bargaining and the grievance process are off limits for QWL; worker participation is a *separate* process.
4. *No one can be laid off or downgraded* as a result of ideas which come from the participation process.
5. The goals of the process include both *human satisfaction* and *economic efficiency*.[1]

These principles are supposed to separate the good QWL programs from the union-busting ones. Watts says they

> ...can be used as a kind of litmus test. If employers accept these principles, in writing, we have a good basis from which to move forward. But if they refuse, we have good reasons for refusing to cooperate.

Since these guidelines are central to most union approaches to QWL, we will examine the five from CWA in detail, as well as two others commonly used, "watchdogging" and "gainsharing."

1. Equal Partnership

QWL advocates argue that union interests are protected when the union is an equal partner in all aspects of the program, from planning to implementation.

The idea of joint union-management activities is not new. Many industries have long had joint apprenticeship committees, joint safety committees, or joint United Fund committees. There has also long been a tradition in the labor movement of distrusting collaboration and restricting it to specific areas, because of the understanding that collaboration tends to subordinate union needs to management policies. One of the accomplishments of QWL is that jointness and collaboration are no longer dirty words in much of the labor movement. Indeed, "more jointness" seems to be labor's solution to many of the major problems confronting it today.

Photo by Jim West

DRIPPING WITH JOINTNESS

In 1984, UAW officials got hold of an internal GM strategy document that projected slashing 80,000 jobs, reducing benefits, and doing more outsourcing. When union officers protested the company's plans, GM Vice-President of Industrial Relations, Alfred Warren commented:

> It's actually talking about jointness, all of those proposals were joint kinds of things.... I don't know what's in there [that they would feel is] not to be trusted.

In fact, according to Warren the document "drips with jointness."[2]

Leaving aside the question of whether or not more joint activities would in fact benefit the labor movement, an equal partnership in QWL programs has not been achieved and is not possible. Even where agreements are carefully worded, equality on paper does not translate into the actual operation of the program.

Union participation in steering committees is not equal. QWL programs usually set up a structure of joint committees to oversee the operation. The structure of these bodies tends to follow hierarchical management structure rather than union structure: lower bodies report to and are responsible to higher bodies rather than the democratic method of higher bodies being accountable to lower ones. All minutes of local QWL groups are supposed to go to upper bodies for review, but the minutes and records of these upper bodies are generally not available.

The union's representation on these steering committees is likely to be less than management's. In Ford's Body and Assembly Division, for example, the Joint Steering Committee which directs Employe Involvement for all plants has 19 members—16 from higher Ford management and 3 from the UAW International. Union leaders explain that since decisions are made by consensus the imbalance is of no consequence.

When the Dearborn Assembly Plant Electricians' EI group presented important proposals on outsourcing and training to this Division steering committee, none of the union members of the committee was present. Nor had union members attended the previous meeting, when the committee planned training for the coming year. When asked about this, a management member explained that the union representatives were extremely busy. The imbalance on the committee is even more exaggerated because, in addition to non-QWL assignments, the union members have to cover union-QWL relations with the entire Ford Motor Company, whereas the management people only work within the division.

Only management has the machinery to make its participation real. Many local presidents complain that although they try to attend QWL steering committees regularly, they are at a great disadvantage. The plant manager can assign whatever staff necessary to keep track of the program and additional staff to deal with special problems. Unions cannot match the resources management has at its disposal. Local union leaders are occupied with other issues and have no union machinery to do anything more than react when something major is called to their attention. Many local leaders will privately admit that they have little idea about what is actually going on in their QWL programs, much less real control.

Access to knowledge is far from equal. Management controls most of the information needed to fully understand the issues that come up in QWL: facts on costs, employment levels, projected products, production methods and the like. The union must rely on management for this information. This means management can keep, hide, feed, or distort the facts as it chooses.

On the other hand, because of the open nature of unions, they have little special information that management needs. The union leaders' single access to valuable knowledge—the eyes, ears and minds of the membership—is undermined by the QWL process, which makes that shop floor knowledge directly available to management as well.

When management does agree to share its knowledge with union leaders, there is often a large price: the leadership is expected to keep it "confidential" from other sections of the union, especially the membership.

Neutral consultants aren't neutral. Most QWL consultants are essentially management consultants, have no understanding of trade unionism, and willingly put their QWL services at the disposal of union busting companies (see letter).

Donald F. Ephlin
Director, General Motors Department
United Auto Workers
8000 E. Jefferson
Detroit, MI 48214

February 12, 1985

Dear Brother Ephlin:

I wish to call your attention to the role of QWL consultants in attempts to defeat union organizing drives.

Onan Corporation has been fighting the UAW organizing drive at its Huntsville plant. The National Labor Relations Board, with later court approval, found Onan guilty of repeated and flagrant unfair labor practices. NLRB documents state that two consulting companies, Baker & Co. of Dallas and Peoples Management Corporation of Chicago, were retained by the Onan Corporation during the drive "to assist it in the possibility of establishing some type of work life program." (ALJ Decision, November 30, 1983, Ona Corporation, a division of Onan Corporation, and UAW and Employee Action Committee, Case 10-CA-19146)

The UAW filed unfair labor practice charges concerning the QWL program, essentially charging the company with setting up a company union, and the Administrative Law Judge found for the UAW. The corporation is appealing to the full board.

Baker & Co. has done considerable consulting work for the UAW-GM QWL program including (with David Kolb) preparing a substantial part of materials used for training UAW members and facilitators.

In the NLRB proceedings on this same case, the International Association of Quality Circles (IAQC) filed an *amicus* brief calling for the Board to substantially weaken union protections under the law so as to protect quality circles unilaterally put in place by employers.

The fact that an employee relations consulting firm works in any way with a union busting company should be enough to demonstrate that it lacks sufficient commitment to unionism to guide the installation of UAW QWL programs.

The fact that the IAQC actively promotes weakening the remaining legal protections for union organizing should lead to similar conclusions and place in question consultants who are members of the IAQC or who use IAQC materials and conferences as part of their training programs.

I understand that the UAW-GM Department and General Motors are currently drawing up an approved list of consultants for joint QWL activities. Since the UAW-GM consultant jobs are often lucrative, excluding consultants who work for non-union companies might help isolate the union busters. I suggest that the union include the following minimum qualifications before a consultant is placed on the approved list:

1) The consulting firm must establish a policy that it does no QWL consulting or other employee relations consulting with any firm which is non-union or seeks to decertify a union.

2) The consulting firm must demonstrate that it has a knowledge of labor history and labor law, and advocates strengthening the role of unions in protecting and advancing the interests of workers.

Fraternally,

Mike Parker
Coordinator
Labor Notes QWL Task Force
Member, Local 600 UAW

Management's power to implement forces the whole QWL structure to adapt to management. Because of the distribution of power, local union QWL practitioners naturally tend to function as though they were in the management structure. At a meeting of QWL practitioners in Detroit, a union and a management facilitator from GM jointly presented a case study which demonstrates this point:

A QWL group in an engineering department was half salary, half hourly. The group was divided over what one facilitator called "union-management" issues. Many of these issues were of a double-standard variety: salaried employees worked flexible hours, could use phones, and had company cars at lunch time. After several meetings, tensions were rising.

The facilitators decided that they had to chance a risky course. They went to the plant manager, explained the situation and proposed a solution. They warned that the proposal was risky and that "the group might blow up." The plant manager agreed to let the facilitators try, and authorized the full eight hours' pay for a special meeting for everyone in the group.

The facilitators held the all-day session with the group. They proposed an exercise called "Intergroup Clearing" in which the opposing groups are separated and each draws up two lists: what you know about the other group, and what you need to know about the other group. The lists are then exchanged, and finally the two groups are brought back together. The danger was that the process could intensify hostilities; the facilitators hoped that instead it would clear the air.

The exercise worked. The group decided to discuss and deal with the "union-management" issues one at a time.

The other practitioners complimented the facilitators on their daring and decisive action. Many commented on how nice it was to have a plant manager with enough "trust in the process" to chance blowing up an already tense situation.

After considerable discussion along these lines, the facilitators were asked, "What was the union's role in all this, especially since the issues are standard union ones? You described asking the plant manager for approval of your plan because it was risky. Did you also ask the union for approval?" After some embarrassed looks and some flustered comments by different people, the hourly facilitator responded, "I told the [steward]

DROWNING IN JOINTNESS

The 1984 UAW-GM contract set up an "Executive Board-Joint Activities" to oversee a number of overlapping joint structures including the National Committee to Improve the Quality of Work Life, the National Skill Development and Training Committee (which also controls most of the funds used by QWL), the National Joint Committee on Health and Safety, the National Committee on Attendance, the National Substance Abuse Recovery Program, the Tuition Assistance Program, the JOB Security Program, the Growth and Opportunity Committee, and other joint activities that the two parties might agree upon.[3]

In addition to regular union responsibilities, local union officials at GM are expected to keep on top of one or more local joint QWL steering committees as well as the joint JOB Security Committee. This new committee evaluates the cause of each layoff and assigns each laid-off worker to an appropriate status in the job bank, oversees training programs, oversees use of workers in areas of "nontraditional work," makes proposals for changes in the local contract to make the plant more competitive, and makes proposals for beginning new businesses to the New Business Venture Development Group set up by the Growth and Opportunity Committee.

Attempts to gain more union influence by increasing the number of joint activities can only make it harder for the union to have real control in any one area. The thinner the union spreads itself in a multitude of committees, the more it will rely on the company to provide it with information, administer the committees, and implement the results.

about the workshop, but he isn't friendly to QWL."

Neither the two facilitators nor the twenty other practitioners discussing the case were out to bypass the union. Many of them were chosen by their unions and they probably all believed that QWL had to be a joint process. Yet the facilitators' way of proceeding seemed natural because it was a natural response to the power set-up. The plant manager's approval was necessary because he had to authorize the eight hours' pay. There was nothing, on the other hand, that the facilitators needed from the union. To avoid a possible union veto, the path of least resistance was to involve the union as little as possible.

The same situation repeats itself in a thousand different ways in the operation of the usual QWL program. If the facilitator is trying to do a good job, he or she is dependent on support from management every day. This support includes little items like room allocations and office supplies as well as major ones such as cost information needed by a QWL group or time off for a group to visit a supplier. Much of the perceived success and morale of QWL programs depends on QWL-generated ideas actually being implemented, which—again—is a management decision. Management will continue support for the program only if it is comfortable with the day-to-day workings, so it is easiest for the facilitator to make management comfortable.

Union approval, on the other hand, usually is not vital for the day-to-day functioning of QWL. The facilitator is under little internal pressure from within the program to involve the union. If the union does not demand to be involved, the path of least resistance for the facilitator is simply to avoid the union.

2. Making It Voluntary

Although most unions make it a principle that individual participation in QWL should be voluntary, this idea has dangerous ramifications. Voluntarism can cause or deepen divisions within the work group or the union. One of the few QWL programs to recognize this problem is the one being developed by the City of Boston and Service Employees Local 285. The proposal submitted by the city notes:

> If in a functionally defined group, some employees join the program and others do not, that fact itself is likely to reflect pre-existing cliques or differences in motivation. The Worksite Groups would then end up exacerbating social and attitudinal divisions among people who work together. These groups should be able to resolve problems that arise among people who work together; but if some co-workers join and others do not, the group might intensify tensions.[4]

Voluntarism can also be dangerous once the groups are in operation. When only a part of the workforce participates in a program, management can use QWL to provide its favored few with extra perks.

When workers criticize the functioning of a group or the whole program, they are often told, "It's voluntary— if you don't like it you can leave." This process often results in an organized polarization between the uncritical supporters of QWL and those on the outside. The outsiders consider the QWLers a group of "company sucks" while the QWL participants dismiss their critics as "lazy do-nothings and professional bitchers." And by saying that participation in QWL is an individual question, the union seems to sanction both.

When problems arise in a department, whether or not caused by the QWL program, the lines are often drawn between the participants and the non-participants. Because of the structure of QWL, and because of the way QWL participants are trained together and share a few special privileges, they often end up functioning as a clique. Management, of course, has no objection to dividing the union.

For the union's purposes, it appears that structures which include entire departments or work groups together, or structures where QWL participants are representatives (elected and recallable by others in their work groups), are preferable to voluntary schemes. These alternatives have their own problems—reinforc-

ing departmental lines can intensify departmental rivalries, for example—but voluntarism appears to create more.

3. Separating QWL from Collective Bargaining

We discussed this guideline at length in chapter 8. The bottom line is that (a) it is just about impossible to keep collective bargaining issues separate from QWL, and (b) the attempt to do so hurts the union.

4. Getting Job Guarantees

The International Union of Electronic Workers (IUE) asks for written guarantees that no jobs will be eliminated as a result of QWL activities.[5] Other unions, such as the Communications Workers, specify that no one can be laid off as a result of QWL—a much weaker position since it allows job loss through attrition. The UAW-GM QWL program explicitly opens all the loopholes:

> There may be no layoffs directly resulting from a QWL activity. This does not mean that layoffs will not occur due to changes in the business, only that improvements resulting from employe participation will not be used to reduce the workforce. This will occur through attrition.[6]

As long as layoffs are allowed for "changes in the business," such language is meaningless. GM's plan to reduce its workforce far exceeds contractual protections and includes plans to replace domestic models with imports. Suppose that due to such "changes in the business," a plant needs 10 fewer employees. At the same time, 10 are retiring. Those 10 retirees will not be replaced, and those 10 jobs will be lost through attrition, but on the other hand no one will be laid off. Now assume that, at the same time, QWL "improvements" make it possible to cut 5 additional jobs. The plant now needs 15 fewer workers, instead of only 10. Ten can be cut through attrition (the retirees) and 5 can be laid off "due to changes in the business"—all without breaking the guideline that says "no layoffs from QWL."

During peak employment periods the lost jobs will not be obvious, but as the long term trend to a reduced workforce sets in, every job eliminated by QWL will eventually put one more person on the street.

Most QWL programs have even less to say about job loss than GM's. The UAW-Ford program includes only the vague guideline that "EI is not a productivity gim-

A bumper sticker at the Ford Rouge plant.

mick.''[7] But Ford President Philip Caldwell is candid about using EI to cut jobs. He explains:

> I can think of one case where we did a little group operation in the assembly of an instrument panel. Instead of having 12 people, the employees themselves found they could do it with essentially 10. We said, ''Well, we would like to eliminate the other two jobs.''[8]

Given such company expectations it certainly makes sense for unions to insist on specific written guarantees on job security in their QWL programs. But contract language alone will not provide protection. The contract can only be enforced if the union is able to track the specific jobs. Factories today are anything but static. In addition to QWL, companies are introducing new ways to organize production (team concepts), new ways to handle inventory (*kan-ban* or ''just-in time''), and new technology. Office and other forms of white collar work are also being reorganized. Since all these innovations cut jobs, it is almost impossible to trace job losses specifically to QWL.

Written guarantees can prove useful if they are specific and if the union is vigilant. But unless a union is prepared to insist that there be no jobs lost *for any reason*, the natural tendency of QWL suggestions to lead to job loss will continue—contract guarantees or not.

___5. Making 'Human Satisfaction A QWL Goal_____

This is a nice sentiment which does nothing to pin the program down. After all, QWL practitioners believe that the best way for workers to gain high level satisfaction is by making productivity suggestions. Any view of ''human satisfaction'' besides ''making a contribution to the organization'' is considered to be low on the hierarchy of values. Most QWL programs allow groups to address ''environmental'' or ''creature comfort'' issues but consider these primitive, mainly for purposes of pulling the group together and developing trust. A group ''matures'' when it moves on to dealing with production issues. The authors of the CWA/AT&T study seem to sum up their own view through the words of a participant they quote:

> The group is getting despondent because mostly domestic things are being worked on. We want to work on profit, productivity, and the customer.[9]

___6. Watchdogging _____

Many local unions, suspicious of QWL, have attempted to protect the union and the membership by ''watchdogging'' it. The union tries to keep close tabs on the program and see that it doesn't go out of bounds. The union assigns stewards the responsibility to monitor QWL groups and to blow the whistle when necessary—if, for example, a group proposal violates a contract provision.

The watchdogging strategy appeals to many locals because it allows them to maintain their suspicions and distance from the program without having to refuse to participate. If QWL is popular, then the union doesn't interfere. If QWL becomes politically unpopular, the union leadership doesn't have to take responsibility for it.

The main problems with the watchdogging strategy are (a) it allows management to keep the initiative while the union can only react, and (b) it is completely ineffective.

" ...and now for step seven in our grievance procedure! "

It is simply not possible for a steward to keep on top of a fully functioning QWL program. There may be ten to twenty functioning QWL groups in one steward's district. While virtually all QWL programs include the right for the steward to be present at meetings, typically the steward rarely or never attends.

Thus when an issue does come to the steward's attention, the QWL group has probably already discussed it several times, and has perhaps even begun to take action on it. If the steward believes that the discussion or the action violates some contractual understanding or union position, he or she is expected to stop it. At best, the group members disappointedly accept that the steward is doing his or her job. More likely they get angry because the union stepped in ''like a bureaucrat'' and stopped them from discussing something they freely chose to discuss.

Although the watchdog role seems to be a politically easy stance when the union is initially establishing its attitude toward QWL, in practice it turns out to be a political liability for the stewards. Whenever the steward steps in to stop an activity, that section of the steward's constituency likely to approve is not immediately affected and not likely to care strongly. But the group that is antagonized is clearly defined, immediately involved, and likely to remember at election time.

On the other hand, a steward closely associated with QWL, or one who doesn't aggressively watchdog when this is the union stance, can quickly get the "in bed with the company" reputation.

Thus the watchdog role turns out unintentionally to be a set-up for the front line union leaders. The path of least resistance is for the stewards to put as much distance as possible between themselves and QWL, shift the responsibility for what happens in circles to someone else, and find out as little as possible about what is going on.

Watchdogging as a general stance defines the union as outside the central part of the process, as if to say: The union is the third party which is watching to protect its own special interests while the employees and management work on common problems. The union is also caught in a contradiction. You need a watchdog to watch what others do, not what you do yourself. If the union really is in full partnership with the company in QWL, then who is the watchdog to watch—the membership?

As a result, unions at the national levels have officially shifted away from the watchdog stance toward that of "equal partnership." But since "equal partnership" does not work in reality, and provides no role at all for stewards and other front line union leaders, most local unions still maintain the watchdog stance for lack of an alternative.

__7. Gainsharing _____

Since increasing productivity has become the central focus of most QWL programs, many unionists have turned to some form of "gainsharing" plan so that workers can benefit from productivity increases as well as management. Some hope that if the company has to give employees part of the savings from cutting jobs, it will be in less of a hurry to reduce the workforce.

Some unions, such as the International Woodworkers, believe that gainsharing should be a part of any QWL agreement. "So-called 'nonfinancial' [participation] programs are lucrative for employers and a rip-off of employees," says IWA Research and Educa-

tion Director Roy Ockert.[10]

Gainsharing plans operate on many levels. Where formal paid suggestion programs are in effect, some unionists urge QWL groups to submit their QWL proposals as suggestions so that the company will not get an entirely free ride. Others have embraced profit-sharing plans. The best known plans used in conjunction with QWL are Scanlon, Rucker, and Improshare. They use local production rather than sales or profits as the basis for calculating gains.

But in anything like their current form, gainsharing plans provide no solution to union problems with QWL. In practice, the amount the company has to pay to employees is so small it does not influence management decisions. But even these small financial rewards are often sufficient to magnify QWL's dangerous tendency to get groups of workers proposing speed-up and job cuts for each other.

✻ ✻ ✻

Most active trade unionists understand instinctively that there is something dangerous, if not absolutely wrong, about QWL. The general trade union approach to QWL reflects this in its guarded, defensive style. Some of the individual parts of the defense, like trying to get contractual guarantees on job security, speak to a central problem, but they are not enough. Other measures, like claiming to be "an equal partner" in a game with a stacked deck, only further disorient the labor movement. The labor movement needs to develop its own strategy based on its own needs and strength. We discuss some possibilities in the next chapter.   □

Notes

1. *Workplace Democracy*, Summer 1982.
2. *Detroit Free Press*, March 22, 1984.
3. Memorandum of Understanding: Joint Activities, UAW-GM Contract, 1984.
4. "Grant Proposal for Funding by the Federal Mediation and Conciliation Service of a Boston Labor Management Cooperation Program," May 11, 1984.
5. IUE 1982 Convention Resolution.
6. *QWL*, UAW-GM Joint National Quality of Work Life Committee, 1983.
7. "Employee Involvement: What's It All About," UAW-Ford National Joint Committee on Employe Involvement, October 1980.
8. "The Automobile Crisis and Public Policy: An Interview with Philip Caldwell," *Harvard Business Review*, January-February 1981.
9. "The Quality of Work Life Process of AT&T and the Communications Workers of America," draft, January 1984, sponsored by U.S. Dept. of Labor.
10. *International Woodworker*, June 26, 1984.

_A UNION STRATEGY FOR QWL

In the hands of employers Quality of Work Life programs are a powerful weapon. They appeal to some of workers' best instincts—to do a good job, to be part of a group, to make a contribution—while they subtly or not so subtly undermine unionism.

As we discussed in the last three chapters, the strategies most unions have developed for dealing with QWL do not effectively counter its destructive tendencies. When locals ignore QWL employers have total freedom to use it to their advantage. Written guarantees to protect workers and the union are at best only a beginning point, since they are only as strong as a membership willing to enforce them. Equal representation on joint committees is an illusion. Playing "watch-dog" by definition removes the union from a central role in the program. And erecting an artificial barrier between collective bargaining and QWL only serves to isolate the union.

A local union really has only two options for facing the challenge of QWL. It can force the company to drop the program altogether. Or it can decide to participate fully, organize its members, and press the limits of the program so that it really addresses the quality of working life, and builds rather than undermines the union.

_1. Getting Out

The first option—getting out—is not as simple as it appears. The employer will bring heavy pressure to continue the program. Often local managers are under orders from on high to implement QWL. Management may make veiled threats to close the plant or subcontract work unless the union agrees to QWL. If a program ends, a determined employer may begin a new program under another name. When workers at General Motors' transmission plant in Windsor, Ontario voted out QWL, for example, GM reintroduced most of the substance in a Statistical Quality Control program. Management at Bethlehem Steel in Indiana tried the same approach.

Although the programs are supposed to be voluntary, contractual provisions may be interpreted to make it difficult for a local to withdraw.

Opposition to getting out may also come from within the union. When international union policy favors QWL, a local may find that top leaders will block withdrawal. Additionally, significant sections of the local may have a big stake in the program. Facilitators, for example, may not be happy about giving up their full or part-time jobs.

In its initial stages, QWL is often popular with a por-

tion of the rank and file. If a local union withdraws, the leadership may face a rebellion from QWL partisans, who will then be drawn even more toward a company viewpoint. The union cannot simply ignore the worker dignity, participation and respect promised by QWL. To withdraw from QWL without shooting themselves in the foot, local leaders must provide an alternative. They must educate the membership about QWL's hidden traps and rebuild union pride and an active union life as the alternative.

Despite the obstacles, a number of local unions have refused to participate in QWL or have withdrawn from the program. Withdrawal usually followed management actions which brought into question the company's real intentions.

At the Pontiac Truck and Bus plant, for example, the company tried to use QWL to change classifications, weaken the local contract, bypass shop floor union representatives, and pit workers against each other. The final straw came when the company closed down an operation, cutting 200 jobs, in a department with an active QWL program.

The local executive board voted to get out of QWL in October 1983. The membership endorsed this action at a union meeting and later reaffirmed their support by re-electing the incumbent officers. When management attempted to keep the QWL program going anyway, a few members continued to attend meetings. But by doing this, UAW Local 594 President Don Douglas points out, "Management is just putting a nail in the [QWL] coffin by showing that it is really a management program."

A union best deals with QWL by understanding that QWL itself is not the problem, just as it is not the solution. As described in chapter 4, management will use QWL as best it can to strengthen its overall policy and goals. The key to a successful union QWL strategy is to deal with those management policies directly to show how QWL is just a piece of a larger picture.

For example, a loose coalition of union activists and committeepersons (stewards) at Ford's Twin Cities assembly plant waged a campaign to rebuild a strong militant union and in the process dealt with their Employe Involvement program.

Employe Involvement started at the plant in 1980 with strong support from both union and management. The staffer in charge of EI for the UAW international, Al Hendricks, had been president of Local 879, and his brother Richard was the current president. For its part, to assure the program's success Ford contracted with a consulting firm and spent an estimated $250,000 for six months.

The program followed a standard pattern: start slowly, put circles in departments where there are few union militants, and expand from there. Union activists who were able to join circles tried to raise issues such as how overwork on certain jobs was affecting quality. They were told these issues were inappropriate and were urged to discuss instead more manageable issues such as water fountains.

While continuing to participate, these activists pointed out to co-workers that the management which was pushing EI was the same management which was cutting quality inspectors, speeding up lines, and harassing and firing militant union officers and activists.

Twice the local membership voted to suspend EI in response to firings, including that of a popular committeeman, Tom Laney. Both times international union representatives told them that the membership could not suspend the program. Since the program was voluntary, argued Al Hendricks, the union had the obligation to assure a member's right to participate.

In 1982 the local voted against the concessions contract which won a majority nationwide. When both management and international union leaders stated that plants with EI had voted heavily in favor of the concessions, EI was further discredited in the local.

EI was finallly left without a leg to stand on when management tried to use it to change the relief system in the plant. Management wanted to replace tag relief (a crew of replacement workers relieves assembly line workers one by one for their breaks) with mass relief (the whole line is shut down and everyone takes break at once). The coalition of activists insisted that the issue was not which method was more pleasant but the fact that mass relief would mean the loss of 250 jobs by allowing Ford to axe the jobs of relief workers. Those working, they said, had an obligation to stand by their laid-off brothers and sisters.

Twice the membership voted against mass relief by large margins. But management and local union officers worked out a 60-day "trial period" through the EI-

Photo by Jim West

UAW member makes his feelings known before the union's collective bargaining convention.

related Mutual Growth Forum. During the trial period management tried to use EI groups to help build support for the new system. At the end of the 60 days, the membership voted to return to tag relief and also to cancel EI for the third time.

When union elections came around six months later, the activists who had opposed EI and mass relief took over the main union offices. Twice-fired committeeman Tom Laney was elected president and another militant committeeman, Ted LaValley, became chairman.

The UAW international representative still insisted that the local could not vote out EI. The company and the EI consultant, Frank Wuest, tried to keep it going. But the new leadership supported the membership's vote. EI quickly faded to a tiny program with some salaried and a handful of hourly participants.

The new union leaders understood that EI spoke to needs which the union had to address. They gave attention to the grievance procedure and, through firmness and persistence, started winning significantly more grievances. In the 1984 local contract they negotiated two new committees to work on specific problems. The Skilled Trades Training Committee is modernizing the training program. The Ergonomics Committee is developing new work procedures and finding new equipment to reduce heavy lifting and other causes of work-related injuries.

The local is finding ways to involve more members by activating the standing committees, electing zone stewards to work with the committeepersons, expanding the newspaper, and holding classes. The local is planning annual conventions as a way to develop union

VOLUNTEERING—ARMY-STYLE

In 1983 Steelworkers Local 1223 in Yorkville, Ohio voted to withdraw from its Labor Management Participation Program with Wheeling-Pittsburgh Steel. But the company, backed by the USW District Director, tried to continue the program. In 1984 the company fired three union leaders, including the president, primarily because they had written articles against LMPT for the union newspaper. The arbitrator in two cases upheld the company's action, arguing that "voluntary" union participation applied only to getting in, not to getting out.[1]

Indications are that the arbitrator will be overturned. The National Labor Relations Board ruled that the third officer should be reinstated, and the other two are appealing to the Board as well.

policy and better prepare members for participation in international union bodies. It has also increased its involvement with other unions, community groups, and farmer organizations in the region.

Descriptions of how three other locals stayed out or got out of QWL programs are reprinted from *Labor Notes* on the next pages.

Management Turns Down 'No Foremen' Plan

by Dave Stock, UE Local 262

When H.K. Porter, a metalworking firm in Somerville, Mass., announced that it was instituting a Quality of Work Life program in 1980, the union leadership in the shop was skeptical.

Their last contract had been settled by a bitter 6½-week strike. In a daily running battle, management missed no opportunity to attack the union (part of Amalgamated Local 262 of the United Electrical Workers). Hard struggle, including "unofficial" job actions, had been necessary to defend the workers' wages and working conditions. Why should they welcome a trio of high-paid management consultants from North Carolina into the shop?

The company made an all-out effort to convince its workers to accept the new program. It sponsored a banquet at a fancy hotel for employees and their families. At "informational meetings" about QWL, they admitted that they had "had the wrong attitude in the past." Their consultants and foremen went around the plant lobbying individual workers. And, of course, they promised to pay everyone for time spent in QWL meetings.

The union executive board soon realized that sections of the membership were attracted to the new program. Some people hoped for peace—for relief from battles with management. Others thought they saw a new opportunity to get themselves noticed and rewarded by the company.

Although most of the workers tended to oppose QWL, the leadership wanted to avoid a potential split in the ranks. The executive board decided to negotiate with management over QWL. The company, which badly wanted the union's support, agreed to delay the formation of quality circles while talks went on.

Since Porter claimed that they had no ulterior motives behind their proposals, the union requested full disclosure of all QWL training manuals and promotional materials, information on the financial set-up, names of workplaces where the consultants had been active in the past, etc.

This proved to be a fruitful avenue. The materials made it clear that the company's main interest was profit, not "employee satisfaction."

The consultants refused to divulge information about their past activities in unionized plants, even though this information had been part of their sales pitch to Porter. This tarnished the image of impartiality and openness.

And in the course of union questioning, one of the consultants let it slip that his firm's services were available to companies trying to keep unions away.

Meanwhile, the union was busy investigating QWL. Their research wasn't very encouraging. QWL advocates appeared to want management-run quality circles to take over many of the union's functions on the shop floor.

The leadership's worst fears about the program were strengthened at the UE District 2 Council in February 1981. Delegate after delegate, from workplaces all over the Northeast, rose to talk about QWL experiences in their own shops.

It was remarkable how many factories in the district had had a program initiated within the previous year or two. Some of the stories about how QWL had been used to turn workers against each other or undermine the union were quite graphic.

Many Porter workers were following these developments closely. Their attitude toward QWL began to harden. But it was events on the shop floor that were decisive. The company never stopped creating confrontations.

For instance, they asked the union to change the dates of two paid holidays.

When the union refused, management closed the plant for two days, causing loss of pay and bitter feelings among the workers. A continual stream of union publicity kept the spotlight on incidents like this.

After about three months of discussion, education and experience with company hypocrisy, the membership was firmly convinced of the potential dangers of QWL. At a membership meeting, they decided unanimously to submit a final proposal to management.

The union expressed willingness to cooperate in solving problems in the plant, but made it clear that they were skeptical of the company's motives. They offered to hold "circle" meetings in the various departments to discuss whatever topics the company requested.

They set conditions, though: no management personnel could be present at the meetings unless invited. All suggestions would be screened by the union leadership, who would pass them on to the company once it had been determined that they wouldn't hurt any union member.

Most Porter workers felt that the union had met the company more than half way. When Porter turned down the proposal on the grounds that "their foremen had to be involved at all levels," QWL was pretty much dead on the shop floor. And for the time being, at least, the company recognized that they had reached an impasse.

Ontario GM Workers Opt Out of QWL

by Mike Parker

Workers at the Windsor, Ontario General Motors transmission plant have voted overwhelmingly to end their participation in the company's Quality of Work Life program. The exceptionally large turnout to the UAW Local 1973 unit meeting came despite the union leadership's support for QWL and an aggressive company campaign to defuse the opposition.

Not long after QWL was voted out, so was the unit chairman who had supported it. Both votes carried by margins of three to one.

Most workers first heard about QWL last summer in large company-called meetings. The plant manager and the union leadership described the program and then held elections for representatives for each department. The reps were taken to the Holiday Inn for a few days for training and returned as boosters. Most workers seemed willing to give QWL a chance.

At first most QWL efforts focused on items such as getting clocks moved, water fountains fixed, radios in the plant, and ventilation. But suspicion was aroused, because these were items the union had been trying to get for years. Suspicion grew when workers discovered from a contractor that some changes in the ventilation system which the QWL program was taking credit for had actually been planned earlier.

SATISFACTION = PRODUCTION

In Department 90, management had been pushing for some time for 2,150 parts per day rather than 2,000. At the department's October meeting, management decided to use some QWL rhetoric. As an inducement for the workers to put out the extra production, the General Supervisor offered to pay up to nine of the machine operators jobsetter's wages if they would adjust their own machines. He made repeated references to "increased work satisfaction."

The Dept. 90 workers realized, of course, that the plan was to do away with jobsetters, both the classification and the jobs.

Dept. 90's response was to get together with the neighboring department, 91, and draw up a simple petition: "We will not participate in any QWL programs and this being the case, as we are the majority, we ask that our representative be removed." Every worker in both departments signed—about 30 people—including the QWL "rep."

The company's response was a combination of "divide and conquer"—overtime for Dept. 90, none for 91—and "police action"—using minor infractions as an excuse for harassment in 91, which management considered to be the ringleaders. But the department stuck together. For two weeks the harassment caused production to drop from 2,000 parts per day to under 1,500. Finally, the company gave up

and the department returned to "normal."

At the same time, workers in 90 and 91 decided to find out what they could about QWL. They wrote away for information. They distributed copies of articles in the plant and initiated a general debate over QWL.

ACCIDENT

Another key event followed a serious plant accident. Because the injured worker was saved by the immediate attention of a nurse, workers became concerned about the lack of professional medical help on the night shift and weekends. The question came up in a QWL meeting and management said no.

This led the chairman of a QWL group to resign, stating, "As long as there are individuals who express these attitudes towards the workers, QWL will never work." Dozens of workers also signed a note endorsing his resignation letter.

As opposition to QWL spread, a motion for the union to get out of the program was submitted to the January union meeting. At first the unit chairman, Ed Whited, ruled the motion out of order. But overwhelming support forced him to schedule a vote for the following month's meeting.

There was intense debate in the plant for that month. The local union leadership distributed leaflets praising QWL. Others argued that the motion should be defeated because the program was voluntary, people should have free choice, and QWL was working in some departments. A supervisor handed out *Time* magazine reprints describing how a Fiat plant had smashed its "militant minority" to solve its problems.

In the leaflet war, QWL opponents argued:

> QWL is dangerous. Things that it accomplishes—coveralls, non-skid flooring, drip pans, etc.—are concerns of the union, not QWL. The company has embarked on a program to destroy the union—pitting plant against plant, department against department, worker against worker, all for profits.

They also circulated copies of the recently publicized "secret" GM documents showing the company plans to cut about 20% of its workforce in two years.

The week before the meeting, the company announced that there would be a nurse, after all, on the midnight shift. Management scheduled Sunday work for several of the departments, particularly the ones that were strongly against QWL. About 50 workers demanded passes, giving up double-time pay to go to the meeting.

The attendance of roughly 300 people made the meeting one of the largest the unit has seen. The motion to end participation in QWL passed 3-1.

WHAT NEXT?

The people most active in opposing QWL had not previously been active in union politics. They plan to become involved now. A number of the plant committeemen have come around to openly opposing QWL.

Although the opponents won the vote, they are not finished with QWL. As Pat Colella says, "We opposed it because we saw it was dividing the union. We are not unified yet because there are still some departments that support it.

"We want the union to bring in speakers and films to educate all the members about how the corporations are trying to bust the unions and how we can be a strong union."

Union to Bethlehem Steel:
'We Won't Help You Eliminate Jobs'

by Nick Contri
Vice President, USWA Local 6787

In the fall of 1983, Bethlehem Steel's Burns Harbor mill decided to start classes which every employee would eventually attend. They were Statistical Process Control and Juran classes. Both dealt with group problem solving. The union, United Steelworkers Local 6787, was neither informed nor involved.

Early in 1984, the union became aware the company was conducting these classes and started involving union officials, who immediately identified them for what they were. They were the tools for "Labor-Management Participation Teams" (LMPT), the steel industry's version of QWL.

The company was choosing facilitators for the classes, and the union knew the company would control whatever projects came out of them.

MUTUAL AGREEMENT

The national steel contract allows LMPT activities only under mutual agreement by the local union and management. In a few months the union collected enough information on the existing programs and filed a grievance charging that the activities were illegal and must stop.

Within a week, the grievance was settled with language that the company would stop these classes. In return, the local union would attend one meeting with the company on exploring the possibility of starting LMPT.

The week before this meeting, the union held a workshop for all its officers, from assistant griever up. We were educated on why LMPTs work so well for the company and not so well for the union.

What transpired at the meeting is something that every union member could be proud of.

More than 30 representatives of the union from all across the plant, both elected and appointed, attended.

Each one in their own way told the company that before the union would consider the type of cooperation the company was desiring: 1) we should be guaranteed job security; 2) all work in the plant should be returned to the hourly workforce rather than outside contractors, and 3) the members should get a piece of the pie if the new system were to be successful.

We all realized that the company is in business not to make steel, but to make profits. We demanded the input to change even this—we wanted control over investments that would keep people working.

I wish the words of our local union president, Dave Sullivan, could be printed as they were said, but the message was clear. The company does a very good job eliminating jobs on its own, and we don't intend to assist them in that endeavor—in any manner.

[Author's Note: Subsequent events in Local 6787 illustrate that a battle against QWL is not an easy one to win. Management persisted in its efforts to install an LMPT-type program, accompanying its campaign with threats of job loss. In April 1985 a new, pro-LMPT administration was elected in the local.]

2. Making QWL Work for the Union

Most locals may decide, for any or all of the reasons cited earlier, that getting out of QWL is not possible. In this case the union's best bet is to take the QWL bull by the horns, take leadership in the program, insist that it meet its promises, and use it to meet real worker needs and to build the union. Attempts to redirect the QWL program may well cause management to cancel it altogether. But if the company does cancel for this reason, it will be clear to the members that it is the union, not management, which is truly concerned about improving the quality of work life and worker participation.

There are several general concepts which are key to a successful union strategy.

1) The union must develop its own goals and strategy before it enters "joint" activities. All too often locals take management and QWL consultants at their word and expect to use joint bodies to work out solutions from scratch. But management holds its own meetings and sets its own goals for QWL before sitting down at the table. Since management is hierarchically structured, management officials will implement predetermined policy in a united fashion.

The union cannot afford to be less prepared than management. The union should decide its goals and attitude toward QWL democratically and be prepared before the joint meeting. The joint body then becomes the place where management and the union, each with its own position, work on implementing the program. There can still be problem solving at joint meetings. But with the union prepared, both parties, not just one, will have clear goals and limits.

Some unions are beginning to recognize the need for all-union mechanisms to train participants and to provide direction for their activity in QWL. The New York State Professional Employees Federation provided union training before beginning a QWL program and

This cartoon appeared in the April 1949 issue of *Ammunition*, a United Auto Workers magazine. The accompanying article ridiculed the "human engineering" advocated by Henry Ford. In a forerunner of modern-day QWL, the magazine reported, "Foremen are attending schools throughout the country to receive training in the art of convincing workers that they really are deeply beloved by the boss."

later held a statewide conference to evaluate the program and plan future union participation. The Steelworkers hold national meetings for LMPT participants and are planning a newsletter and a weeklong educational conference. A number of UAW locals have put on a series of meetings or conferences to enable the union to get a handle on QWL.

The union must insure that their members do not lose their union identity when working in joint projects, and that the union's interests are not reduced to the lowest common denominator with management. In one local the education and QWL coordinators had signs by their desks supporting another union's strike. The company insisted the signs come down because "it was an office for the joint project"!

Finally, participation in joint committees should be truly equal or the committees should be abandoned. It is not enough that the numbers from union and management be equal. Often management members work full-time on these committeess while union members are part-time and have many other responsibilities. Under these conditions at best the union members have veto power, but more often are nothing more than tokens which legitimize a management committee.

This is particularly intolerable in the case of a joint steering committee which is supposed to oversee the entire QWL program. If the union president or chairperson cannot make this committee a priority, then another strong union person should be appointed instead. If necessary, union funds should be used to insure full participation. This is not the place to be asking management for help in funding. The last thing the union needs in this critical position is a person whose position depends on maintaining what management considers a successful QWL program.

2) The union leadership must be united. A union program will only be taken seriously if the union appears committed to it. The union leadership—officers, stewards and facilitators—must act together. The union-appointed facilitators must see themselves as part of the union team and responsible for implementing the local's QWL policy.

3) The union should do its own long range planning. Management, after all, has a business plan. The union must understand management's plan and develop its own. Otherwise it will always be in the position of reacting to immediate events while long range goals slip away.

Companies often present QWL as the road to job security. The union should have its own plan for saving jobs, and a strategy for winning it. The members are more likely to choose to march with the union when they know where it is going.

4) The union should get independent help and expert advice when determining union goals, training, and materials. It cannot rely on the consultants hired "jointly" to install and advise the QWL program. Their interests lie with keeping the program going, not with the union's needs.

University labor studies programs may be helpful.

There are also a number of independent labor institutes which work with local unions in different parts of the country. See chapter 20 for some resources.

The union should also demand to see the "union label" on the consultants who advise the joint program. The union has a right to full references for the consultant and should reject any who are union busters or who do consulting work for non-union companies. Locals can check with their own internationals, with the AFL-CIO Organizing Department in Washington, and with the unions at other companies which have used the consultant.

5) The union has to be prepared to bargain hard for its interests in QWL. Don't assume that the union has no bargaining power over the structure or procedures. QWL programs differ greatly even within the same corporations. It may not even be legal for a company to maintain a QWL program if the union objects (see chapter 12).

Union leverage can be particularly great in the large corporations which have committed themselves to QWL programs and have developed expensive PR campaigns around them. The middle levels of management in many corporations are under tremendous pressure from above to install QWL. As the current management fad, a showcase QWL helps someone rise in management and a failure can block an otherwise promising career. UAW Vice-President Donald Ephlin describes the changes that took place when the president of General Motors became committed to QWL:

> When Jim McDonald says, "I want QWL," every manager says, "You got it." Many didn't even know what it is.[2]

If a QWL program creates bitter feelings or public controversy, a major part of its benefits to management is lost.

If the program hasn't yet begun, bargain for what the union needs *before* it begins. Insist on sufficient time and money for the union to allow its leaders and members to become familiar with QWL, determine local policies, and complete any necessary training. The union shouldn't feel bound by management's proposals or schedule.

There may be contractual or guideline provisions which can be used to insist on certain union procedures. For example, the December 1984 GM-UAW leadership guidelines include the statement that before "the parties jointly explore the meaning of QWL . . . it may be useful for the parties to go through a separate self-examination stage first."

If the program is already under way but is out of control (from the union's standpoint), it is probably best to put the program on hold while the union gets organized. One option is to demand that the program be dismantled and restarted from scratch.

6) Don't be defensive about the union. QWL's emphasis on direct communication between individuals and its "we're all family here" style tends to put the union in the role of outsider in the program. But unions can take credit for almost everything workers have today which gives them a decent life at work as well as a decent life outside of it. While unions need considerable improvement, there is much to be proud of.

___3. Steps to Building a Union QWL

What follows are some suggestions developed from working with a number of locals. Two cautions here: First, every suggestion will not be appropriate in every workplace; they must be adapted to the situation. Second, the worst strategy is to dabble in QWL. A few isolated union successes within QWL may only serve to give an entire program legitimacy, even as it continues to operate mainly as an anti-union program.

1) Begin by organizing a leadership conference to work out the union's position on QWL. Appendix I at the end of this chapter gives a sample agenda for such a conference. Include both facilitators and first line stewards. Allow enough time so that differences can be brought out and worked through.

This is a good place to use the QWL training methods described in chapter 2 and the appendix. First, these exercises give union leaders who are not familiar with QWL an excellent introduction to its attractions. Second, the "ice-breaking/team-building" features do work—this time for the union. Third, the problem solving skills are genuinely useful. If the conference focuses on the real problems facing the union (rather than artificial problems like "the sailor and the girl"), the union can make considerable progress on pulling together and developing its own strategy.

It is critical that the key union officers be at the conference and participate fully. Perhaps the most important outcome of the conference is a team which can handle initial problems and future ones as well. This will not happen if the key players are not present.

2) Provide for union structures that can lead union QWL activities on an ongoing basis. It may be sufficient to assign responsibility for QWL to the union executive board, the shop committee or some other union body. But in many cases a small working committee which includes QWL facilitators, key stewards, and the union president (or designate from the executive board) would be a more effective working body. This committee may want to meet regularly with all the facilitators.

QWL is a complicated and decentralized program. One of the first things a leadership committee needs is solid and regular information. A good way to gather information systematically and to measure progress is to develop a checklist or survey such as the one at the end of this chapter (Appendix II). One of the values of such a survey is that it focuses on the goals of QWL from a union point of view. The survey helps to identify trouble areas and to pick out the positive ideas that should be spread to other circles.

3) Bring the union QWL facilitators on board. If they function as part of a union team, facilitators are potentially a great resource. In many industries, the decline in union membership has meant a decline in the number of union stewards and officials. This in turn has reduced the number of openings in the union structure for aggressive new blood. Many of the people who might have looked to union involvement are ending up as QWL facilitators instead.

Conversely, if the facilitators do not see themselves as part of the union structure, they can pose a grave danger. They can form a highly-motivated, well-informed pro-company body which rivals the union for influence on the shop floor.

Facilitators must be part of the union leadership. They should participate in developing the union's policy and be responsible for carrying it out. Part of this can be done structurally: facilitators can be made part of the executive board (with or without vote); they can have regular meetings with the shop committee; and/or they can participate in a QWL leadership committee as described earlier.

Treating facilitators as part of the leadership should be done informally as well. Facilitators should be consulted regularly, be given regular union briefings like other union leaders, and be involved in union activities other than QWL.

Facilitators should of course get thorough QWL training from a *union point of view*. But given the kinds of problems that facilitators handle, they also need to get traditional union training in the contract, grievance procedure, union history and union structure. One of the most valuable forms of union training is "on the job." By functioning occasionally as alternate stewards, facilitators will have a much better idea of the problems union representatives face.

In order to train circles effectively facilitators may also need training in certain substantive areas, such as health and safety, new technology, or the company's products or services.

The union should be clear that the facilitator's job is to represent the union point of view in QWL. The facilitator's job description should be written with this in mind (see the example in chapter 6). The local union must have the power to select, to direct and, if necessary, to replace the facilitator. If a facilitator is in trouble with management because management is not getting its way in QWL, the union must back him or her up. And if a facilitator is running a program that undermines the union, that facilitator should be replaced.

The union must make it clear to the company that the facilitator is not a company "go-fer"; he or she must have sufficient equipment, material and cooperation to do the job right and without harassment. In one Ford local the union leadership had to insist that the company could not time-study the union facilitator.

Finally, the union should work out a position regarding the facilitators' special status. For example, how do overtime rules, bumping rules, promotion rules, and wage rates apply to facilitators? Should facilitators be prohibited from running for union office because their job provides an unfair advantage? Or would such a prohibition work against the need for facilitators to think of themselves as part of the union leadership, and would it tend to keep union activists from becoming facilitators? Answers to these questions will vary from local to local. The important thing is to make sure that the union has worked out a procedure to handle them as they arise so they will not become big problems or create personal bitterness.

4) Bring the stewards into the program. The stewards should be represented in the QWL leadership described earlier. The discussion in chapters 8 and 9 showed how the "watchdog" role puts the steward in an impossible position. Most QWL programs have too many circles for the steward to be an active member in all of them. But he or she can be actively involved in one or two, and can be brought in when the circle is dealing with an issue in which union help and involvement is essential. Stewards can lead task forces to deal with subjects of plantwide interest such as noise reduction or outside contracting.

The steward can use the QWL structure to build the union network by designating one person in each of the QWL circles as an alternate steward. These alternates should get union training and occasionally be called on to function as stewards.

Stewards and facilitators should be encouraged to develop a close working relationship. They might issue periodic joint reports on shop floor developments.

The union can reduce the tendency for QWL to undercut or demoralize the stewards by insisting that all

" See how well our automatic grievance machinery works! "

facilities available to QWL facilitators such as office equipment and computers should also be provided to stewards.

5) Involve the membership. The union leadership must develop a clear attitude toward QWL which it communicates to the membership. This can be accomplished by preparing and distributing a candid policy statement which includes what union leaders hope to see QWL accomplish, what they see as its problems, and proposed solutions. Any reservations about QWL should be openly acknowledged.

As the program continues, the union should develop its own channels for reporting what is going on in QWL. Members and leaders should report problems and successes so that the entire membership can see the whole picture. Personal recognition is one reward from QWL. The union should recognize QWL achievements according to its own pro-union criteria rather than let members depend on management channels for recognition.

The union has to make it clear that the issues that come up in QWL will affect all workers, and therefore every union participant in a QWL group should see him or herself as a representative of the other workers and the union. Members who have a healthy skepticism about the program should be encouraged to participate and raise their problems for groups to deal with. If only the most pro-company workers participate in QWL, it is guaranteed that the program will be pro-company and undermine the other workers and the union.

If possible, departments should elect their QWL representatives. While election of QWL representatives is not common, it has been done. In fact, one of the highly publicized QWL success stories, involving the

Newspaper Guild in Minneapolis and St. Paul, is based on committees of elected representatives. These departmental elections are sometimes hotly contested.

A local union may not have control over training programs developed by joint national committees. But it should be able to have its own local orientation for all members who participate in the program. Especially when joint training is of the heavily emotional kind described in chapter 3, it is important that participants be prepared before training begins. One of the benefits of a union QWL orientation is that the team-building effects of QWL-type exercises accrue to the union instead of to management.

The orientation program also allows the union to put joint QWL training in its proper perspective. It is quite possible to gain useful skills and even to enjoy the exercises at joint QWL training. But the mistake is to believe that relating to management officials as equals in a hothoused "family" atmosphere has anything to do with the relationship when there is production to get out.

Much of QWL's appeal to union members is that it appears to fill a vacuum; it provides workers with the opportunity to have some control at work. Union members often perceive the union as just another bureaucracy or a service agency. Union leaders and members must take the time to examine their local carefully. Is the union actively pursuing the kinds of issues that affect life in the plant? Are there ways for rank and file members to get involved easily? Can members be heard in the union newspaper? Do the members make the big decisions or are union meetings held just for the record? Does the union offer members a chance to learn new skills? Does it offer pleasant social relationships? Are newcomers welcomed?

Union leaders must maintain membership confidence that union involvement in QWL does not mean they are in bed with management. Leaders should avoid "off-site" conferences with management at plush resorts. Meetings between the leadership and management can be cordial but they should keep to union business and not turn into social events. Likewise the union should check that the handling of grievances, union bargaining and other union activities do not wither while attention is paid to QWL.

6) Develop a clear understanding on how to handle the collective bargaining/QWL overlap. There are a number of different approaches:

a) *Establish union-management negotiating sessions to screen topics proposed by QWL groups.* Problems can be settled in these sessions as in regular negotiations, or if both sides agree the topic can be sent back to a QWL group. One of the advantages of this system is that it tends to take the "fans, water fountains and common sense" issues out of QWL. Management either responds to the union in good faith or it does not, but is not allowed to bypass it. It also makes it possible for the union to plug stewards into particular group activities at an early stage. This procedure is being used at Ford's Dearborn stamping plant.

b) *Communicate to management a clear union policy that what it refuses in collective bargaining it cannot give through QWL.* This should make management more careful about turning down items in bargaining discussions and the union will be able to use bargaining to cover broader areas. Many leaders of the United Auto Workers including Vice-President Donald Ephlin have said they are supporting this policy.

c) *Regard QWL as a first step in the collective bargaining process.* Both stewards and members can take advantage of the informal and problem-solving atmosphere of QWL to resolve problems that come up in the workplace. But if they are not resolved then the union can take them to the grievance procedure or contract negotiations. Similarly, if a QWL group develops a proposal which is rejected by management, the union can carry the proposal to the bargaining table.

Whichever general strategy a union chooses, it should also:

Insist that groups have the right to meet without management representatives when necessary. Meetings without management are necessary, for example, when members in a QWL group begin to complain about fellow workers. When a worker at Ford's Chicago assembly plant brings in a particular gripe against another worker, the EI group calls for a union representative and asks the management representative to leave. Without management present, the problems are discussed by the workers themselves and frequently resolved.[3]

Keep the membership informed about what is happening in collective bargaining. The union can hold regular classes to train members in the contract and the grievance procedure. It can publicize grievances in process and settled, and post proposals for contract demands or for periodic mid-contract negotiating sessions.

7) Take leadership in choosing QWL projects. Although circles usually choose their own problems to work on, the union can develop a list of suggested topics. Part of the job of leadership is to expand the

SUGGESTIONS FOR QWL PROJECTS

WORK LIFE ISSUES

Some good union sources for information on many of these topics are listed in the appendix to this chapter.

Health and Safety

Job stress. Studies show that stress is highest for workers who have no control over the design or pace of their jobs. After training in this area, circles could identify stressful jobs and propose solutions (see chapter 13).

Noise control

Ergonomics. This is the science of designing jobs and tools so that they fit human beings.

Chemical hazards. Groups could research all chemicals used in the workplace and make proposals for elimination, safe handling, screening exams, and tracking medical histories.

Video display terminals. Problems range from uncomfortable machine design to health hazards to employer monitoring of performance.

Special health problems. Almost every industry has some special health problem, such as "white lung" in textile or exposure to particular diseases in medical professions.

Problems of specific groups of workers. Women at GM's Livonia Spring and Bumper Plant have formed a women's QWL group to deal with specific problems that women face in the plant. A group could form to address problems of workers with physical disabilities.

Equal Treatment With Management

Parking facilities

Time clocks

Discounts on or free use of company products

Doing a Good Job

Circles can propose better tools, better techniques and better training to do higher quality work. Frequently, however, proposals in this area can lead to indirect job loss so union attention is particularly necessary.

Attending trade shows

Visiting supply or tool manufacturers

Organizing on the job training sessions

Work as Part of Life

Flextime and absenteeism. A circle could do a survey and make a proposal for work time to be organized around the workers' needs (see chapter 13).

Childcare arrangements

Job transfers. People will find more satisfying jobs if they are allowed to transfer until they find the one best suited to them. Circles could make proposals to reduce transfer restrictions.

Sabbaticals or leaves. Circles can work on proposals for extended leaves of absence for education, travel, family, or even trying a different kind of job.

"Creature Comforts"

Heating and cooling

Locker rooms

Waiting areas

Lunch rooms and food services

Physical fitness

JOB SECURITY ISSUES

Reduce "outsourcing." Circles could examine parts brought in from non-union companies and make proposals for creating additional jobs in the bargaining unit by producing these in-plant.

Reduce subcontracting. Circles could examine services provided by non-union service or repair companies and propose training so that these could be done within the bargaining unit.

A welder-repair EI group in Ford's Dearborn assembly plant proposed that additional workers be hired to repair expensive valves and hydraulic cylinders rather than replace them. Electricians in the same plant took over repair of electronic weld controls that had previously been shipped out for service. The benefit to Ford was a $100,000 savings in repair costs over nine months, faster turnaround time, and a higher quality of repair. The benefit to the union was better training for electricians and supposedly more jobs. (In fact, it turned

"realm of the possible." QWL training is useful here. The purpose of the Nine Dots problem (see chapter 2) and the brainstorm technique is to help participants break through unnecessary limitations on their thinking. See the list of QWL project suggestions in this chapter.

Note that in many QWL programs, problems are specified first and then task forces are formed to solve them. Members with special interests can initiate task

forces to deal with them.

8) Deal directly with the job loss problem. As we discussed in chapter 8, most circle proposals which save money do so because they will mean fewer jobs. Fewer rejects, for example, means fewer items have to be manufactured to get the same number out the door. The savings result because fewer work hours are needed to produce the reduced number of goods. Similarly with reduced "downtime," improved office procedures, or

out that more maintenance jobs were not created—just more work.)

The Machinists-Eastern Airlines agreement included a "Contracting-in Committee" to find jobs that could be done by bargaining unit members. In 1984 a large number of major jobs that had been farmed out (such as the repair of jetways) was brought into the bargaining unit. A welder developed a repair process for heat shields which previously had been thrown away. Through the committee's initiative several printing jobs, such as the company's carbon forms, are done in-house, requiring additional equipment and three more people.[4]

Technically, the Contracting-in Committee was separate from the EI program, though it was introduced at the same time. As IAM stewards Rusty Brown and Paul Baicich point out, it demonstrates that "we don't need 'Employee Involvement' to work on the issue of contracting-in. A shop floor union structure can do the work in tandem with a contracting-in committee on the District level." But a QWL program could use the Contracting-in Committee as a model. Indeed, before Employee Involvement was seriously damaged by Eastern management's actions in January 1985, some of the Action Committees also worked on contracting issues.

There are some pitfalls in contracting-in type activities. For example, Brown and Baicich suggest that certain projects brought in to IAM workers at Eastern may have been done previously by IAM mechanics at United Airlines. Unions need to develop safeguards so that contracting-in activities do not end up pitting one group of unionized workers against another.

Propose job intensive solutions. The union can help groups search out solutions which will increase jobs. For example, an LMP Team at McLouth Steel proposed that certain supplies be bought in bulk rather than prepackaged. The money saved by buying in bulk paid for the extra person hired to do the handling.

Training. Circles can propose training to main-tain and enhance skills. The more skills a worker has in a trade (as opposed to knowledge required only for a specific machine), the easier it will be to find a job elsewhere should the plant close down. If a particular occupation is being phased out by new technology, a circle can propose a retraining program.

New technology. See chapter 13.

Alternative plant use. The fate of most individual plants or offices is often decided by corporations far removed from the workplace and the community. To help forewarn of or prevent closings, circles can investigate the facilities to make sure that the parent company is not stripping the local plant. With knowledge of the plant's capabilities, circles can investigate the needs of the surrounding community to assess the possibilities for producing alternative products.

COMMUNITY SERVICE

One more area for QWL that is often overlooked is community service. Sometimes QWL groups take responsibility for blood drives or United Fund contributions. This could be expanded to cover other community needs such as programs for children, or organizing for decent public services like garbage collection and street repair.

reduced maintenance: a significant part of the money saved will be from reduced labor time.

Protecting jobs should be one of the union's main concerns in QWL. Where the program includes guidelines which prohibit job loss, the union can propose specific procedures to make the guidelines work. Here are examples:

a) Build into the QWL procedure a *job impact evaluation.* Just as the government requires an "environmen-tal impact study" before certain construction projects can be started, a standard part of every circle's problem solving should be to examine the effect that any proposal will have on jobs. Circles could be required to hold a meeting with stewards to brainstorm and discuss the job impact, and post their preliminary findings for comment by others. Or the QWL group could make a presentation to the stewards committee on job impact.

The advantage of this kind of procedure is that it

focuses the group on looking at the problem from a union point of view. No circle would seriously consider a proposal without looking at its dollar cost (the management perspective). Neither should it seriously consider a proposal without looking at its cost in jobs (the union perspective).

b) Encourage groups to *choose problems and solutions which create jobs*, as discussed above.

c) *Make up for lost jobs with specific new projects.* As discussed in chapter 9, vague guidelines about "no loss of employment as a direct result of QWL" need specifics if they are actually to protect jobs during a time of constant technological change. One way is to assign labor saved by specific QWL proposals to other QWL projects directed at improving work life quality.

For example, suppose a group makes a proposal that would cut one job. Before the group's proposal could be adopted it would have to be tied to another QWL or union proposal which required additional labor hours such as child care or contracting in. This is a variation of the "earned jobs" arrangement used between 1978 and 1981 by IUE Local 717 and GM Packard Electric.

d) *Transfer savings in labor time to training.* When a QWL proposal results in loss of work time, the time lost could be added to a "training bank." The time thus created could be used for training programs on company time. Alternatively, QWL labor savings could be applied to shortening the work week. An experiment at Harmon Industries in the 1970's featured an "Earned Idle Time" provision.

9) **Take control of QWL training.** There are two possible kinds of training involved. First is the standard QWL *procedural* or *organizational* training in problem

---

8 PROBLEM SOLVING STEPS

1. State the problem.

2. List possible causes.

3. Choose most likely cause.

4. List possible solutions.

5. Choose best solution.

6. **Post for comment. Evaluate job impact. If unacceptable go back to Step 5.**

7. Implement solution.

8. Evaluate results.

---

solving and organizational skills. Under most programs, these courses teach people to think "company" and not "union" (see chapter 3). Unions should carefully, possibly with expert help, examine the training program. They should consider who actually gives the training, the content of the exercises and examples, and the structure. Relevant questions could include: What is the ratio of management to union trainers? Are union members expected to temporarily suspend their union identity during training? Who trains the trainers? The union should insist that union history and procedures be

included in the course.

The union might want to propose to do all the training of its members. The agreement between the United Paperworkers and Westvaco Corp. provides that union and management train their own people separately. UPIU stewards and officers teach both QWL and grievance handling to union members of the Labor-Management Committees.[5]

The second type of training is *substantive* and deals with specific workplace problems. For example, QWL could provide training in noise control, handling dangerous chemicals, reducing stress, VDTs, or installation of new technology. Many unions have excellent materials in these areas, and some useful publications are listed in Appendix III at the end of this chapter.

10) Reestablish the union "mission." An important appeal of QWL is that it offers an idealistic long run vision. All too often employers have portrayed unions as privileged, narrow, special interest groups. Unions have a mission to provide power to the powerless and create social justice for all. Unions need to proudly put forth their own vision. They need to remind their members of labor's history as well as taking action today to reclaim the vision. As a beginning unions must reestablish active solidarity between unions and provide full support for all struggles to organize the unorganized.

To make its point the union should insist on union labor for all QWL materials. UAW Local 909, for example, demanded that all QWL paraphernalia (buttons, jackets, printed materials) be made in union shops. Carrying this principle one step further, circles can refuse to voluntarily discuss quality problems that involve non-union suppliers when there are union suppliers available. Secondary boycott laws do not apply to QWL groups.

11) Arrange cross-union contacts for QWL participants. One of the most valuable resources a union has is the experience of other unions. Such contacts also lessen the pressure to buy into the "local against local" mentality that QWL fosters, and reinforce the common interests of labor. If unions adopt common guidelines for QWL then the programs themselves will not become the basis for pitting unions against each other. Locals could get together and request their international union to sponsor a conference, or could work through the local Central Labor Council to set up a cross-union discussion.

For all the reasons outlined in earlier chapters, current QWL programs are naturally and heavily biased toward management. A union attempt to gain some control over QWL is extremely difficult. Occasional dabbling is the worst alternative—the union appears to take responsibility and management gets its program.

However hard the union is willing to work to reshape QWL, it must still be prepared to get out. If the union is not capable of withdrawing from QWL in a unified and organized way, with the support of most of the leaders, members and facilitators, then it is in a weak position to deal with management in the program. If management

believes that significant sections of the union are dependent on the QWL program for patronage jobs, funding, office space, or a political benefit, it may not take seriously the union's willingness to pull out.

Management may well exercise its own option to withdraw. Where unions have taken serious steps to reshape a QWL program and institute some degree of union control, many employers have responded by allowing the program to collapse with red tape, delays, and lack of funds. While unions have some leverage, it is a mistake to assume that management is always blind or stupid. When the program stops doing what the employer intends, the employer will stop funding it. □

Notes

1. *Labor Notes*, August 23, 1984.
2. Donald Ephlin, Speech, Michigan QWL Council Conference, November 11, 1983.
3. Albert R. Verri, *The New Industrial Relations*, Master's Thesis, Roosevelt University, Chicago, 1983. Verri is a former UAW international representative.
4. "A Report From the Contracting-In Committee," District 100, International Association of Machinists, December 4, 1984.
5. Edward Cohen-Rosenthal and Cynthia Burton, "Labor-Management Cooperation," *The Paperworker*, June 1984.

__Inside the Circle: A UNION GUIDE TO QWL___
Labor Education and Research Project, P.O. Box 20001, Detroit, MI 48220. (313) 883-5580.

APPENDIX I

A QWL Conference for Union Leaders

Following is a suggested outline for a local union leadership conference on QWL.

OBJECTIVES

- ✓ Understand how QWL works.
- ✓ Examine the experience of other unions with QWL.
- ✓ Understand the positive features of QWL.
- ✓ Identify and analyze problems posed for the union by QWL.
- ✓ Identify possible union strategies.
- ✓ Strengthen union team functioning.

SESSIONS

A. Introduction and welcome
1. Overview of conference
2. Introduction to QWL
3. Team building exercises

B. History of QWL ideas
1. History of international union's position on QWL
2. History of local union-management discussions on QWL

C. Understanding the QWL process
1. Problem solving methods
2. What is attractive about QWL
3. What goes on in QWL training
4. What goes on in QWL groups

D. Problems QWL poses for unions

E. Relationship between collective bargaining and QWL
1. Permissive and mandatory issues
2. Possible union strategies

F. Functioning on "joint" committees

G. Problem solving groups

The problem solving groups' activities should be divided into several sessions and interspersed with the other conference sessions. The conference is broken down into smaller working groups and each group is assigned a specific problem. Examples:

1. Generate a list of the ways jobs might be lost directly or indirectly through QWL.

2. Generate a list of suggested projects for QWL groups to work on. Make them specific to your workplace.

3. Generate a list of the ways QWL might threaten the stewards or other union representatives.

4. Generate a list of general problems QWL poses or might pose for unions or the ideas of unionism.

5. Generate a list of problems union members who have QWL responsibilities (facilitators, coordinators, group leaders) have or may have in carrying out their responsibilities.

These groups should function as QWL circles do. After lists of possible problems are developed, the groups should work on finding solutions. Since many of the participants will not have had experience with QWL before, and part of the purpose of the exercise is to introduce unionists to the QWL process, the exercise should be highly structured. For example, the first topic would be structured along the following lines:

1. Use brainstorming to generate the initial list of ways jobs might be lost through QWL.

2. Select six important ones.

3. Select the one which appears most serious.

4. List the possible ways the union might deal with this problem.

5. Discuss solutions and prepare a recommendation on the best solution or combination of solutions.

6. Prepare a presentation to the whole conference summarizing the issue and describing the proposed solution in detail.

H. Identifying possible union strategies

I. Deciding union position

J. Next steps

K. Review and evaluation of conference

APPENDIX II

A QWL Survey

The union's first step toward getting on top of an already-functioning QWL program is to find out what is going on. Gathering the information in a systematic way by using a checklist or survey sheet helps the participants look at areas they may not have considered. It also makes it easier to compare different experiences.

On the next pages are lists of questions developed in a Wayne State University labor studies class. The first list covers the basic descriptive facts about the program. The second list raises questions for evaluating QWL from a union point of view.

The checklists should be modified to take into account differences in industry, occupation, union, and QWL structure.

I. Descriptive

1. Background

Labor-management relationships

Plant problems

2. Structure of QWL Program

Steering committee (how many, who, frequency of meetings, responsibilities)

Coordinators (how many, who, how selected)

Groups (how many, how selected, size)

Other structures now existing or planned (e.g., business teams, self-managing groups)

3. Implementation

How did program get started?

How was joint steering committee established?

Initial surveys?

Consultant? Who, how selected?

Communication system? (e.g., QWL newsletter, company newsletter)

Physical facilities (office, telephone, parking permits)

4. Policies and Procedures

"Mission" or "policy" statements or "statements of purpose"

Guidelines or rules

Contract language (national and local)

5. Projects and Activities

Completed

In progress

Rejected by group

How were projects selected?

What was disposition of projects presented to management?

6. Training

How conducted?

Who does it?

Who gets it?

What is its content?

Where do training materials come from?

II. Evaluation

(Note: Some of the answers may be different for different circles.)

1. What is role of union QWL coordinator, facilitator, leader? What is his or her relationship to local union policies and leadership?

2. What is relationship of stewards to QWL?
   (uninvolved, watchdog, QWL advocate, union advocate)

3. What is relationship of union officers to QWL?
   (uninvolved, watchdog, QWL advocate, union advocate)

4. What is international union's role in program?
   (international reps, steering committees, conferences, materials)

5. What is attitude of QWL participants?
   (enthusiastic, demoralized, detached) Why? What are attractive or negative features?

6. What is attitude of non-participants toward QWL and toward QWL participants?

7. How is the relationship between QWL issues and collective bargaining handled in practice?

8. Does the union have a strategy toward QWL? How is it expressed? How is it communicated? Is it known and understood by the membership?

9. What are the company's goals with regards to its workforce? How does this fit with its QWL involvement?

10. What specific problems has QWL caused the union?

11. How has QWL benefited the union?

APPENDIX III
Resources for Union QWL Projects

New Technology

Work Transformed: Automation and Labor in the Computer Age, by Harley Shaiken. 1985. 306 pages. Holt, Rinehart and Winston. Shows how social choices are made in the introduction and use of automation. $17.95.

Labor and Technology: Union Response to Changing Environments, edited by Donald Kennedy, Charles Craypo and Mary Lehman. 1982. 209 pages. Department of Labor Studies, The Pennsylvania State University. A collection of papers by union staff researchers which provides valuable data on the effects of new technology in several industries as well as proposals for union response. Dept. of Labor Studies, 901 Liberal Arts Tower, University Park, PA 16802. $6 plus $.90 postage.

Job Design—Ergonomics

Sprains and Strains—A Worker's Guide to Job Design. 1982. 36 pages. Shows how jobs can be redesigned to avoid stress and injury. United Auto Workers, Purchase and Supply Dept., 8000 E. Jefferson, Detroit, MI 48214. Publication #460. $2.

Noise

Noise Control—A Worker's Manual. 1978. 47 pages. Includes detailed technical information. UAW Health and Safety Dept., 8000 E. Jefferson, Detroit, MI 48214. $1.25.

Sexual Harassment

Stopping Sexual Harassment: A Handbook, by Elissa Clarke. 1981. 51 pages. Shows how to deal with harassment from supervisors and co-workers, from a union member's point of view. Includes a sample survey. Labor Education and Research Project, PO Box 20001, Detroit, MI 48220. $2.50 plus $.75 postage.

Chemicals

Work Is Dangerous To Your Health, by Jeanne Stellman and Susan Daum. 1973. 448 pages. Classifies chemicals by occupation, explains measuring and monitoring, and how to keep records. Women's Occupational Health Resource Center, Columbia University School of Public Health, 21 Audubon Ave., 3rd floor, New York, NY 10032. $4.95 plus $1 postage.

NIOSH/OSHA Pocket Guide to Chemical Hazards. 1978. 191 pages. Easy to use. Order Publication #017-033-00342-4 from Superintendent of Documents, U.S. Government Printing Office, Washington, DC 20402. $7.50 payable to Supt. of Documents.

Stress

Occupational Stress: The Inside Story, by Aaron Back, Michael Lerner, Lee Schore. 1982. 103 pages. Discusses the sources and methods of dealing with stress at work. Institute for Labor and Mental Health, 3137 Telegraph Ave., Oakland, CA 94618. $3.

"Bosses Face Less Risk than the Bossed," *New York Times*, April 3, 1983. Summary of extensive study, led by Dr. Robert Karasek, which shows that lack of "job control" is strongly linked to heart disease.

Video Display Terminals

Office Work Can Be Dangerous To Your Health, by Jeanne Stellman and Mary Sue Henifin. 1983. 239 pages. Includes sample surveys, lists results of radiation testing on some VDT's. Women's Occupational Resource Center, Columbia University School of Public Health, 21 Audubon Ave., 3rd floor, New York, NY 10032. $6.95 plus $1 postage.

This Booklet Is For Office Workers. 1983. 21 pages. Good for overall office health and safety strategizing. Southeast Michigan Coalition on Occupational Safety and Health (SEMCOSH), 1550 Howard St., Detroit, MI 48216. $2.

Health Protection for Operators of VDTs/CRTs. Good information on the VDT itself. New York Coalition on Occupational Safety and Health (NYCOSH), 32 Union Square, Room 404, New York, NY 10003. $1.

General Health and Safety

A Worker's Guide to Documenting Health and Safety Problems. 1978. 68 pages. Labor Occupational Health Program, 2521 Channing Way, Berkeley, CA 94720. $6.

Workplace Health and Safety: A Guide to Collective Bargaining. 1980. 68 pages. Labor Occupational Health Program, 2521 Channing Way, Berkeley, CA 94720. $7.

This Booklet Is For Health Care Workers. 1984. 22 pages. What the hazards are and what to do about them. SEMCOSH, 1550 Howard St., Detroit, MI 48216. $3.

How To Inspect Your Plant. 1982. 36 pages. Checklists for various hazards. United Electrical Workers, 11 E. 51st St., New York, NY 10022. $1.

Information About Your Company

Spying On Your Employer. 1980. 4 pages. How to use the library to discover your employer's true financial condition. Labor Education and Research Project, P.O. Box 20001, Detroit, MI 48220. $.50.

Resources: Digging Out Facts On Your Employer. 218 pages. Shows how to use the library, includes a checklist for evaluating an employer's "ability to pay." Labor Center, External Programs, College of Business Administration, Oakdale Hall, University of Iowa, Iowa City, IA 52242. $10.

CROSSROADS: LABOR COOPERATION OR COMPETITION

In the middle of the LTV Steel complex of plants on Cleveland's Cuyahoga River, a new galvanizing plant is under construction. Technically the plant will belong to a new company owned 60% by LTV and 40% by Sumitomo Metal Industries of Japan. But the chief executive officer of L-S Electro-Galvanizing Co. is also the president of LTV. He describes his new labor agreement with the United Steelworkers union as "pioneering."[1]

The plant will contain the newest technology and employ only about 70 workers, all of whom will be "salaried." Starting salaries will be the equivalent of $8.50 per hour, at least $1.80 below rates at the other LTV plants in the area. Management points out that part of the pioneering agreement is the absence of built-in cost of living increases.

A letter to laid-off LTV employees offers an opportunity to apply to work in the new plant—"a participative environment unlike any other in the steel industry." Those who successfully complete the probationary period will give up their seniority and callback rights at LTV Steel. Management promises employees:

> ...a unique work life system and unique job versatility features. For example, Operating and Maintenance duties will be integrated and work stations and work routines will be flexible and developed through participative efforts.[2]

LTV's agreement with the Steelworkers is a perfect illustration of how management links "employee participation" and QWL to job loss and weakened unions.

But while QWL is not just a corporate fad, neither is it a corporate goal. From the corporate viewpoint, QWL is just a short stretch of road on the way to the larger goals of bigger profits and greater control over the workforce. When these goals have been reached, QWL and its baggage—the circles, the facilitators, the training—will be discarded. In a sense the labor movement is at a critical crossroads. It can allow itself to be dragged down management's road, or it can take its own independent path.

In this chapter we will discuss what lies ahead down management's road, and why following this road is a losing strategy for the labor movement. Then we will suggest some independent steps for labor, the beginning of an alternate road.

Briefly, we will argue that:

1) The main purpose of QWL is to channel unions into adopting "help-my-company-compete" as their primary strategy.

2) The competitive strategy is a guaranteed long run disaster both for individual unions and for labor as a whole.

3) The only long-range plan that will work in the interests of labor involves a conscious decision and attempt to alter economic forces rather than being at their mercy.

4) Such a plan requires building cooperation inside the labor movement rather than competition, and alliances with workers and communities outside organized labor's ranks.

5) QWL hurts efforts to build labor strength and alliances by carving up the labor movement into competing "special interests."

6) The labor movement can call upon its traditional cooperative values and formulate a new plan appropriate to the new economic challenges.

Corporate Strategy: Beyond QWL

One of the biggest problems for unions in the "new industrial relations" is that they have allowed management to develop long term plans and take the initiative, leaving labor to fight brush fires while the forest burns. It is only recently that unions have begun to develop any strategies at all for dealing with QWL, let alone good ones.

But while unions are groping for a way to deal with QWL, management is planning the steps which will follow it. From management's point of view QWL does a good job of weakening the union, but by itself does not create the new, stable relationship that management seeks to make its planning more efficient. In addition, QWL is expensive and does not seem to work well for long.

Thus management and many professional QWL practitioners look for current QWL programs to evolve to what they consider a higher level, which includes "semi-autonomous work teams" or the *Socio-Technical Systems* (STS) approach.

These are not new ideas. Some companies, including General Motors, experimented with them extensively at non-union plants during the 1970's, before QWL became popular. Now, however, they are presented as the logical outgrowth of QWL.

Like QWL itself, the STS approach seems perfectly reasonable when first explained. The underlying idea is that work organization, technology and employee relations interact and, to be effective, must be planned together. To take a commonly used example: a company might want to organize work for "zero defects," so that no assembly line worker knowingly allows a defective part to go by. This requires that every worker have a stop button, as well as "banking" of parts so that every time an individual needs to stop the line, hundreds don't have to cease work. But it also requires a cooperative spirit and a feeling of responsibility on the part of the workers, since it would be counterproductive to provide every worker with a stop button if their attitudes were "bad" and they used it to create breaks for each other.

STS in practice usually means some form of "semi-autonomous work team." In theory the team has no "supervisor," although it probably has an "advisor." The teams work within a framework established by management, which determines production quotas, production methods, and materials to be used. Frequently teams have some disciplinary power over members and some say over their pay increments. Work is often reorganized so that each worker does several tasks. Team members may rotate jobs and the teams meet regularly to discuss their work.

Several features of these STS systems pose a serious challenge to unions.

1) The collective bargaining agreement becomes less relevant as each team sets its own standards for the pace and methods of work. Previously bargained agreements on workloads for specific jobs, for example, are out the window.

2) Job classifications are replaced by a "pay for knowledge" system. Under this system workers who can do all the jobs in a team earn an additional ten or twenty cents per hour. In some programs there are additional increments for learning other teams' jobs. But the extra pay isn't actually for knowledge —a metal finisher who

"So long, partner!"

studies metallurgy receives no extra money. It is a cheap way for management to buy out the classification system, with significant loss of both jobs and job control (see chapter 4).

Pay-for-knowledge is extremely divisive. When management determines who is to get the extra pay, pro-management attitudes are rewarded. When workers are allowed some influence within a management-controlled framework, cliques are encouraged to reward each other. Experienced trade unionists sometimes refer to it as "pay for scabbing" or a shop talk version of "pay for apple polishing."

3) The team is often responsible for assignment of duties and evaluation of individual members. Workers take on the tasks of managers and naturally end up shafting fellow workers. As a Canadian study noted:

> Thus, the union is sometimes faced with a situation in which it is forced to ... contest decisions no longer made by a management representative but rather by [its own members].[3]

4) Large disparities in working conditions develop between different groups of workers, further breaking down solidarity and the union's ability to establish decent working conditions.

5) STS creates a direct link between the work groups and management, excluding the union.

QWL practitioners propose various methods to defuse expected union opposition to work teams. They suggest early consultation with the union, giving union leaders some "stake" in the process, or forcing hesitant union leaders to cooperate through direct appeals to the rank and file.

Some Ford Motor Co. and many General Motors plants are introducing team production slowly through QWL programs, both by indoctrinating facilitators (see chapter 6) and by trying to channel QWL activities into what are termed "natural work groups," usually departmental units. Defining QWL groups by their production tasks naturally focuses them on dealing with immediate production problems. In this form it is easier to pass to the group responsibility for meeting management's production goals.

General Motors has used its new plants to establish precedents for STS (as well as to put competitive pressure on existing plants). For example, when GM opened its new assembly plant in Lake Orion, Michigan in 1984, the company put all production workers through a three-week orientation to teach them the "Orion Concept." For most of the orientation there were no union representatives present; the tone was set by a set of "Policies and Procedures" which began:

> In as much as we are a new plant, there are no local agreements at Orion and non-skilled trades employes are compensated in accordance with a Management Pay for Knowledge policy.[4]

In the "Orion Concept," 10 to 16 employees who work in the same geographical area form a work group. Each work group selects one hourly person to be the "work group coordinator." Up to four groups are responsible to a "work group manager," who "should be viewed as a co-worker."

The Work Group Manager's job is to assist your Work Group in meeting schedule requirements and in helping the Work Group maintain high quality at a competitive cost. Your Work Group Manager needs your cooperation and loyalty in order to accomplish these goals.

The work group managers meet regularly with the hourly coordinators, who are widely regarded as assistant bosses.

In theory, the work groups run their areas by means of compulsory weekly meetings. But a group of 10 to 16 people does not make many serious decisions in the half hour per week the company allocates. Almost the entire meeting is taken up by a standard format: presentation and charting of the group's absenteeism statistics, charting of scrap statistics, and questioning of the need for any materials "bought" from the supply crib (e.g., gloves, brooms, cleaning materials). The fact that all work group meetings are held at the same time means that union representatives cannot attend most of them. Thus the group meetings are nothing more than a transmission belt to establish the management framework and management values within which employees are supposed to function.

There is also a QWL program in the Orion plant. But unlike the elaborate QWL programs in older GM plants, it has little structure, staff or activity. Except for a sports program, QWL is practically invisible in Orion, as management now works through the team organization. Two other GM assembly plants, in Wentzville, Missouri and Shreveport, Louisiana, have essentially the same team structure with similar problems. Their QWL programs are also little more than paper.

Corporations are looking for ways to rid themselves of levels of management as well as production labor. Work teams are a perfect solution. They get workers to carry out the policies of top management. They do not offer real influence in making policies and indeed weaken the union's power to restrict management's policy choices.

QWL Is About Competition

The rhetoric of QWL speaks to real needs. It seems reasonable that after more than a century of industrialization we could pay attention to the quality of life on the job rather than to productivity alone. Indeed, most QWL programs used to begin with the promise that worker satisfaction would be their priority.

But with few exceptions, unionists now recognize and accept that increasing productivity is the main goal of QWL. Now worker satisfaction is seen as perhaps a welcome by-product. The main reason that unions go along with QWL, despite its obviously pro-management objectives, is that they have adopted it as a strategy for job security. QWL has been sold and bought mainly in the hope that through it the union might be able to salvage some jobs. The rhetoric of worker satisfaction and participation is little more than fluff on this hard kernel of "realism": *The union must help the company reduce costs, so the company can be competitive, so we can save some of our jobs.*

THEIR SATISFACTION AND OURS

A decade ago, the labor movement had a clearer understanding of what management meant by worker satisfaction. Former UAW Director of Special Projects Nat Weinberg put it well:

Management, with few if any exceptions, is concerned about job satisfaction *only as a means to an end*. The end is higher profits through higher productivity, reduced absences and turnover, etc. To workers, job satisfaction *is an end in itself* even if it should result in somewhat *lower* productivity. When the UAW won increased relief time for assembly line and certain other workers, it compelled the auto industry to hire literally thousands of other workers to get out the same volume of production. That obviously meant lower productivity, but what was wrong about it?[5]

This is the reason that QWL advocates slide so readily into accepting every management demand—including those which actually destroy decent working conditions. The argument that we have to contribute our *ideas* to help our company compete applies equally well to giving up our breaks, giving back our wages, cutting jobs, and allowing speedup. Economist Harry Katz suggests that workers protect their jobs by giving up shop floor power. He argues that:

...modifications in work rules can lead to lower costs which in turn, lead to reductions in the price of autos, an expansion in auto sales and eventually to an expansion in auto employment. Yet it appears that workers do not always see these connections. Instead management's initiatives on the shop floor center around efforts to convince workers and their unions that such a correspondence in fact does exist.[6]

The essential "theory" underlying QWL turns out to be not a psychological one about "the hierarchy of needs" and "self-actualization" after all. Rather, it is a simplistic economic theory, a union variant of "trickle down" Reaganomics: throw money at the companies in hopes that they will do something that may let us keep our jobs.

While unions are naturally resistant to the competition strategy, they face enormous pressures. Faced with declining memberships, employer aggression, and threats of shut plants, and isolated from the rest of the labor movement, many local unions have felt that there was no choice but to hop on the competition bandwagon.

Why Competition Won't Save Jobs

Even forgetting for a moment the damage that competition does within the labor movement, attempting to make a company competitive in the marketplace is not a viable strategy for saving jobs.

MOVING JOBS

Most of the U.S. jobs initially lost to foreign competition were relatively *low* wage jobs. The garment industry lost more than 50,000 jobs between 1956 and 1971. The electronics industry lost over 100,000 in just the six years starting with 1966.

Until recently, economic barriers made it unprofitable for the high-wage industries to run away. But now modern technology is pulling down those barriers.

For example, the auto industry did not move earlier to export jobs because production requires what management calls an "infrastructure," including financial services, engineering, and marketing skills. Now technology makes possible "world infrastructures." A Detroit-based General Motors can house its design engineers in California and through computer and satellite communications keep on top of production lines in South Korea. Headquarters can approve a design change and with the speed of light a computer-operated machine tool halfway around the world can begin producing the new part. Thousands of miles away, the mating part is also changed so that when the two are assembled, the fit is right.

These systems don't work perfectly today, but corporations are moving as fast as they can to refine them. General Motors has forced development of an industry-wide standard, a "Manufacturing Automation Protocol," so that different brands of computer-operated machine tools can be connected together and directly to central computers. One of the main reasons GM bought Electronic Data Systems in 1984 was to provide for central control over all its computer operations. One of the key features of the company's Saturn project will be to perfect this kind of control, which will in turn open a world of possibilities for flexibility in manufacturing.

1) Working cheaper will save jobs only if it means reducing our standard of living to something comparable to that of the "competition." Workers in the U.S. are being pitted against workers who earn one-tenth as much, who work without free unions, and who live under dictatorships in countries such as Korea, Taiwan and the Phillipines. As long as this kind of wage differential exists, U.S. corporations will continue to seek cheap labor elsewhere, as they have for the past 20 years.

The technical, political, and economic barriers to capital mobility are coming down as the industrial capabilities of other countries rise. The U.S. labor movement cannot agree to reduce workers' standard of living "just this once" like a single bitter pill. Once the competition strategy is adopted, the wages of American workers will continue to be reduced until they are in the same ballpark as wages in whatever underdeveloped

country sets the standard. There will always be some barriers to complete equalization, like transportation costs and the costs of keeping the pipeline filled. Even so, if the Korean or Mexican workers' wage and benefit package is $2.50 per hour, then the "competitive" U.S. package will be continually pushed toward $5.00.

2) Working smarter will not save jobs. A constant theme of QWL is that by using our minds and giving our suggestions to management we can improve productivity to such an extent that we can compete successfully in the market against cheaper labor. This is one of the biggest illusions about QWL. Knowledge shared with a multinational corporation is readily transportable across national boundaries. Indeed, any (but the most mismanaged) corporation is organized to take ideas developed by a Cleveland QWL group and introduce them into its plants in Mexico or Korea or even offer them to supplier companies. In fact, the more worker knowledge is articulated, polished and presented in a formal package to management, as happens in QWL, the more likely that those techniques will be used in the "competing" operation.

Only a misplaced sense of national pride would lead us to believe that U.S. workers are smarter than those in other countries. A U.S. engineer and consultant to the auto industry who has worked in Korea says there would be no problem transporting techniques there because Koreans are extremely hard working, entrepeneurial and technologically astute.[7] Tremec, a Mexican company which is competing to produce transmissions for Ford, has an employee participation program which reports the same kind of successes that U.S. companies like to claim.[8]

3) Going with the flow won't save the labor movement. There is a variant of the competitive strategy which says: allow the market to shift investment away from the old, noncompetitive industries into new goods

and services which are needed. Unions should then shift gears, emphasize retraining for the new high-tech industries and for clerical and service jobs, and organize them.

Of course labor should be organizing rising industries and demanding retraining. But by itself this is no strategy for labor. First of all, the robotics and automation industries themselves create very few jobs compared to the number they displace. GMF, a leading robot manufacturer, brags that its robot motors are themselves assembled by robots in a Japanese factory.

Second of all, although service jobs are indeed being created, they are also threatened—by the very same technology which is supposed to be the American worker's lifesaver. It is now profitable for American Airlines to fly used tickets to Barbados, where low-paid clerical workers enter data on computers. This data is then beamed back by satellite to corporate headquarters in the U.S. Cheap labor combined with advanced technology produces automatic banking machines competitive enough to replace $6.00 per hour tellers.

Grocery checkouts with talking computers, machines that do blood pressure checks, teaching machines, and computerized shopping services—these innovations indicate the range of threatened jobs. Some displaced workers are being retrained to be word processor operators. But word processor operators are already losing some jobs to optical print readers. And devices are now being developed that can directly convert verbal dictation to computer input.

In addition, technology will produce a new breed of clerical worker who will be harder for unions to organize. A 1984 study found that current technology could allow 7,000,000 workers to "telecommute"— do at least part of their work from their homes using a computer terminal. Up to now these have been mainly professionals, but Blue Cross and J.C. Penney have been experimenting with a cottage industry system for data entry clerks. Despite vigorous union objections, the Reagan administration is trying to clear legal obstacles.[9]

Labor Has Leverage

The flight of jobs and the advance of technology combine to paint a frightening picture of the future. The industries on which the labor movement has traditionally been based are in decline. A multinational diversified corporation can easily withstand a prolonged strike by one of its unions in one of its companies in one of its countries. New technology is proving to be an effective strikebreaker, as in the telephone strike of 1983. But some corporate plans which have put the labor movement on the defensive also provide unions with increased leverage.

Building new plants in new areas and installing new technology both require considerable capital outlays. International production also requires complex political and economic arrangements. Therefore corporations must stretch their investment plans over years. The threat to move an entire industry overnight is not credible in a bargaining situation. If the unions involved refuse to be blackmailed and use coordinated bargaining, they can resist employer demands and buy time to develop long run strategies.

Unions have another lever in the fact that the successful introduction of new technology requires worker cooperation to iron out the bugs. As corporations become more capital intensive (fewer workers compared to machines), strikes, slowdowns, or lockouts become more expensive because the machinery must be paid for whether it is producing or not. This means that the workers who program, operate and maintain the new technology, although fewer in number, have greater power in dealing with management. This will be especially true if unions organize the unorganized technical workers now, and resist management attempts to transfer control from workers to management.

Similarly, although the growth of conglomerates has enabled corporate giants to better withstand pressure from any one corner of their empires, the structure of the conglomerates and their interlocking business connections give labor additional pressure points as well. Unions can run successful corporate campaigns like the one against J.P. Stevens.

Indeed, the international competition which is driving corporations to squeeze labor has also forced management to drop some of its traditional defenses against union power. In the past companies have stockpiled materials as a defense against work stoppages. To cut inventory costs management has turned to *kan-ban* or "just-in-time" systems modeled after Japanese methods, in which companies arrange to have parts delivered only as they are needed. The problem with kan-ban, of course, is that it presumes a cooperative workforce. Even a short work stoppage at any point in the process, from supplier to final assembly line, tends to halt operations both upstream and downstream very quickly. Under kan-ban workers' power to win demands through direct shop floor action is greatly enhanced, as is the ability of the best organized sections to aid the others.

Corporations are spending such large amounts of money to tame their unions through QWL because they understand very well that unions still have the power to derail their plans. But the time to use this power is limited. Time wasted while the labor movement checks out the empty promises of employer cooperation means opportunities for the labor movement permanently lost.

A New Course

The forces of competition are destroying industries which provide decent wages and working conditions for large numbers of workers and the political base for the major unions. As these forces continue to operate, there will be no competitive strategy clever enough to maintain U.S. jobs at $12.00 an hour against rates of $2.50 an hour and conditions of dictatorship.

If the labor movement wants those jobs to survive, we have to oppose those market forces *as a matter of policy*. If we want to maintain "smokestack" industries with decent jobs in the U.S., we have to force the policymakers to act. If we want to convert old factories to produce mass transit, or prefabricated housing, or fuel-efficient furnaces or anything else, we have to make those decisions also.

In other words, we have to reject competition as the primary basis for making economic decisions and insist instead on economic planning.

In our personal lives, we think that someone who just sits back and lets life happen to him or her is pretty stupid. When we want to achieve certain goals we make plans that will get us from point A to point B. The same applies to the economy—we will never achieve job security or decent working conditions by waiting for the competitive market to make it happen.

The corporations would have us believe that "economic planning" is a dirty word in American political dialogue. But elements of economic planning already exist in different forms. Corporate tax breaks which encourage or discourage certain types of investment are a form of indirect or "indicative" planning. So are import controls. The problem is that the plans are made not in the interests of workers and their families, but in the interests of multinational corporations.

One example of pro-worker and pro-community economic planning in its infancy is the "Steel Valley Authority" proposal for the Monongahela Valley area of Pennsylvania. In the last few years the steel towns around Pittsburgh have been devastated as U.S. Steel has switched investment out of steel into other, more profitable fields, such as oil. Over 25,000 jobs have been lost at U.S. Steel alone since 1980, and a number of steel mills and related facilities have shut down completely.

Union members and community activists in the Steel Valley are organizing to keep steel production in the area. They are creating a local Steel Valley Authority which will have the power of "eminent domain." Cities and states have long used eminent domain to confiscate private property to build roads or public housing. The citizens of the steel towns say that now it may be necessary for local governments to take industrial facilities away from the companies that no longer seem to want to use them.

Communities have passed resolutions, held town meetings, and hammered out by-laws for the proposed Authority. They are conducting feasibility studies to determine how steel production can be continued. They are interested in converting old facilities for new uses. As two of the organizers wrote:

> Now communities are looking at abandoned blast furnaces and seeing regional trash incinerators, boiler houses as self-reliance in utility production, and abandoned real estate as something they can control.[10]

Rather than allowing themselves to be at the mercy of U.S. Steel's decisions about how to respond to the market, these communities are trying to take their fate into their own hands.

Uniting the Underdogs

The Steel Valley Authority is just one idea, and it is far from perfection or realization. Today the labor movement lacks the political clout even to slow down the installation of corporate and Reaganite plans for its future, much less impose its own plan.

In the last 30 years union membership has dropped from 35% to 18% of the workforce. Organizing is meeting more resistance and bringing in fewer members. Traditional economic muscles are weak from disuse.

As a result, organized labor's political muscle turns out to be mainly flab. Unable to pass a single one of its legislative priorities in a Democratic-controlled Congress with Democrat Jimmy Carter as President, it has become completely disoriented by the Reagan offensive. Politicians now seriously question the value of labor's endorsement. Unions are seen as nothing more than a "special interest" trying to protect overpaid, lazy members. Worse, significant numbers of union members and even some union leaders have bought this anti-union package of ideas.

The dilemma facing organized labor is how to convince those not immediately reaping the benefits that they too have a stake in defending the gains made by unions. Why should a typist who makes $5 per hour defend the jobs of auto workers who make more than $10, especially if the typist thinks doing so might add to the cost of the car that he or she buys? If there are not enough jobs to go around, by what right does a job belong to a Pennsylvania steelworker rather than to an unemployed worker in Alabama or a starving peasant in Korea?

When an employer tries to break a union and advertises for scabs, thousands show up. Many have heartbreaking stories about how they would prefer not to scab but have been unemployed for months and need medical care for their children. Why should we choose sides and try to stop such people from taking jobs?

To win support the unions must demonstrate that to defend the power of the union movement is to defend the interests of all workers.

Until unions began leading the way in making concessions, the high wages and working conditions of unionized workers set the standards for everyone. It is no secret that nonunion companies come as close as they do to matching wages of union companies in order to keep unions out. By a ripple effect, high union wages have boosted the standard of living of whole communities.

But even more important, the labor movement has been the most powerful political force representing the interests of all workers and "underdogs." From minimum wage laws and occupational health and safety standards to sweeping economic policies or civil rights legislation, reforms have had no chance without active labor support. It is true that Reagan has weakened labor. But it is also true that labor's weakness has been one of the main reasons for Reagan's success.

In politics, talk is cheap. Labor has to prove again in action that it is committed to a broad social program. Labor's political power depends on its ability to mobilize its own members to in turn lead a crusade for all working people.

QWL Helps Make Labor a 'Special Interest'

Here we return to the issue of union support for Quality of Work Life programs. Not only does QWL undermine the union on the shop floor, it undermines the union movement as a political force. QWL's stress on identification with the company and company solutions to economic problems makes it harder for a union to unite and mobilize its members on issues that go beyond the individual firm.

Consider, for example, how critical are campaigns to organize the unorganized. As long as companies believe that they can get work done cheaper by "outsourcing" it, they will continue to run away from unions. But if companies can be taught that an aggressive organizing drive will follow any work moved, outsourcing ceases to be so attractive. The logic of QWL makes organizing drives more difficult.

One discussion at a QWL conference sponsored by the U.S. Department of Labor centered on multiplant corporations which have QWL at one plant and an anti-union campaign at another. One participant suggested using the QWL program to "leverage a change at plants where the union is working to gain representation rights." But the UAW's representative objected:

> Joe Desmond questioned that strategy, however, saying existing cooperative programs have an obligation to the people participating in them and should not be used as a pawn in other representation struggles.[12]

The logic of QWL establishes a certain priority. Struggles to organize the unorganized come to be viewed as special interests—and you certainly wouldn't want to disturb a QWL circle in order to support those outsiders who are trying to organize a union against our cooperative boss.

Indeed, many union leaders hope that QWL will demonstrate how useful unions can be and that therefore management resistance to unionization will be reduced. It's not a new strategy. It's the old maxim which is rediscovered in every period of labor weakness—if you can't lick 'em, join 'em. In the 1920's the AFL tried to build its reputation by working with the Taylor (scientific management) Society and publicizing its commitment to union-management cooperation. As professor of management Sanford Jacoby describes it:

> The AFL also hoped that its attempt to portray itself as a responsible partner in management would appeal to nonunion employers. For example, since the AFL had been unable to organize the automobile industry from below, Green made overtures to executives of Ford and General Motors in 1926 and 1927, suggesting that they permit organization of their craft workers by the AFL.

THE POLITICAL CHOICE

Labor's current course in the Democratic Party is QWL writ large in the realm of politics. Labor has come to a political crossroads similar to the one it faces in union-management relations.

One political alternative is to continue as a junior partner to the corporate interests who run the Democratic Party through control of the money, seats on crucial committees, and most important, their ability to set the terms of the political debate. This course means burying labor's identity as a political force. In response to just a slight exercise of independent political muscle in 1984, even the supposedly most pro-labor wing of the Democratic Party, led by Ted Kennedy, is now holding organized labor at arm's length.[11]

The other political alternative is for labor to stop depending on these kinds of friends and to rebuild its own active political base. The only way to put pro-labor economic planning measures on the agenda is through an independent labor party unbeholden to corporate interests. Such a party could champion once again the interests of minorities, women, and senior citizens, rather than treating these forces as competitors for crumbs within the Democratic Party. It could also make new alliances where now the labor hierarchy sees enemies—with environmentalists and the peace movement.

The labor movement in virtually every industrial country in the world with the exception of the U.S. has its own political party to bring labor's interests into politics. Such a party does not solve all labor's problems, but at least gives unions an independent voice. A labor party is one of those old ideas— like the notion that business and labor are adversaries—which seem relevant once again now that labor is getting its teeth kicked in by its supposed friends.

cont. next page

Green repeatedly used the Taylorist argument that only a unionized firm would be able to achieve the organized consent necessary for effective cooperation and increased productivity. He thought that Ford management would be so impressed by the AFL's new philosophy and the results of its experiments in cooperation that the firm would be willing to pursue the AFL's suggestion.[13]

In 1929 to 1931 a similar direct approach to southern textile mill owners, to let the AFL organize unions to improve productivity, also met with failure.

But for some, the 1980's are different. General Motors' Saturn Project to build small cars in the U.S. and the advance recognition of the United Steelworkers at the new LTV-Sumitomo plant are cited as fruits of a cooperative relationship. In chapter 4 and in this chapter we have noted how costly these acts of cooperation will be not only for workers in those plants, but as precedents which will threaten union gains throughout U.S. industry.

By increasing the union's identification with the specific company, QWL contributes to the notion of the union as a special interest, and further divides the union movement from the political forces it should be leading. For example, an often cited success story in the annals of QWL is that the UAW local at General Motors' Tarrytown, New York plant now lobbies in the state capital for lower utility rates for GM.

The Tobacco Industry Labor/Management Committee sponsors an advertisement which presents a caricature of a union as a "special interest." The ad pictures three members of the Bakery, Confectionery and

Tobacco Workers Union, and warns:

> We want you to know our industry is threatened—not by foreign competition or old fashioned technology but by well-meaning people who haven't stopped to consider how their actions might affect others.... [A]ttacks on the tobacco industry threaten the livelihoods of thousands of working Americans who have marched, worked, and struggled for causes we all believe in.[14]

It's true that tobacco workers should not have to pay the penalty because we now understand the dangers of smoking. One reasonable solution would be to use industry profits and the government subsidies now maintaining the tobacco industry to pay for retraining tobacco workers and conversion of tobacco plantations and factories to other products. But the logic of the cooperative relationship leads to the special interest mentality instead.

A union commitment to cooperation with the corporations sends mixed messages both to union members and to potential supporters outside the labor movement.

For example, in 1984 the UAW made the defeat of Ronald Reagan its principal political goal. In July Reagan made a campaign swing through Michigan, to the heart of UAW country, to demonstrate that he had the backing of union members despite their leaders' position. The focal point for his visit in Warren, Michigan was a presentation by UAW and GM spokesmen about their cooperation on the Saturn project. Later, a videotape of the joint presentation to Reagan, and Reagan's approving response, was shown

several times at conferences during the election campaign. Reagan could not have asked for a better campaign tape.

Sometimes the messages about cooperation are not even mixed. Former UAW director of government affairs Steven Schlossberg argues that the new relationship with corporations means that unions must no longer "berate management on 'Big Business Days'" (a 1980 union campaign to mobilize against the political power of the big corporations).[15]

The EI program at Ford's Rawsonville, Michigan parts plant is frequently held up as an outstanding success. The success, as *Business Week* describes it, lay in creating a relationship which enabled the union, UAW Local 898, to lead the way in making contract and work rule concessions that the company wanted.[16] In January 1985 the local made retiring Ford Chairman Philip Caldwell an honorary union member.

No UAW international officer took public exception to the ceremony nor suggested that perhaps there were UAW members who did not wish to sing "Solidarity Forever" with Caldwell. Al Gardner, president of the Local 600 Tool and Die Unit, summed up the feelings of many:

> Here is a corporate boss who has presided over cutting the workforce in half, demanded concessions, closed numerous plants and shipped our work to scab and low wage shops here and abroad, and he gets a medal from the union.
>
> Unions were formed to stop economic and social blackmail but now we seem to have come full turn at

kissing the bosses' ass again for a few crumbs.

It's little wonder that there is confusion in the ranks. One minute we are told to vote against the boss at election time and the next minute we are making the boss an honorary member of our union.[17]

A Plan for Labor

The U.S. labor movement continues to flounder in an ever-widening spiral of defeat. Against powerful market forces it chooses a strategy of narrow self-interest as it identifies with individual companies. In doing so it pits union against union over jobs, unions against minorities and women over affirmative action, unions against environmentalists over environmental protections, unions against taxpayers over tobacco industry supports, and unions against consumers over import restrictions. As a result the unions get more isolated and politically weaker. In greater desperation they tie themselves to the very companies whose main goals are to weaken labor.

As unions throw in their lot with the companies they weaken possibilities for political coalitions with other forces. And since union members themselves are taxpayers, consumers, minorities, women, and environmentalists, unions in effect are telling their own members that unions are relevant only to narrow job interests.

This is not to say that unions should wage a broad political struggle instead of fighting for the immediate needs of their own members. The two cannot be separated. The main resource that unions have in politics is an active, informed membership which strongly identifies with the union. Members who do not respect what a union does on the shop floor will hardly follow its lead in politics. A union which demobilizes its members and allows them to be divided and demoralized in the plant or office cannot muster an army to go out and spread the union word in community or national politics.

Rebuilding the base of the union requires more union organization (not more joint union-company committees), more union training (not more training in company values), more participation in the union (not more participation in a version of ''Junior Achievement''), and more solidarity among workers (not more company identification). At the same time time unions need to point to long-term solutions which lead to worker unity and greater control over the corporations.

Here are some areas where aggressive union activity could begin to rebuild the solidarity of the union movement. Some of them would require challenging the laws which were put in place to strip labor of its power, which underscores the need for a combined political and bargaining offensive.

1. Industry-wide coordination

a) Maintain and extend master agreements throughout each industry. Standardize working conditions. Coordinate bargaining, with common expiration dates.

b) Develop industry-wide union councils with enforcement power, to prevent substandard conditions and to make it difficult for employers to pit one plant against another.

c) Reduce the penalty that workers have to pay because of poor management in one company or because of market shifts, by making pensions and benefits portable throughout the industry. Recall rights should be industry-wide with unlimited recall time.

2. Labor solidarity

a) Massive demonstrations of support for union struggles. Corporations need to fear that they will provoke general strikes if they use courts to break unions,

advertise for scabs, or blackmail unions with threats of plant closings.

b) Secondary boycotts. Refuse to handle products of companies involved in labor disputes.

c) Corporate-wide union councils of rank and file delegates to apply maximum pressure on conglomerates. Use union power as leverage to help organize the unorganized within the conglomerates.

d) Active involvement in and support for the struggles of minorities and women. In particular labor needs to clean its own house and give special support to correcting past employer discrimination through affirmative action.

e) Active involvement in community issues such as school improvements, tax policies, and neighborhood services.

3. International solidarity

a) Force the government to withdraw all military and political support to governments such as South Korea and South Africa which suppress free trade unions.

b) Develop multinational union strategies for dealing with multinational corporations, particularly to oppose shifts of operations from one country to another.

c) Support all attempts to organize and improve working conditions of workers in other countries through job actions and other pressures on employers. The international solidarity campaign which forced Coca-Cola to reopen its Guatemala plant is an example.

4. Controls on investments

a) Require the union's permission for contracting out.

b) Require that the ratio of jobs to production be maintained. Such a requirement would guard against both speedup and outsourcing. (A start on this was made by the UAW at International Harvester in 1985.)

c) Require that profits be reinvested in such a way as to maintain and advance jobs for the workers who earned those profits before they are invested anywhere else. For example, a union could negotiate a clause mandating no overseas investment while anyone is laid off.

d) Limit corporations' ability to milk viable operations. Get rid of all tax write-offs for shutdowns. If a corporation wants to withdraw, it must turn over all plant and equipment to the community which supported it.

e) Require that full information on company operations be made available to the union. The union can work with community groups on plans for alternative products or services should the company want to pull out.

f) Negotiate strong successor clauses which limit the companies' ability to sell operations to others (or in some cases themselves) without carrying over full union conditions.

These kinds of demands would be useful short term solutions for the crisis facing working people. And organizing around them, rather than dividing and weakening unions as most QWL-type cooperative strategies do, would unite and strengthen the union movement to become a potent political force capable of winning the long term solutions.

There will undoubtedly be many defeats along the way to rebuilding a militant social unionism with a political program to take control of a runaway economy. But the labor movement as a whole has no other reasonable choice. The non-adversarial, help-them-compete alternative means certain weakening and defeat.

Today the corporations appear to be in such a strong position and unions so weak that it is hard to imagine a turnaround. It is easy to understand why many unionists have simply given up or have pinned their hopes on promises of company compassion rather than on union strength. It is also easy to understand why so many commentators have declared the labor movement dead as a significant factor in U.S. politics and the economy. One such prediction by the president of the American Economic Association explained:

> . . . American trade unionism is slowly being limited in influence by changes which destroy the basis on which it is erected. It is probable that changes in the law have adversely affected unionism. Certainly the growth of large corporations has done so. But no one who follows the fortunes of individual unions can doubt that over and above these influences, the relative decline in the power of American trade unionism is due to occupational changes and to technological revolutions....
>
> I see no reason to believe that American trade unionism will so revolutionize itself within a short period of time as to become in the next decade a more potent social influence than it has been in the last decade.[18]

These words were printed in 1933, just before American workers took it upon themselves to find their own answer to the Depression, and organized the CIO. We can use historical perspective to remind ourselves that the labor movement has been counted out before, only to be reborn as a bigger and stronger force.

That same history also warns us that labor's comeback will not happen automatically. In the 1920's the labor movement chose between two strategies.

One strategy was cooperation with the employers to try to save some jobs. As we read earlier, most employers treated union overtures with contempt, and the few experiments failed to survive the depression of the 1930's.

The alternative aggressive strategy seemed even more hopeless at the time. The United Mine Workers pursued a policy of militant demands, and they suffered some serious losses. Attempts to organize industrial unions were smashed, "proving" to the commentators that industrial unions were impossible. Yet there were some small successes, and union organizers learned from their defeats. When the successful labor upsurge came in the 1930's, it was the Mine Workers and the militant rank and filers and organizers who had stuck their necks out who provided the troops, the leadership, and the inspiration for the CIO. Those who had chosen the pragmatic expedient of cooperation in the 1920's proved to be roadblocks who had to be swept aside.

Labor's comeback in the 1980's can happen only if leaders and rank and filers refuse to float with the conservative tide, and once again assert labor's values as the ones worth defending. The majority of working people will not be attracted to a warmed over version of management values or to union leaders who see their main job as helping the boss.

What made the labor movement strong was that it offered the human dignity that comes from working together with others and a vision of real cooperation—sisterhood and brotherhood. The labor movement was truly a social movement where members willingly made huge sacrifices for each other. This intensity of commitment to unionism as a just cause, shared by hundreds of thousands of workers, gave the labor movement its impressive strength.

In "cooperative" QWL-type labor-management relations, on the other hand, real human cooperation is destroyed. Workers are encouraged to view workers at other companies as mortal enemies. Within companies, as the union disintegrates it becomes every person for him or herself. Workers are left scrambling to protect their own jobs, win cash awards, or climb to a management position at the expense of their brothers and sisters.

In 1985, the year of the "yuppie," the notions of brotherhood, sisterhood, and solidarity seem out of date. Consumption and selfish individualism are in. At stake is not just the survival of unions as organizations but the values of the entire society. When the labor movement relies on its own strength by building solidarity, its values again become serious contenders in the society as a whole. That is an essential part of the union mission. □

Notes

1. Crain's *Cleveland Business*, March 11, 1985.

2. Letter from LTV Steel to laid-off employees, February 15, 1985.

3. Michel Brossard, "North American Unions and Semi-Autonomous Production Groups," *QWL: The Canadian Scene*, Vol. 4, No. 1, 1981.

4. Quotes are from management orientation handouts and a handbook used during employee orientation.

5. Nat Weinberg, Speech at the 27th Annual Conference on Labor, New York, June 14, 1974.

6. Harry C. Katz, *Shifting Gears: Changing Labor Relations in the U.S. Auto Industry*, MIT Press, 1985.

7. Richard P. Hervey, "Internationalization and Autoworkers' Jobs," presentation at conference sponsored by Labor Studies Center, University of Michigan and UAW Local 600, March 2, 1985.

8. *Business Week*, December 10, 1984.

9. *PC Magazine*, January 1985.

10. Judy Ruszkowski and Jim Benn, "Tri-State Coalition Fights to Save the Mon Valley," *Labor Notes*, April 1985.

11. *Detroit Free Press*, March 30, 1985.

12. "Report on the Secretary of Labor's Symposium on Cooperative Labor-Management Programs," U.S. Department of Labor, 1982.

13. Sanford M. Jacoby, "Union-Management Cooperation in the United States: Lessons from the 1920's," *Industrial and Labor Relations Review*, October 1983.

14. The ad ran in several publications including *In These Times*, *The Progressive* and *The Nation*.

15. Stephen Schlossberg, "Burying the Picket," *The Washington Monthly*, October 1982.

16. *Business Week*, July 30, 1984.

17. *UAW Facts*, UAW Local 600, February 1985.

18. George Barnett, "American Trade Unionism and Social Insurance," *American Economic Review*, March 1933.

LEGAL CHALLENGES TO QWL

by Ellis Boal

I. Introduction and Definitions

This chapter will discuss legal challenges to employee participation plans.[1] The legal literature is sparse on the subject. No reported case explicitly discusses the modern QWL committee widely used in industry today.

The law involved is federal labor law under the National Labor Relations Act (NLRA, or Wagner Act),[2] as amended and expanded by the Labor Management Relations Act (LMRA, or Taft-Hartley Act),[3] and the Labor-Management Reporting and Disclosure Act (LMRDA, or Landrum-Griffin Act).[4] The NLRA is administered by the National Labor Relations Board (NLRB) which has regional offices throughout the country. One need not have a lawyer to file a charge at the NLRB and there is no cost. An unfair labor practice charge is timely if filed and served within six months of the illegal act.

State common law is also involved in the interpretation of union rules.[5] This law will vary from state to state and union to union, so few generalizations can be made about it. But most courts are inclined to uphold any but the most unreasonable interpretations of union rules made by the union officers.

A formal QWL program is normally defined by its charter as the recruitment of rank and file participation into problem-solving operational discussions ordinarily reserved to management. The overall goals usually are to enhance (1) quantity and quality of goods or services produced and (2) worker morale. Typically, the plan will involve periodic meetings between supervisors and selected workers where an agenda of production problems is thrashed out. Recommended solutions are forwarded to higher management. A QWL committee operates on company time and premises with input and support from management. Committees are limited to advisory capacities. Management may veto every committee recommendation.

A key legal element of many QWL programs lies in their claimed tightly restricted jurisdiction: They do not deal with "mandatory subjects" of collective bargaining as that phrase is interpreted under NLRA Section 8(d).

There is extensive legal literature as to what a mandatory (as opposed to "permissive") subject is. Gener-

ally, mandatory subjects comprise negotiable and grievable subjects: wages, hours, and working conditions. In particular, the NLRB has held that work standards and work rules,[6] work hours,[7] work schedules,[8] work loads[9] and work assignments[10] are mandatory subjects.

Contrasted are management prerogatives, such as dealings with suppliers, product design, job design, and quality control. The company is permitted but not required to bargain on these subjects. That is why they are called permissive subjects.

Thus, a union can ask a company to renegotiate a contract that still has a year to run. It can ask for a seat on the company's board of directors. It can ask that the company improve product quality. But it cannot demand these things or threaten to strike over them. On the other hand, if the company does bargain and reach agreement on any permissive subject, the agreement is binding during the contract term.[11]

Theoretically, then, a company could have staff meetings to discuss work, counsel employees about their work technique, or conduct time-study tests, all without advance notice to, or bargaining with the union (if there is one). These are called management prerogatives. If the company wanted to, it could call such communications a participation or QWL program, and it would be legal.[12]

But most participation programs do not actually have their jurisdiction limited to permissive subjects. Whether in the written charter of the program itself, or

Ellis Boal is a lawyer in Detroit and a contributor to Labor Notes. *He is the author of* Teamster Rank & File Legal Rights Handbook.

in day-to-day practice, most programs do discuss such mandatory subjects as safety, morale, communications, work conditions, production ceilings or floors, and the like. Every legal commentator to study this question has concluded that this is the tendency of these programs.

The legal significance of the mandatory/permissive distinction will be seen in the next section. Apart from this consideration, a company steps over the line into illegality when it uses a QWL plan to interrogate an employee in the absence of a requested steward,[13] establishes a plan in order to avoid a union,[14] or intimidates or discriminates against employees who organize against the plan.[15]

II. QWL Where There Is No Recognized Union

As with many aspects of labor law, QWL committees are most easily understood by considering them first in the hypothetical situation where there is no recognized union.

In a nonunion context, the employer can be subject to an unfair labor practice charge under NLRA Section 8(a)(2) if it establishes a QWL program which oversteps proper bounds. Section 8(a)(2) was inserted in the law to outlaw company-dominated unions. It forbids an employer to:

> dominate or interfere with the formation or administration of any *labor organization* or contribute financial or other support to it . . . . [emphasis added]

It contains a proviso permitting the employer to confer with employees on company time, but such employees cannot have official or unofficial representative capacity.

Most QWL committees would be considered "labor organizations" as that word is defined by NLRA Section 2(5). This is because they meet three conditions: (1) employees participate in them, (2) they exist "in whole or in part" for the purpose of "dealing"[16] with the employer, and (3) the subjects of the dealings are mandatory bargaining subjects. The definition holds even though supervisory people may also participate in the QWL committee, and even though it may have no officers, constitution, bylaws, dues, regular meetings, rules of order, or other formal attributes of a union. It is irrelevant that the committee may not consider itself a labor organization.

A real union (or individual worker), recognizing the threat to concerted action, can ask the NLRB to have the committee "disestablished." The NLRB would consider the committee as being in effect a company-dominated union. The facts of supervisory participation, supervisory involvement in selection of employee members, use of company time and premises, management veto power over subjects of discussion, and clerical and financial assistance would establish unlawful domination and support. It is not necessary to show that the company has an anti-union attitude to win a case. Further, the committee itself can be charged

under NLRA Sections 8(b)(1)(A) and 8(b)(3) for restraint, coercion, and bad faith bargaining.[17]

A nonunion employer might try to establish a QWL committee and hope that the employees would be sufficiently cowed or impressed that no one would file charges. This has been the main way that companies have avoided legal liability with QWL up to this point.

The company could also try to restrict the committee's "dealings" in order to avoid liability. If the committee was just a crew working together on one task, there would be no legal objection.[18] If the committee only existed to passively hear pep talks or explanations of policy by company officials, it could not be said the committee was "dealing" with the company.[19] Another approach would be to expressly authorize the committee to discuss complaints or grievances, and give it final authority to act as management's agent in deciding them; this would preclude the argument that it "deals" (as a separate entity) with management on behalf of workers.[20] Absent such unusual restrictions, any QWL committee is eminently vulnerable under traditional notions of labor law.

There is a good historical reason why the law is written so strictly. At the time the NLRA was passed in 1935, companies often organized their workers into phony "inside" or "company" unions and then used them as a buffer against militant organization. Some companies established "Production Committees" during World War II and tried to continue them later, in order to control employee organization. But the NLRA and its subsequent amendments took it as a given proposition that labor and management "proceed from contrary and to an extent antagonistic viewpoints and concepts of self-interest."[21] Labor had been burned badly by management trying to sit on both sides of the bargaining table. Section 8(a)(2)'s cherished protection thus established an "adversary model" of labor relations.

The Supreme Court and legal commentators have

repeatedly taken note of this model. It simply reflects the understanding of Congress when the laws were passed that there are fundamental underlying differences between management and labor. This is not to say that the negotiations and grievance procedure is set up for representatives of management and labor to vent personal hostilities. The differences are institutional and collective. The law prudently recognizes this fact of life, rather than trying to gloss it over. The adversary model survives in the written law today.

But, as will be seen below, this model is now being challenged.

III. QWL Where There Is A Recognized Union

A. QWL WITH UNION AGREEMENT

Nothing can stop a company and a union from agreeing to a tightly restricted QWL program described above. Nor is there anything legally wrong with a union-agreed unrestricted plan (e.g. a plan where committees do discuss mandatory subjects, such as safety) as long as the union keeps a hand in its operation.

Of course, any agreement to establish QWL is subject to the same membership ratification rights that apply to any other collective bargaining contract. Ratification rights derive, if at all, from the union's own rules. If there is a traditional right in a particular union to ratify contracts, local riders, plant practices, and the like, that right will apply to a QWL program. Though the law on this point is in flux, the courts do not otherwise recognize a membership right to ratify. If denied the right to vote on a QWL agreement, workers could file suits under Title 1 of the Landrum-Griffin Act, the common law of union rules considered as contracts with the members, and NLRA Section 9(a).[22]

Ordinarily, the bargaining representative of the employees is a local union affiliated with an international union. Thus, it is the local union which alone has the right to decide (with membership ratification if that is the union's ordinary procedure) whether to accept or reject a QWL program. The local is not required to follow the wishes of the international. Though the international may negotiate the contract, this is only by virtue of specific authority delegated by the local to the international. The authority may be either in the union's written rules or in a convention resolution drawn up for that purpose.

Without such authority, the international could force QWL on the local only through its powers of trusteeship or administratorship. This would require the following of strict procedures under the union constitution. Compliance with Title 3 of the Landrum-Griffin Act is also necessary. In practice, there would be slight chance of any trusteeship based on such grounds.

What if the union negotiates an unrestricted (in name or in fact) participation plan, and then allows it to discuss working conditions and past practices without policing the discussions? For example, suppose a plan is set up that discusses safety conditions and improvements, and the union does not participate? It is easy to see that such a set-up would undermine the union's power to win good contracts or even good grievances. Moreover, the company could more easily manipulate recommendations and resolutions of the committee if experienced negotiators weren't involved on the side of the workers.

There would still be nothing legally wrong, if the committee were considered an arm of the union, and the discussions were considered side-table negotiations. Without such a claim, it is apparent that bargaining (and "dealing") authority would have been handed over by the union to a committee, and that the committee would be a company-dominated "labor organization."

But the union is supposed to be the exclusive bargaining representative. In such a situation, the union would have abandoned its responsibility to bargain and deal for its members. A union may not waive rights concerning the identity of the bargaining representative.[23] The company would have violated Section 8(a)(2) and the union would have breached its duty to represent its members under Section 8(b)(1)(A).[24]

B. QWL WITHOUT UNION AGREEMENT

If a company attempted to establish QWL without union agreement, it would probably not be very successful.[25] If it tried to establish "work crews" or change job assignments, it would have to bargain with the union first. And if the program had the intent or effect of bypassing the union to bargain directly with workers, the company would be subject to a refusal-to-bargain charge under NLRA Section 8(a)(5).[26]

A successful company defense to such a charge could be "union acquiescence," if in fact the union had been informed about the program and failed to protest. An individual member, as well as the union itself, would have standing to file a refusal-to-bargain charge.[27]

If a local union finds itself threatened with unilateral company imposition of a QWL program, it is perfectly legal to block it by ordering members under threat of union discipline to refuse to cooperate.[28] That is, faced with a company order to attend a meeting on company time to discuss product quality, an employee would have to attend the meeting, and answer specific questions concerning his or her operation. But unless the employee's job description required the employee together with others to creatively brainstorm productivity schemes, a refusal to cooperate further would not be insubordinate.

IV. Legal Challenges

Given the state of the law, it might be wondered why dissatisfied workers haven't filed NLRB charges against QWL programs to have them disestablished. Surely not everyone exposed to them is convinced that labor-management cooperation will produce a better work life. Surely some believe that helping their own company to succeed at the expense of other companies which employ other union workers undercuts unionwide and classwide solidarity.

One answer, though not a satisfactory one, is that there are legal arguments in support of QWL programs. Employer attorneys and even some courts have suggested that if certain conditions are met, a QWL scheme might be found legal. The suggested conditions are: (1) the employer has acted with benign intent, (2) the scheme is supported by a majority of employees, and (3) the employer only potentially, rather than actually, dominates the committee.[29]

But under traditional interpretations of Section 8(a)(2), these factors are irrelevant. The Supreme Court ruled in several early cases that company-dominated employee organizations could be disestablished despite the presence of all three of these factors. Every Supreme Court case to consider Section 8(a)(2) has interpreted it expansively. Concerning liability under Section 8(a)(2), every Supreme Court opinion has been unanimous.[30]

The Wagner Act sought to secure equality of bargaining power for workers in hopes of diminishing industrial strife. It did that by establishing unions as exclusive representatives of workers who freely vote for them. But QWL committees are not free of company influence. Senator Wagner said at the time of hearings on his bill: "[T]o argue that freedom of organizing for the worker must embrace the right to select a form of organization that is not free, is a contradiction in terms."[31] The House of Representatives tried to weaken Section 8(a)(2) in 1947 to expressly permit domination of in-plant committees at the time that it passed the Taft-Hartley Act, and that attempt was defeated. No change has been made in the law in 50 years, and the Supreme Court, despite invitations, has never held otherwise.

However, everyone knows today the direction of the NLRB and the Supreme Court. Political pressures on both bodies will be enormous to "modernize" the law or "accommodate" it to perceived changing conditions. Both have done so with regard to other areas of law in the past. Perhaps they will see enactment by Congress of the National Productivity and Quality of Working Life Act of 1975[32] or the Labor Management Cooperation Act of 1978[33] as signals.[34]

If the prospects for legal challenge are speculative, there are some points that should be emphasized if a case were brought. If the QWL program was suggested by the company rather than the union, if the union got little or nothing in exchange for it, if there is confusion on what the committee in practice may discuss, if there is confusion as to whether the committee is the company's agent, the union's agent, or a separate entity, if the company controls the committee membership and agenda, if the committee starts to look like management's pointman in implementing decisions, if the committee is being used to undercut the union, if the union surrenders to the committee its obligation to represent members on working conditions, or if there is organized opposition to the QWL program among employees, then the case will be stronger.

In these circumstances, it is not difficult to construct a good test case to knock out a QWL plan. The strongest argument against the plan would be that it simply flies in the face of established traditional labor law. Even the employers realize this.[35]

In view of the invitation by the letter and spirit of the law, QWL programs will undoubtedly soon be subjected to legal challenge. The more effective challenge, of course, would be organization of workers into and within strong unions. Until then, the law can be of some assistance.

BRIEFLY

The Labor Education and Research Project, producers of this book, filed a brief in an important QWL case before the National Labor Relations Board involving the Ona Corporation and the United Auto Workers. Ona had set up an "employee action committee" with QWL overtones to block a union organizing drive.

The brief, researched and written by attorney Ellis Boal, argues that the Board should retain the assumption of an adversarial relationship between workers and employers, and the prohibitions against employer-dominated labor organizations.

Copies of the brief are available from LERP for $10.00.

Notes

1. The laws covering public employees will not be discussed because they vary widely from state to state. However, the principles explained here carry over into the laws of most public jurisdictions.
2. 29 USC 151 et seq.
3. 29 USC 141 et seq.
4. 29 USC 401 et seq.
5. Union rules include the constitution and bylaws of the particular union, together with any other written or unwritten codes, practices, convention resolutions, or the like.
6. *Miller Brewing Co*, 166 NLRB #90, 65 LRRM 1649 (1967), enf'd 408 F2d 12, 70 LRRM 2907 (CA9, 1969).
7. *Meat Cutters v Jewel Tea Co*, 381 US 676, 85 S Ct 1596, 59 LRRM 2376 (1965).
8. *Inter-City Advertising Co, Inc*, 61 NLRB 1377, 16 LRRM 153 (1945), enf denied on other grounds, 154 F2d 244, 17 LRRM 916 (CA4, 1946).
9. *Beacon Piece Dyeing & Finishing Co*, 121 NLRB #113, 42 LRRM 1489 (1958).
10. *Charmer Industries, Inc*, 250 NLRB 293, 104 LRRM 1368 (1980).
11. The line between mandatory and permissive subjects is not always clear, and subjects can change

from one category to the other because of a particular history at a company or in an industry. See for example, *Fibreboard Paper Products Corp* v *NLRB*, 379 US 203, 85 S Ct 398, 57 LRRM 2609 (1964).

12. Even when the company makes a change which is not bargainable, it must still bargain afterward about the effects of the decision. *First National Maintenance Corp v NLRB*, 452 US 666, 101 S Ct 2573, 107 LRRM 2705 (1981).

13. *NLRB* v *J Weingarten, Inc*, 420 US 251, 95 S Ct 959, 88 LRRM 2689 (1975).

14. *Alta Bates Hospital*, 226 NLRB #65, 93 LRRM 1288 (1976).

15. *Eastex, Inc v NLRB*, 437 US 556, 98 S Ct 2505, 98 LRRM 2717 (1978). The right of an employee to organize against QWL was evidently held to have been waived by a local union when it agreed to a QWL program, according to an arbitrator in *Wheeling-Pittsburgh Steel Corp Yorkville Plant* and *Steelworkers Local 1223*, _____LA_____ (Leahy, 1984). This incoherent opinion also held that the local could not vote to withdraw from the QWL program. The NLRB's General Counsel overruled the latter holding. The former is still pending at the NLRB and in separate federal court litigation. Another arbitrator considering similar facts disagreed with the first arbitrator. *Wheeling-Pittsburgh Steel Corp Yorkville Plant* and *Steelworkers Local 1223*, _____LA_____ (Fisher, 1985).

16. "Dealing" is a looser concept than "bargaining" with management. If the committee merely makes recommendations about workplace problems without trying to reach agreement with management about them, it is dealing with the company, even if not bargaining with it. *NLRB v Cabot Carbon Co*, 360 US 203, 79 S Ct 1015, 44 LRRM 2204 (1959).

17. In a case involving a committee of university faculty members with combined duties representing both management and employees, a Board majority suggested in a footnote that the set-up "could raise questions both as to the validity and continued viability of such structures under our Act," particularly if there were a union, and more particularly if such facts arose in a commercial setting. *Adelphi University*, 195 NLRB #107, 79 LRRM 1545, 1556 n 31 (1972).

18. *General Foods Corp*, 231 NLRB #122, 96 LRRM 1204 (1977).

19. *Republic Drill & Tool Co*, 66 NLRB 955, 17 LRRM 369 (1946).

20. *Mercy Memorial Hospital*, 231 NLRB 1108, 1118-21, 96 LRRM 1239 (1977).

21. *NLRB* v *Insurance Agents Union*, 361 US 477, 488, 80 S Ct 419, 427, 45 LRRM 2704, 2709 (1960).

22. *Trail v IBT*, 542 F2d 961, 93 LRRM 3076 (CA6, 1976).

23. *NLRB* v *Magnavox Co of Tennessee*, 415 US 322, 94 S Ct 1099, 85 LRRM 2475 (1974); *Ford Motor Company (Rouge Complex)*, 233 NLRB #102, 96 LRRM 1513 (1977).

24. In *NLRB* v *Cabot Carbon Co*, 360 US 203, 79 S Ct 1015, 44 LRRM 2204 (1959), the Supreme Court upheld a Board order disestablishing, among others, several illegally dominated employee committees functioning in unionized plants without objection from the unions. In some instances union members served on the committees and/or meetings were held jointly among the union, the committee and management.

25. If the program were of the unrestricted type, the company could be required to abolish the program, return to the status quo, and bargain with the union to agreement or impasse before reinstalling the program. *Defense Logistics Agency, Defense Depot Tracy* and *Laborers Local 1276*, FLRA Case No 9-CA-20241 (1983) (ALJ decision adopted in absence of exceptions).

26. *Medo Photo Supply Co v NLRB*, 321 US 678, 64 S Ct 830, 14 LRRM 581 (1944).

27. *Vee Cee Provisions, Inc*, 256 NLRB #125, 107 LRRM 1416 (1981), enf'd 688 F2d 827, 111 LRRM 2833 (CA3, 1982).

28. *Scofield v NLRB*, 394 US 423, 89 S Ct 1154, 70 LRRM 3105 (1969).

29. See for instance *Hertzka & Knowles v NLRB*, 503 F2d 625, 87 LRRM 2503 (CA9, 1974); *NLRB v Homemaker Shops, Inc*, 724 F2d 535, 115 LRRM 2321 (CA6, 1984); *NLRB v Northeastern University*, 601 F2d 1208, 101 LRRM 2767 (CA1, 1979); *Chicago Rawhide Mfg Co v NLRB*, 2221 F2d 165, 35 LRRM 2665 (CA7, 1955).

30. *Garment Workers (Bernhard-Altmann Texas Corp) v NLRB*, 366 US 731, 81 S Ct 1603, 48 LRRM 2251 (1961); *NLRB v Newport News Shipbuilding and Drydock Co*, 308 US 241, 60 S Ct 203, 5 LRRM 665 (1939); *NLRB v Cabot Carbon Co*, 360 US 203, 79 S Ct 1015, 44 LRRM 2204 (1959); *NLRB v Pennsylvania Greyhound Lines, Inc*, 303 US 261, 58 S Ct 571, 2 LRRM 599 (1938); *Machinists v NLRB*, 311 US 72, 61 S Ct 83, 7 LRRM 282 (1940); *NLRB v Link-Belt Co*, 311 US 584, 61 S Ct 358, 7 LRRM 297 (1941); *H J Heinz Co v NLRB*, 311 US 514, 61 S Ct 320, 7 LRRM 291 (1941); *Fansteel Metallurgical Corp v NLRB*, 306 US 240, 59 S Ct 490, 4 LRRM 515 (1939); *NLRB v Falk Corp*, 308 US 453, 60 S Ct 307, 5 LRRM 677 (1940); *Consolidated Edison Co v NLRB*, 305 US 197, 59 S Ct 206, 3 LRRM 645 (1938); *NLRB v Southern Bell Telephone and Telegraph Co*, 319 US 50, 63 S Ct 905, 12 LRRM 677 (1943); *NLRB v Foote Bros Gear & Machine Corp*, 311 US 620, 61 S Ct 318, 7 LRRM 325 (1941); *Westinghouse Electic & Mfg Co v NLRB*, 312 US 660, 61 S Ct 736, 8 LRRM 460 (1941). The dissents in *Garment Workers* and *Consolidated*

Edison concerning Section 8(a)(2) dealt with the question of remedy only.

31. Hearings before a Committee on Education and Labor on S 1958, 74th Cong, 1st Session, at 41 (1935).

32. 15 USC 2401 et seq.

33. 29 USC 173(e).

34. See *National Steel Corp, Weirton Steel Division*, Cases 6-CA-16246. 6-CB-6012, NLRB Ad Mem (June 30, 1983) (General Counsel declined to prosecute a company-union committee where the company members were a minority of the committee, and in any event represented fellow managers rather than the company itself in a contemplated worker buy-out of the company); *Jet Spray Corp*, 271 NLRB #32, 116 LRRM 1379 (1984) (NLRB declines to rely on prior case which found a violation despite fact in prior case that employees and not employer initiated employee committee).

35. Thomas J. Schneider: *Quality of Working Life and the Law*, speech at Kennedy School of Government and Public Policy, Harvard University, as part of Harmen Lecture Series (November 19, 1981) (copy in possession of author).

WORKING TOWARD REAL QUALITY OF WORK LIFE

Three office workers, Lily Tomlin, Jane Fonda, and Dolly Parton, hold their tyrannical boss hostage for several weeks. To cover for his absence they run the office and use the opportunity to make some big changes. For the first time the employees have a say in how their work is organized. They set up a childcare center near the office. They begin to set their own hours (flextime). Two workers split the responsibilities and the hours of a single full-time job (job sharing). Everyone decorates her own work area. With the employees in charge, the quality of life at work improves dramatically.

—*9 to 5* (The Movie)

The language of QWL is laced with concepts like humanization of work, people-oriented labor relations, and respect for the dignity of the worker. One way to evaluate these "people-oriented" programs is first to determine what changes would be needed to improve the quality of life at work, and then see whether QWL programs are moving in that direction.

From this vantage it becomes obvious that QWL is not truly about improving the work experience. While QWL enthusiasts are praising management for humanizing work and showing new respect for the worker, the actual policies of the corporations are proceeding in the opposite direction. In fact, part of the employers' QWL agenda is to reverse gains that unions fought for years to win.

We will look at four aspects of daily work life and see how QWL fits in.

Worktime

The first step toward humanizing work would be to recognize that individuals have widely different needs. Older workers suffer more medical problems and usually have less stamina then younger workers. Parents need to spend time with their children and be with them when they get sick. Young single workers want time to socialize. If management wanted to "recognize the individual," it could start by asking each person how much he or she wanted to work and then organize the work around those desires.

Employers could also consider workers' individual schedules. The pressures on working parents, for example, are enormous. Often work starts at 7:00, but nursery school doesn't start until 8:30. It is not easy to find someone who will babysit at 6 a.m. and then take your child to school.

Employers' scheduling practices make life even more difficult. In many companies shifts can be changed with only a day or two's notice. You may not know until late in the workday what time you will get off. With forced

GUESS WHO'S ON ROTATING SHIFTS?

overtime, your days off are yours only if the company decides it can't use you. In some jobs ranging from steelworker to nurse, the only thing you can count on is that your shift and days off will be changed monthly.

These practices all reflect management's attitude toward workers: that they have no lives worth considering off the job. Any plans or obligations outside work are inconsequential.

Flexible worktime would be one of the first goals of a real quality of work life program. The technology exists to organize work around people's needs; in fact, worktime is already flexible and scheduled by computer.

UNIONS AND FLEXTIME

While some unions have championed flextime, particularly those representing many women and clerical workers, significant sections of the labor movement have been suspicious. Unions have feared that flextime might, "lead to flexible job classifications or other losses to employees."[1] Indeed, employers' flextime proposals have often been packaged with attempts to eliminate overtime pay after eight hours' work. In several industries, flextime is just the code word for employer flexibility to replace full-time jobs (and benefits) with part-time jobs (and no benefits). Unions need to find ways to achieve employee flexibility without sacrificing other union conditions.

ARE YOU THAT SICK?

In its 1982 concessions contract with the UAW, General Motors won an "irregular attendance control program." Among other features, this program provides that if a worker misses 20% of the work days in a six-month period, his or her benefits will be cut by 20%. The kicker is that the policy applies to both excused and unexcused absences, unless the worker provides satisfactory details of his or her private medical treatment.

In September 1982 a "not for publication" list entitled "Purification Guidelines" was circulated among officials charged with enforcing the new attendance policies. Absences from gastric ulcers ("proven by objective findings") would not be counted against you. Absences for tooth disorders would. Back problems would have to be proven by a myelogram (a highly uncomfortable, expensive, invasive procedure with risk of serious complications). A psychiatrist's note specifying psychosis or schizophrenia would save you from the absence control plan, but a diagnosis of depression or hysteria would not. Late syphilis would not count against you in the absentee procedure, but early syphilis, herpes, or gonorrhea would.

It is just that management's view of production demands is used as the input to the computer, and the worker's schedule is assumed to be the easily adjustable output.

Far from recognizing individual needs for work flexibility, many corporations are now running campaigns to crack down on absenteeism. Many of the same corporations which conduct elaborate QWL programs have also instituted draconian measures to force workers to fit exactly into production time slots. The very technology that could make flexible worktime possible is used instead to police attendance. Old-fashioned time clocks are out, replaced by computer systems that track absenteeism, initiate disciplinary action, and notify foremen about habitual offenders.

According to QWL theory, an improvement in worker participation and morale will lead to a decline in absenteeism as a by-product. As one of the union pioneers of QWL, the UAW's Irving Bluestone, put it, "If absenteeism declines because workers are more interested in their jobs, and find them more satisfying, all parties stand to benefit."[2] The fact that the companies have felt the need for elaborate campaigns against absenteeism suggests that QWL has failed in this regard.

QWL theory says that workers are absent because work is unsatisfying. But rather than dealing with the causes of absenteeism, many QWL structures have joined in the campaigns against absenteeism itself. An Ohio Bell QWL circle studied attendance patterns and proposed a plan, now on trial in Cleveland, which provides for an incentive payment for those with perfect attendance.[3] The UAW-Ford National Joint Committee

on Employe Involvement mailed every union member a booklet entitled *Absenteeism Hurts! Coming to Work Helps*. The EI newsletter published in Ford's Dearborn frame plant featured "A Critical Look at Absenteeism." The article complained that the company had to maintain 100 additional employees to cover absences (including vacations and medical leaves as well as unexcused absences).[4]

It is a bit unseemly that a union-sponsored publication in a plant with hundreds of people on layoff should complain that the company has to have more people on the payroll than it would like. To suggest that workers' vacations are part of the problem, and to do this all in the name of Employe Involvement, is a demonstration of the real direction and logic of most QWL-type programs.

Most of the QWL arguments for the absentee crackdown are couched in terms of hurting other workers. For example, the UAW-Ford booklet states:

> Absenteeism causes quality problems [which is] a sure way to lose sales. Lost sales, of course, mean lost jobs.
> Absenteeism upsets normal relief patterns.
> Absenteeism disrupts the lives of other fellow employees who have to be shuffled around to cover the jobs of absent employees.[5]

All of these arguments are bogus. One might be moved by the company's concern for the unfortunate employees who have to be "shuffled around to cover jobs," until one remembers that Ford is also pressing to break down classifications and work rules to give management more freedom to shift people around at its own will or whim.

The companies like to say that "no replacement can do your job as well as you can" (the worker's heart swells with pride). In fact, the employers design and

organize jobs so that workers are as interchangeable as possible. A National Research Council's study of absenteeism in the auto industry concluded:

> Given the nature of the jobs and the organization of the work, industry sources generally view work disruption as a minor factor, with redundancy in the relief pool of much greater importance.[6]

In other words, management's real concern is the expense of having extra workers on the payroll to cover for absences.

Even here, management could spend less "extra" money if it allowed workers to schedule their absences in advance. When management makes it tough to get a day off in advance, in effect employees are encouraged to wait until the day and call in sick. So management never knows how many people will be off and has to carry "redundant" workers to compensate.

Similarly, the facts do not support the product quality argument. A study of 18 General Motors assembly plants during the 1970's showed that higher product quality seemed to be associated with *higher* absenteeism.[7] Although the study's authors wish to dismiss this data, the relationship makes sense. A person who feels sick, has a personal problem, or for any other reason does not want to be at work on a particular day, is less likely to pay attention and do a good job. To use peer pressure or threats of discipline to force such a person to work will likely make the quality worse.

With computers most plants could easily adapt production schedules to accommodate a slight variation in attendance, especially if the variations were known in advance. In fact most plants already make major adjustments of this sort, not for workers' needs, but to accommodate machine breakdowns, delivery problems or the like.

Despite QWL rhetoric, the corporation's authority depends on insisting that company needs take priority over all else in life. Maintaining this authority and control is a big part of the reason that management is not interested in humane policies on working hours or absenteeism. The irony is that QWL programs end up as part of the management campaign to save money or maintain authority rather than promoting true improvements in these working conditions.

__Stress_____

While the popular image is that stress is the burden of top executives, studies have found that "top executive" does not even make the list of the most highly stressful occupations. A National Institute for Occupational Safety and Health study found that, of the jobs considered, the most stressful were inspectors of manufactured products, warehouse workers, public relations workers, laboratory technicians, machinists, laborers, mechanics and structural-metal craftspersons.[8]

Research over the last several years has demonstrated that stress is a killer. It is an important risk factor in heart disease. Other medical problems linked to stress include ulcers, high blood pressure, alcoholism, and depression. In addition stress contributes to accidents, family problems, and drug abuse.

The stress reaction, the body's natural defense against danger, is often called the "fight or flight" reaction. A perceived threat triggers production of hormones, such as adrenalin, which in turn cause the heart to speed up and other organs to prepare for exceptionally high effort. Stress is often credited with enabling people to perform "superhuman" feats such as lifting a truck off a trapped child.

Stress becomes a medical problem when it becomes

the body's "normal" state, when the body is continually prepared to meet danger and is continually releasing high levels of hormones.

What causes stress on the job? Occupational stressors include working around dangerous equipment, high noise levels, temperature extremes, uncomfortable working conditions, and shift work (particularly with rotating shifts). But physiological stress is also triggered by mental pressures. Fear of job loss produces the stress reaction, as do lack of respect, conflicting job demands, and sexual or racial harassment.[9]

One of the most important causes of stress is lack of control over one's job, particularly when the job is very demanding. Studies of Swedish and American workers ranked jobs according to the amount of control workers had over them. The researchers then compared the amount of control at work with the occurrence of heart disease. They found that workers with the least control over their jobs were five times as likely to develop heart disease as those with most control.[10]

The most stressful jobs turn out to be the ones which combine high psychological demands with severe restriction on the worker's ability to respond. As Dr. Arthur Vander, professor of physiology at the University of Michigan, explains:

> If the executive at General Motors is very much in control of the situation and feels comfortable with what's happening, he's under no stress at all. You contrast that to a blue collar worker who might be in an assembly line in a speedup, who has no control whatsoever over what's happening—that person's under a great deal of stress.[11]

Most companies ignore evidence that conditions of work contribute mightily to a person's stress. If they attempt to deal with stress at all, they approach it as a personal problem and perhaps offer the "troubled worker" some counseling. To be sure, work does not cause all problems and the assistance can be helpful. But such

assistance does nothing to identify or eliminate the powerful stressors that exist on the job. Indeed, to the extent that counseling places the responsibility for the work problems on the worker, it may even make things worse.

New policies that companies are now trying to implement will actually increase occupational stress. Management "flexibility" in job assignments, which gets rid of classifications (see chapter 4) or skilled trades lines of demarcation (discussed later in this chapter), greatly increases stress. It decreases the limited control workers presently have over their jobs and increases the conflicting demands and unclear expectations under which they work.

Similarly, despite volumes of studies on the stressful nature of shift work,[12] there have been only a few attempts to consider human needs rather than production needs in scheduling.

Identifying and eliminating sources of stress at work would certainly seem to be appropriate tasks for QWL groups. Some groups have in fact reduced noise or danger or other physical stressors. But in most programs these tasks are usually tolerated only as "first steps" and groups are urged to move on to the more serious questions of quality and productivity.

A major idea associated with QWL is that workers must take more responsibility for quality, for the company's success in the marketplace, and for their own job security. Circle members are told that their jobs depend on quality work or on the ability of the company or plant to be more competitive.

At the same time, as we discussed in previous chapters, QWL gives workers no control over either their immediate jobs or company policy. Management carefully guards its prerogatives *to make the decisions.*

In fact, QWL contributes to decreasing worker power by undermining the union and reducing union and worker control on the shop floor. QWL thus becomes the classic formula for *increasing* occupational stress—high psychological demand and little power.

New Technology

New technology could be a real breakthrough for an employer truly committed to improving the quality of working life. New technology designed to enhance worker control of the job could liberate workers from tedious, dangerous jobs and improve skills. Yet there is little evidence that this is what happens and much which demonstrates the reverse.

The form that technology takes is not a given. Companies' choices about technologies are related to their other strategic considerations. Is the purpose of Numerical Control (NC) machine tools to increase product quality, or to decrease the control of the skilled machinist?[13] Is the purpose of a centralized computer to increase the productivity of office workers directly by providing them with better tools, or does management have in mind gaining greater control over the office workforce?[14] Management's goals for new technology determine whether it will be used to enhance or destroy the quality of working life.

Consider the telephone industry, which has an extensive QWL program. The introduction of technology has made work more unpleasant. Operators no longer control when they pick up calls. When one call is finished, the computer automatically connects the operator to the next one. The same computer switching system also monitors the length of each call and the time between calls. Operators who average more than 30 seconds per call are subject to discipline. Naturally, customers who get the required "short treatment" respond hostilely to the operators. The net result is poorer service and unpleasant conditions of work. In 1984 AT&T Communications in Baltimore fired an operator of 16 years experience who insisted that she had a moral obligation to take the time to assist elderly or confused callers.[15]

The phone companies also use new technology to reduce the skill level and judgment required of testers and repairers. Previously, skilled workers would take a complaint, test the equipment, diagnose and repair the problem, and then check the equipment once more. Nowadays, a clerk with no technical knowledge enters the complaint into a computer, which analyzes the problem and issues instructions for a repairer to replace a specific module. The computer then tests the system again and decides whether to issue further instructions.

In effect, the craftworker becomes the tool of the computer. The computer is programmed to use as little of the craftsperson's observation or judgment as possible. But there is nothing in the technology that *requires* it to be programmed that way. Better and faster service would result if a skilled person took and analyzed the original complaint directly instead of an untrained person forcing it into a predefined category. If the craftsperson were taught the computer program and allowed to intervene to adjust it, situations not foreseen by the original programmers could be resolved more quickly. But AT&T used the opportunity of the new technology to take control of the job away from the unionized craftsperson.

Similarly with office automation: word processors have the potential to relieve tedious tasks like retyping. But a study of a large engineering office found that the technology:

> reduced task variety, meaning, contribution, control over work scheduling and boundary tasks, feedback of results, involvement in preparation and auxiliary tasks, and communications with authors.[16]

WHY THIS JOB?

The Man-mate gave way to the Unimate robot at Ford's Dearborn assembly plant in July 1984. "Old Man" Brown was still employed but his favorite job was gone.

The body sides for Ford's Mustang are assembled and welded on two large oval-shaped conveyor systems. When they are finished the 70-pound sides have to be lifted off the assembly conveyors and placed on an overhead conveyor, which takes them to another work area where they are attached to the floorpan.

For as long as most people can remember the job was done with the Man-mate, a 20-foot swinging yellow arm with a claw on the end which looked like it was left over from a grade B mad scientist movie. The operator sat in the Man-mate, manipulating hydraulic controls to move the arm and claw and swing the machine around to load left and right body sides alternately onto the overhead conveyor.

The day shift operator, William Brown, was well respected not only for his 31 years seniority but because of the way he could operate the Man-mate. Old Man Brown was the area repair and utility person. Over the years he had trained a number of Man-mate operators, but "it took six months before someone was really good."

The first two weeks in July, the assembly plant took its scheduled vacation shutdown. On the first weekend the Man-mate was removed, the area was stripped, and the new Westinghouse Unimate robot was installed. Replacing the human/Man-mate combination was exceptionally difficult. The Unimate itself rode on an automated carrier and all its motions had to be coordinated with three independent, old and cranky conveyor systems so that it could pick up and place parts "on the fly" (while everything was moving). In addition, all kinds of safety interlocks had to be provided to insure that no one could accidentally come within reach of the moving robot's mighty but unseeing arm.

One more Unimate robot by itself was hardly noteworthy. The plant already had some 25 Unimate welders, some AMF Versatran robots, and two new Tokiko robots in a paint spray booth.

Yet many workers knew that this robot was different. Other robots took away jobs that were dirty, dangerous and unsafe. Few people missed breathing in paint fumes or facing weld flash. But the Man-mate involved skill, coordination, judgment. It was a sit-down job—one of the few production jobs in the plant which did not leave you physically drained at the end of the day. It was a central job which involved a lot of responsibility. Some say there was also a special pleasure in that job because the machine responded to the person, in a factory where most of the time the person responded to the machine.

In fact, the Man-mate job was considered one of the best jobs in the plant. Not because it was easy, but because it was skilled and it was special. And its loss was mourned. As one worker summed up the feelings of many: "With all the shitty jobs in this place they had to take that one."

There is an Employe Involvement program in the Dearborn assembly plant. But no one ever asked any of the EI groups to consider which jobs should be replaced by automation. Management reserves decisions in this area for itself.

While repetitive and boring jobs may be obvious candidates for automation, sometimes jobs are automated because they require *too much* skill like the Man-mate job described in the box. Employers regard jobs that depend on worker skill or experience as restrictions on their ability to control production and they are willing to pay to maintain that control. The total cost of buying and installing the robot which replaced Man-mate was more than $150,000. Yet the robot replaced only one person on each shift in an operation which the company

skilled tradesmen also wired in a new electronic apparatus to automatically check the electrical systems of cars, and did away with three inspector jobs.

Where does QWL fit in? Ronnie Straw and Charles Heckscher, two researchers for the Communications Workers of America who are supporters of QWL, are candid:

> Though the QWL process has led to improved relations and less burdensome supervision in many offices, it has not reached to the fundamental policies which

expects to close down within a few years.

Automation now threatens many factory jobs that are considered the more desirable ones—jobs that are less repetitive, require more skill, are not as physically taxing, and give some sense of control over the work process. The new targets include fork-lift drivers, material handlers, inspectors, and machine operators. These jobs can now be eliminated because of larger computer memory, more sophisticated software, and "vision" and "touch" senses for the automation. One of the fastest growing areas is automated parts storage, records, and retrieval systems which can handle full pallets or the tiniest parts. Driverless "trucks" roam modern plants under computerized instructions, picking up and delivering parts. At the Dearborn assembly plant, the same week that the Man-mate was removed

shape the development of new technologies. It seems that for every improvement in individual locations, a dozen systems come after from Bell Laboratories reinforcing the dehumanizing patterns which we are battling.

> As for the Technology Change Committees, their effectiveness has been limited both by the resistance of management, which sees this area as a crucial bastion of "managerial prerogatives," and by the lack of experience of union participants. As a result, membership attitude surveys over the past three years have shown, if anything, increasing levels of discontent with job pressures.[17]

The CWA hopes that the cooperative relations developed in QWL will develop into increased participation in the planning of technology. But it isn't as though no one has ever pointed out to AT&T that its use of technology takes control away from workers. AT&T knows exactly what it is doing and will not voluntarily give up its prerogative to make the decisions.

However, corporations like AT&T would appreciate cooperation from unions and workers in the introduction of new technology. When such technology is first installed it contains many "bugs." Engineers depend on machine operators and plant maintenance personnel when they are debugging and getting a new system fully operational, to observe and report problems and suggest solutions. Under the best of circumstances these can take weeks to years to work out. The speed and cost of installing equipment is determined by the extent of cooperation from the workforce.

Once managers have made the important decisions about new technology, they frequently involve QWL groups in the final stages. For example, a QWL group may visit a manufacturer to examine the machine before it is delivered and make suggestions, such as where controls should be placed. Management hopes to take advantage of worker knowledge and suggestions to smooth off the rough spots. But more importantly, management hopes that this involvement will give workers a sense of "ownership" in the new equipment which will motivate them to cooperate fully in its introduction.

Management also looks to QWL to help create a general climate of cooperation. Ford Chairman Philip Caldwell explains:

> We at Ford have had few problems implementing new processes in technology. We have had some unwillingness at the local level to let achieved economies flow through to the bottom line. But we believe our employee involvement programs being developed with the UAW will help change this attitude by letting everyone see the benefits of productivity gains.[18]

Skilled Trades Work

Some jobs provide much greater satisfaction than others. A reasonable approach to improving the quality of working life would be to identify these jobs, determine what features make them satisfying, and then expand these features.

Skilled trades jobs in industry, including millwright, electrician, toolmaker and others, are among those satisfying jobs. The work requires considerable skill, a long period of training, and continued learning. The nature of the work requires a great deal of cooperation within trades, across trades and across shifts. Compared to production work, skilled work is varied, it is often self-paced, often interesting. While it sometimes involves heavy work, it rarely requires the continued

PAY FOR KNOWLEDGE

The company was proud of its million-dollar automated hydraulic widget machine. But one day, as these things often happen, the machine failed just after the warranty ran out. The company tried everything, but no one was able to get the machine running again. The company was losing hundreds of thousands of dollars in lost production. Finally they called in a well known hydraulics expert who flew in from New York the next morning. She took one look at the dials and gauges, and another look at the machine. She picked up a hammer and gave it a whack. The machine sprang into operation. The expert left and was on a return flight before noon.

The company was happy to be back in business again. But a few days later it received a bill from the expert for $30,000. The company immediately telegraphed her: "$30,000 is an unreasonable amount. You were here less than 15 minutes and all you did was hit the machine with a hammer. There must be some mistake. Please send an itemized bill."

In the next mail the company received the itemized bill: "Travel Expenses—$500. Travel Time—$300. Hitting the Machine—$5. Figuring out where to hit the machine—$29,195."

physical stress of many production jobs. While it entails considerable responsibility, there is (or has been) corresponding control over work decisions. A tradesperson can take the abstractions of physics or geometry and immediately translate them into physical actions that bring results in the real world. Thus the skilled trades should be a QWLer's model: people involved in their work, with a fair degree of interest, creativity, autonomy, and teamwork built in.

It is precisely these positive features of skilled work that the corporations have chosen to attack. They understand that skilled work is a mixture of more routine kinds of operations and highly specialized skills.

A high proportion of the work that a tradesperson does, perhaps 80%, could be done by someone with only six months' training. But the other 20% requires years of training and experience. And even though the tasks in the lower 80% do not require that much skill, knowing *when* to use them does.

The corporations' strategy is to separate the skilled trades' 80% routine work from the 20% expert work. They want to reduce the skill level of the trades so that they are trained only for the 80% part. Then management can rely on an entirely different group of workers to handle the remaining 20%. This elite group would be either a part of management, classified as salaried engineers or designers, or outside contractors. The strategy is as old as Frederick Taylor's "scientific management" attempt to remove "all possible brainwork" from the shop floor.

Management's *deskilling* strategy takes two seemingly contradictory forms. One strategy is to break a complex job down into a series of highly specialized tasks. The other is to increase the number of tasks a tradesperson is expected to do so that it is impossible to acquire any depth of skill. In this case the "jack-of-all-trades, master of none" adage applies perfectly. In other words, deskilling is the result of either severely narrowing or broadening the scope of work. The companies have been pushing both.

DESKILLING THROUGH SPECIALIZATION

In the metalworking or tool and die trades, the companies' attack on skill has historically taken the form of over-specialization. Rather than an all-round machinist with well developed theoretical knowledge, the companies want operators of specific machines. Where they have been able to get away with it, they have reduced the jobs to "mill hands," "lathe hands" and "grinder hands" because it is the hands they want. Even where, through union pressure, the official standards for a tool and die maker apprenticeship require broad training, often the apprentice is tracked into a very limited subfield which may continue for his or her entire career.

One journeyman tool and die maker's experience is typical. Most of his apprenticeship and all of his work for the next four years were spent on "die tryout." (Dies are matching metal pieces which are mounted in stamping presses. The press forces the dies together to cut and shape a steel sheet.) The journeyman spent his whole day bent over or curled up in huge press dies with his hand grinder, making the finishing adjustments so that the dies meshed properly. But he wasn't just a die

COLOR BY NUMBER

"Let's take my trade, machining, as an example. You learn certain basic types of operations, each simple and relatively easy to learn, and you combine them with an indefinable ingredient, your own skill, to create what is often a tribute to your vision and experience. Being a skilled machinist eliminates the division between manual and mental labor. One of the real satisfactions of skilled work is that, like an artist, your hands produce what your mind conceives.

"Today more and more of the work process is being organized to limit your vision to the narrowest possible execution of someone else's plans. If Michelangelo, for example, had to paint in this way, he would have painted the Sistine chapel by numbers, filling in the colors of someone's neatly laid out design...." —*Harley Shaiken*[19]

---

tryout specialist—he was further specialized to one specific kind of die called a draw die. When GM closed his plant he realized that he had lost touch with his trade. He had become so specialized that he was no longer qualified for most of the work done by tool and die makers.

DESKILLING THROUGH BROADENING

In the steel industry management has made considerable headway in combining the jobs of its skilled maintenance workers into two general classifications or "supercrafts"—general mechanical and electrical. Such supercraft workers are not actually trained in all the trades, but they are taught enough to do the 80% routine jobs in some of them. The key point is that just about any kind of work is now part of the worker's job description. In the auto industry management has gotten around the old classifications by creating and expanding new ones with such broad jurisdictions that they amount to "supercrafts."

For example, the auto companies have been most successful in expanding a classification usually called Welding Machine Repair (WEMR). An automated welding apparatus requires much regular maintenance—such as changing, dressing and adjustment of weld tips—as well as electrical, hydraulic, millwright, tool maker, and pipefitter maintenance skills. Why, the companies argue, do we have to have one person from each of these trades available when we can train one person to take care of the whole machine?

Instead of highly skilled workers who thoroughly know their crafts and can easily apply them to new situations, the companies prefer jacks-of-all-trades who learn on and know a particular machine. When a machine goes down they are not interested in a worker with a theoretical understanding. They want somebody who knows what relay to push or pressure switch to bypass, even if he doesn't know why.

Broadening maintenance classifications turns out to produce much the same results as the overspecialization of the machining trades. Workers' knowledge is tied to specific machines and they become a new breed of machine operator.

A side benefit to the companies is that the new broad classifications have pitted sections of the trades against each other and created tremendous bitterness. Often, to get the union's permission to create the Welding Machine Repair trade the companies agreed to pay it a higher rate than many other trades.

Despite management's frequent claims, it is not likely that efficiency in production is even the real reason for amalgamating the trades. It certainly sounds more productive to have one Welding Machine Repairer assigned to a line rather than, say, a group of four including an electrician, a pipefitter, a machinist, and a millwright. But much of this difference disappears when the territory is enlarged so that the group of four tradespersons covers four lines.

Further, the real issue in efficiency is how long the machine is down and how well it is fixed so that it stays in production longer. No one would propose to staff a hospital only with general practitioners. Highly skilled experts are more likely to identify the problem quickly and make the proper repair. A couple of extra tradespeople make little difference compared to the costs of downtime for a $10 million production line, 20 idle production workers, poor quality parts, and the effects of possible shortages downstream.

Nor is the new organization of work safe. Maintenance work can be extremely dangerous. It involves working around lethal voltages, pressures and weights, often when the nature of the malfunction is unknown. Of the 14 UAW members killed in industrial accidents in 1983, 11 were in the skilled trades. Often skilled tradespersons have to call on all of their experience and training to avoid serious accidents. It is

also unsafe for production workers to have people with limited knowledge doing whatever they can simply to get a machine running again, since often the easiest way is "jumping out" safety features originally designed into the machine.

Photo by Jim West

A s industry automates, the proportion of skilled trades will rapidly increase as production workers are cut back. Since skilled jobs represent the future of industrial work, the conditions set today will be the mass conditions of tomorrow. The corporations are clear that they want these jobs to become as much like production jobs as possible, with workers as interchangeable as possible.

In many industries the main hope for young workers for job security and a decent work life is to get into the skilled trades. Every skilled trades job lost is one less opportunity for a "quality" job. The loss of skilled jobs particularly hurts women and black workers who have only broken the barriers to entry in these jobs in the last few years.

The corporations want to deskill the trades because management finds them troublesome. Their sense of skill, the discretionary elements, the feeling of job control translate into a sense of power and a demand for respect from management. Workers whose jobs depend mainly on their ability to operate one or two specific

By Carol ★ Simpson

LINES OF DEMARCATION

Corporations have convinced the public that unions have forced them to operate by unreasonably restrictive skilled trades work rules called "lines of demarcation. This is *Business Week's* example:

> If an electrician can use a screwdriver to take the cover off an electrical contact instead of waiting for a millwright to perform the nonelectrical task, you save a lot of money in terms of downtime, and that's the name of the game.[20]

This kind of ignorance about what goes on is repeated until it becomes accepted. In the first place, electricians do use screwdrivers to remove covers of electrical boxes. Secondly, skilled trades voluntarily use their common sense about lines of demarcation in the course of cooperating in regular work. Thirdly, the companies through contract and arbitrators' decisions have established the notion of "overlapping and incidental work"—trades can be required to do work that might normally belong to another trade if it is an incidental part of, but necessary to, their main assignments.

Management uses all of these in pressing for ever greater flexibility. For example, an electrician can mount a small electrical panel as an "incidental" operation using his or her standard tools and skills. But as the panels get bigger the point is reached where it is difficult to install them by hand and much easier to do with a power lift truck or other rigging equipment. Once electricians start using this equipment, however, the companies declare the equipment "tools of the trade" and start requiring electricians who have inadequate training in rigging to mount larger and larger panels.

Workers are forced to draw the line because management is always in a rush to get productivity in the short term, whatever the long term consequences to safety, contracts or quality of working life. As with the non-skilled classifications described in chapter 4, the issue is not whether work can be done flexibly, but whether the flexibility is all management's.

In practice, management violates lines of demarcation daily. A foreman can order a worker to take action and despite the popular image, a worker has no right to refuse (except in certain cases where injury is likely). In the most blatant cases that get to the higher levels of the grievance procedure, the worst that happens to the company is that it gets told it was naughty and has to pay a few hours' extra pay.

---

machines are tied to those machines and to the company which set them up. They do not have the self-confidence and power that comes from having readily marketable skills.

In other words, it is precisely those aspects of work that QWL pretends to be about that companies are seeking to destroy in the skilled trades.

And QWL's role is to help the company do just that. *Business Week*, for example, lauds Ford's use of its Employe Involvement program in "smoothing the way" to break down lines of demarcation:

> EI "opened up lines of communication" [plant chairman Dave] Curson says, enabling the two sides to collaborate on cutting costs and outbidding competitors. Last March the members of Local 898 ratified a precedent setting agreement that calls for experimentation with new forms of work organization, such as production teams, and, in a major cost-cutting move, consolidates 24 skilled trades into 14.[21]

In addition, the agreement allows production operators "to perform minor maintenance" and to assist skilled trades so that only one skilled tradesperson need be assigned where formerly two were needed. In language that clearly "communicates" a direction, the agreement concludes:

> ...it is expressly understood that [these examples] are not intended to be all inclusive.[22]

Management usually tries to be careful not to bring up lines of demarcation directly in QWL meetings. But the corporations' propaganda about the lazy, "featherbedding" tradespeople combines effectively with QWL discussions of making the company competitive. In operation QWL often pits production against skilled.[23] The net result is greasing of the skids for a successful attack on the skilled trades.

* * *

It cannot be said that Quality of Work Life programs have nothing to do with the quality of life at work. Some of the projects that QWL groups commonly work on, such as fans and water fountains, or getting management to address workers respectfully, are real work life issues too. The reason groups are allowed to pursue them is that they cost little and do not challenge management's control. The real test of QWL is on the issues which could *fundamentally* alter the quality of life at work. A few QWL efforts do achieve real improvements. But for the most part, QWL programs turn out to be either a dull tool for labor or a sharp one for management to cut in the opposite direction. □

Notes

1. George Strauss, "Quality of Worklife and Participation as Bargaining Issues," in Hervey A. Juris and Myron Roomkin, eds., *The Shrinking Perimeter*, D.C. Heath, 1980.

2. *Viewpoint*, AFL-CIO Industrial Union Department Quarterly, Volume 8, No. 3, 1978.

3. *QWL Newsletter*, Ohio Bell, December 1984.

4. *Ford Facts*, column by Al Gardner, November 21, 1983.

5. *To Compete: We Need Each Other. Absenteeism Hurts! Coming to Work Helps*, issued by UAW-Ford National Joint Committee on Employe Involvement, October 1981.

6. National Research Council, *The Competitive Status of the U.S. Auto Industry*, National Academy Press, 1982.

7. Harry C. Katz, Thomas A. Kochan, and Kenneth R. Gobeille, "Industrial Relations Performance, Economic Performance, and QWL Programs: An Interplant Analysis," *Industrial and Labor Relations Review*, October 1983.

8. *Psychology Today*, January 1979.

9. Aaron Back, Michael Lerner, and Lee Schore, *Occupational Stress: The Inside Story*, Institute for Labor and Mental Health, 1981.

10. *New York Times*, April 10, 1983.

11. Dolly Katz, "Boardroom Toll from Stress Less Than That on the Line," *Detroit Free Press*, February 11, 1985.

12. See, for example, J. Carpentier and P. Cazamian, *Night Work*, International Labour Organization, 1977.

13. See David F. Noble, *Forces of Production* , Alfred A. Knopf, 1984.

14. These kinds of choices are analyzed in depth in Harley Shaiken's *Work Transformed: Automation & Labor in the Computer Age*, Holt, Rinehart and Winston, 1984.

15. *Detroit Free Press*, April 6, 1984.

16. David A. Buchanan and David Boddy, "Advanced Technology and the Quality of Working Life: The Effects of Word Processing on Video Typists," *Journal of Occupational Psychology*, March 1982.

17. *QWL Focus*, Ontario Ministry of Labour, Spring 1984.

18. "The Automobile Crisis and Public Policy: An Interview with Philip Caldwell," *Harvard Business Review*, January-February 1981.

19. Harley Shaiken, "Craftsman into Babysitter," in Ivan Illich et al., *Disabling Professions*, Marion Boyers, 1977.

20. *Business Week*, April 26, 1982.

21. *Business Week*, July 30, 1984.

22. Letter of Understanding, March 12, 1984.

23. Robert Thomas, "Participation and Control: New Trends in Labor Relations in the Auto Industry," CRSO Working Paper #315, University of Michigan, 1984.

__Inside the Circle: A UNION GUIDE TO QWL__

Labor Education and Research Project, P.O. Box 20001, Detroit, MI 48220. (313) 883-5580.

USING QWL TO KEEP UNIONS OUT

Instead of a Union

Industry publications such as *Forbes*, *Business Week*, and *Iron Age* can scarcely contain their glee as they note the downward slide of labor's ability to organize. They give much of the credit to employers' new emphasis on the "carrot" instead of the "stick" in labor relations—using psychology and a human approach rather than open threats, goon squads, and Pinkertons.

In practice, the stick seems to be gaining in popularity these days just as much as the carrot—witness the scab-herding at Greyhound, the teargassing at Phelps Dodge, the rise in union decertification elections.

But employers are nothing if not flexible. Many are following the example set by John D. Rockefeller in 1915, who, after the Ludlow, Colorado strike massacre, developed a plan for "Joint Committees on Industrial Cooperation and Conciliation." Today there is an explosion in the number of corporate consultants, labor relations specialists, lawyers, workshops and publications all available (at a hefty price) to advise in using "communication" and "participation" to crush any attempt to organize a union.

Scores of management consultants regularly bombard non-union employers with offers to apply the latest techniques in union busting. J.W. Hickey and Associates of Columbus, Ohio sends out the following letter after a representation election has occurred:

> We were happy to learn . . . that you beat the union in the last election. Congratulations are certainly in order! . . .
> J.W. Hickey and Associates has developed a number of professional programs to prevent the union from

NLRB ELECTION RESULTS

	UNION VICTORIES	MEMBERS ORGANIZED
1972	54.9%	286,000
1973	52.0	224,000
1974	51.0	190,000
1975	49.6	208,000
1976	49.7	160,000
1977	46.4	204,000
1978	48.1	158,000
1979	47.2	195,000
1980	47.9	175,000
1981	46.0	147,000
1982	43.8	88,000
1983*	46.6	72,000

*1983 estimated based on partial figures

Source: AFL-CIO Dept. of Organization

Note that a union election victory does not mean that a contract will be signed. There are so many ways an employer can continue to resist that fewer than two out of three election victories ends up with a collective bargaining contract.

DECLINING ORGANIZATION

	% of Labor Force Organized	% of Private Sector Organized
1958	24.2	36
1968	23.0	30
1978	19.7	24
1980	20.9	NA
1982	17.9	NA

Source: U.S. Labor Department

EMPLOYER RESISTANCE TO UNIONS ON THE RISE

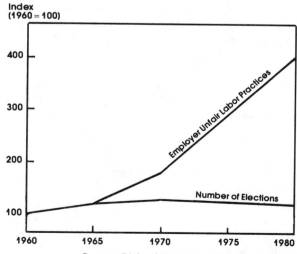

Source: Richard Freeman and James Medoff,
What Do Unions Do?

One measure of employer resistance to unionism is the dramatic increase in employer unfair labor practices during organizing drives.

returning.... We have found that employees are impressed that management is interested in their feelings and willing to make some changes for their benefit. As you know, employees today are interested, want to be involved in, and feel they are a part of forming decisions having an effect on their job or working conditions.

QWL programs and quality circles have become one of the most popular weapons of the new union busters. One consultant told a workshop sponsored by the California Hospital Management Association:

> In recent years, methods such as the Quality Circle (QC) have been proposed and used to give employees a greater say in how their jobs are performed. The perceived benefits of such "shared management" include greater employee job satisfaction, less turnover, improved communications between management and employees, less absenteeism, higher productivity, and less employer susceptibility to union organizing.[1]

The Council on a Union-Free Environment (CUE) established by the National Association of Manufacturers has a series of publications promoting quality circles. They include case studies of "successes" at nonunion plants of Sundestrand Aviation, the TRW conglomerate, and Coors Brewing.

There are companies which have used QWL to fight off unions in every sector of American industry, including ones thought of as highly organized. The president of Viking Freight, Richard Bangham, says that complaint airing sessions help keep his trucking company union-free. "One of the company officers goes out to each terminal every month to sit with the employees and explain the company's performance in the previous month," Bangham says. "Then we have a suggestion and 'bitch and gripe' session afterwards."[2]

The new Nissan truck plant in Smyrna, Tennessee and the Honda plant in Marysville, Ohio are both nonunion. Wage-benefit packages are lower than UAW scale. But both plants have elaborate employee participation programs which undercut the union's appeal so effectively that there is little chance of successful organizing drives for the present.

QWL has also been employed to keep the so-called "sunrise" industries—high tech and services—nonunion. Texas Instruments, IBM, and TRW are among the successful users of QWL.

Few management consultants or companies openly proclaim that they are using their QWL programs to keep unions out. The programs are supposed to create the appearance that there is natural communication, goodwill, and participation, and that the union is not necessary. To announce that they are a response to the threat of unionization gives credit to the union and is self-defeating for the union buster. Thus the smart consultant will describe his QWL program in more neutral language. The notorious union busting firm Modern Management, Inc. (previously MMM) touts quality circles as an aid to productivity:

> As today's emphasis upon participative management has grown, the "Quality Circles" technique has proven particularly productive in combining principles of communication, management, and employee relations to

produce astounding results in productivity and profitability. During the past five years, American organizations literally have saved millions of dollars by implementing the employee suggestions which have come out of Quality Circle meetings.[3]

However, the primary value of QWL, according to the union busters, is to undercut reasons that workers might turn to a union in the first place. Woodruff Imberman, a well known Chicago-based union busting consultant, claims to have done extensive research into quality circles and specializes in preparing employees so that QC programs will be successful.[4] He explains:

> We're interested in improving employee morale.... We would rather help a company avoid an election than win one.[5]

NO S.O.B.'S HERE

Loren D. Barre, the shirt-sleeved president of RTE Corp., stepped to the microphone to tell about 60 production workers who had packed a smoky cafeteria that sales and earnings were right on target for an upbeat year. After the brief presentation, the head of the Waukesha (Wisconsin) electrical transformer maker turned the meeting over to the employees. What he got was an earful.... "If the rank and file worker can express himself like this, he doesn't need to go to the union steward to complain about those SOBs in the front office," said Barre later.

Such freewheeling meetings ...have become a cornerstone of a strategy to remain nonunion.... The effort has paid off: RTE has not even faced a serious organizing drive since 1965 despite its proximity to heavily organized Milwaukee.

—*Business Week*, December 4, 1978

Union organizers and union busters alike refer to this strategy as "union substitution." The company seems to provide unilaterally the channels of influence and group feeling that come with unionism, without giving up any real power.

Should a union organizing drive begin, the participation groups have additional anti-union uses. The groups provide management with a ready forum for conducting its anti-union campaign in the most favorable circumstances. Observers credit the General Motors' QWL program for salaried workers as key to beating back the UAW's 1983 organizing drive.[6]

An AFL-CIO study of organizing drives in 1982-3 found that the existence of a grievance procedure or medical insurance did not significantly affect a union's ability to win a representation election. According to Charles McDonald, the editor of the AFL-CIO's *Statistical and Tactical Information Report*, "The one major company 'benefit' that drastically affected union organizing drives was the quality of work life plan, particularly in manufacturing establishments."[7]

Of 225 organizing campaigns examined by the study (in units greater than 50 people), most did not have substantial QWL programs. In these the unions won 47% of the elections. At the workplaces which did have QWL, unions won only two out of six campaigns in service industries and only one out of twelve in manufacturing. If anything, these figures underestimate the effects of QWL programs, since elections were only held where the unions had some initial success and felt strong enough to request the elections in the first place.

AFL-CIO Secretary-Treasurer Thomas Donahue says that almost all union organizing directors believe that QWL programs make organizing more difficult.[8]

In some cases companies use QWL-type groups for more than just propaganda. A rare inside look is pro-vided by researcher Guillermo Grenier, who spent several months in the Johnson & Johnson Ethicon plant in Albuquerque, New Mexico. The plant was organized into work teams. Grenier describes how they operate:

> . . . Facilitators (supervisors) are expected to remain in control of their teams while employees are made to feel that the system is "open" to their suggestions and decisions. According to Jaramillo [a social psychologist who is the plant personnel manager], teams are used as part of a strategy to "isolate" pro-union employees from their fellow team members. The "isolated" individual can then be dealt with in some fashion: he or she can be fired for not having "team support" (one of the "objective criteria" for termination at Ethicon), or for a poor "attitude" or other factors ostensibly unrelated to union support. . . .

Where union members are not fired, their personal isolation from other team members can be used by management (or by anti-union employees acting on behalf of management) to make union members look like ''losers'' to their fellow workers and discredit the union itself. [9]

The key to union avoidance strategies is to remove as many of the *appearances* of the employer-employee authority relationship as possible without challenging the substance of the rules. At the same time the union is painted as an outsider whose involvement can only turn informal, friendly human interaction into a formal, bureaucratic relationship. At the anti-union Honda plant in Marysville, Ohio, bosses and workers alike are all ''associates.'' Many plants have abolished grating distinctions like separate and unequal lunch rooms or parking spaces. Management at the new Nissan plant in Tennessee puts the emphasis on ''communications.'' As President Marvin Runyon explains:

> We honestly believe our employees do not want or need a union or any third party to speak for them. If you have to go through a third party to talk to someone you lose something. The guy in the middle might hear things a little differently and distort meaning. [10]

Challenging Legal Restrictions on QWL

Since they have been so effective in keeping unions out, why haven't QWL programs been used more extensively? As described in chapter 12, the main reason is that the NLRB has interpreted the National Labor Relations Act to limit the kinds of QWL programs a union busting employer could get away with.

But now QWL supporters are trying to chip away at this traditional pro-labor interpretation. The International Association of Quality Circles (IAQC) has asked the NLRB to reinterpret the law so that quality circles (using the IAQC definition) cannot be effectively challenged by unions. The IAQC describes itself as ''the largest professional organization in existence devoted to promoting the Quality Circle concept'' and claims 6,000 members, including many consultants and corporations. In an *amicus* brief the IAQC demands that the Board:

> reflect a recognition of contemporary developments i.e. recent efforts by management to embrace employees in a participative decision-making process. No longer can the Act be interpreted as presupposing a natural and basic conflict between employers and its employees.

The IAQC argues that the Board should even endorse such programs as ''mandated by today's National Labor Policy.'' Significantly, the IAQC's brief was submitted in a clear case of union busting. The Ona Corporation in Huntsville, Alabama was found guilty of 59 flagrant unfair labor practices during a UAW organizing drive, including threats of blacklisting, plant closures, loss of benefits, and loss of promotions. While these violations were on appeal, the parent corporation instituted a QWL-type program at all of its plants. The company established an "Employee Action Committee," picked its members from volunteers, and provided the committee with a short list of problems from which it could choose (breaktimes, floating holiday, vacation schedule, telephone usage, shift preference, and safety apparel). The UAW charged that the committee was clearly an employer-dominated labor organization and thus in violation of the NLRA. The Administrative Law Judge who heard the case agreed. Ona appealed to the full NLRB.[11]

In response to the popularity of QWL and in reasoning similar to that of the IAQC, several scholars and lawyers have also proposed "reinterpreting" labor law. They propose to weaken unions' traditional exclusive bargaining rights or prohibitions against employer domination, thus making it more difficult for unions to control or challenge QWL programs.[12]

The combination of a Reaganized Labor Board and pressure from supposedly neutral QWL practitioners will likely force significant changes in the accepted legal interpretation of "company unions"—and thus create new obstacles to organizing.

_The Union Response_____

T he fact that QWL is used by union busters has not escaped the attention of the labor movement. The AFL-CIO Department of Organization has produced extensive material on the use of employee participation schemes to keep unions out, and manuals to help union organizers deal with these programs.

The use of QWL for anti-union purposes has also fueled the debate which is raging in the labor movement over such schemes. After all, many large and influential unions, such as the UAW, CWA, IUE, and USWA are heavily commited to QWL. Unionists who favor QWL often feel they must justify their position in light of QWL's popularity with the union busters.

One pro-QWL line of argument says that QWL programs established with full union participation and appropriate safeguards are significantly different from unilateral company programs, and actually strengthen the union involved. When a union organizer is confronted with a company-run QWL program, he or she should explain the difference between union _busting_ QWL and union _sponsored_ QWL.

In actual practice, however, there is little difference between non-union QWL programs and union-co-sponsored ones. The training, the procedures, the materials, and the topics dealt with by circles in union and in non-union companies are almost exactly the same.

Most of the consultants who set up programs in unionized companies happily provide the same services and set up the same programs for non-union employers (see chapter 9). In their descriptions, the difference be-

tween union and non-union programs is often only a detail. Typical is an article by D.L. Landen, well known QWL consultant and president of the Michigan QWL Council, a prestigious group with heavy union involvement. Landen mentions the difference only once, in describing the employee involvement steering committee:

> In a unionized setting, this is a joint union management committee; in non-represented organizations the committee consists of management and non-management employees.[13]

The union busters are quick to point out: if the program is the same, then why pay dues and bring in outsiders instead of letting the employees themselves handle it?

In theory, one way that a union organizer could expose a union busting QWL program would be to point out its lack of real decision making power. But most union QWL programs also reaffirm full management rights to make final decisions. In fact, non-union QWL circles frequently appear to have wider latitude than union circles because they are not limited by the restrictions sometimes imposed by the unions.

Because the similarity between union and non-union QWL programs is easily apparent, unionists who are committed to QWL fall back on another argument. The fact that union busters use QWL, they say, does not prove that QWL is bad for the labor movement. After all, union busters often recommend that companies pay higher wages in order to discourage unionization, and union organizers do not denounce higher wages. QWL is a benefit for workers in and of itself, they say, and unions should take the credit when management introduces QWL to keep unions out.

But QWL is not just another benefit. Participation schemes are not only about how management relates to workers. They are also about the way workers relate to management. QWL programs claim to give workers influence over their work environment by organizing them in a special way—small groups working directly with management. This is put forward as the alternative to the union way of providing influence. QWL offers communication and individual recognition and participation in place of the _power_ that can only come from acting collectively—unionism.   □

__Resources

Report on Union Busters: RUB Sheet, published irregularly by the AFL-CIO National Organizing Coordinating Committee.

Quality Circles: An Organizing Manual, AFL-CIO Department of Organization and Field Services.

"We Are Driven," script of January 23, 1984 PBS documentary on Nissan Motor Co. in Smyrna, Tennessee. Available from WGBH Transcripts, 125 Western Ave., Boston, MA 02134.

Ron Chernow, "The New Pinkertons," *Mother Jones*, May 1980.

Richard B. Freeman and James Medoff, *What Do Unions Do?*, Basic Books, 1984.

Guillermo J. Grenier, "Twisting Quality Circles to Bust Unions," *AFL-CIO News*, May 14, 1983.

Steve Lagerfeld, "The Pop Psychologist As Union Buster," *AFL-CIO American Federationist*, November 1981.

Charles McDonald and Dick Wilson, "Peddling the 'Union Free' Guarantee," *AFL-CIO American Federationist*, April 1979.

Notes

1. Larry Curtis of Musick, Peeler & Garrett, "Quality Circles and the Taft-Hartley Act," October 22, 1981.
2. *Transport Topics*, American Trucking Association, January 31, 1983.
3. Modern Management, Inc. brochure, no date.
4. *Management Review*, September 1982.
5. *Industry Week*, April 2, 1984.
6. *Detroit Free Press*, November 8, 1983.
7. *Statistical and Tactical Information Report*, AFL-CIO, April 1984.
8. *AFL-CIO News*, November 20, 1982.
9. *AFL-CIO News*, May 14, 1983.
10. *Detroit Free Press*, July 11, 1983.
11. Ona Corporation, Case No. 10-CA-19146. The Labor Education and Research Project, publisher of this book, submitted an *amicus* brief answering the IAQC.
12. See for example Donna Sockell, "The Legality of Employee-Participation Programs in Unionized Firms," *Industrial and Labor Relations Review*, July 1984, or Thomas J. Schneider, *BNA's Employee Relations Weekly*, May 6, 1985.
13. *Work Life Review*, Michigan Quality of Worklife Council, April 1984.

THE FEDERAL GOVERNMENT AND QWL

In response to growing concern about world competition and U.S. productivity, in the 1970's various federal agencies and legislators dabbled in Quality of Work Life. They took several initiatives:

• In 1973 a Department of Health, Education and Welfare special task force reported on its study of the "blue collar blues," which was published as the widely read *Work In America*.[1]

• In 1975 Congress passed the "National Productivity and Quality of Working Life Act." The major goal of the act was to reverse what was believed to be a significant decline in the rate of productivity growth. All concern for "a healthy environment for collective bargaining" or the "role of the worker in the production process and the conditions of his working life" were couched in terms of their effect on productivity.

The act created a National Center for Productivity and the Quality of Working Life consisting of cabinet officials and five presidential appointees from industry, labor, and state and local governments. Vice-president Nelson Rockefeller chaired the center and $7 million was allocated for demonstration projects and field research for the next three years.

Neither organized labor nor the Carter administration took much interest in the center. Vice-president Walter Mondale declined to take over as chairperson and it withered away.

• During the 1970's the Department of Commerce's Economic Development Administration gave grants to begin several experimental Quality of Work Life programs. The U.S. National Institute for Mental Health made a few similar grants.

• In the early 1970's the Federal Mediation and Conciliation Service (FMCS), which originally had been formed to provide third party intervention in the settlement of strikes, began to develop a program to improve labor management relations before they reached the strike stage. In 1974 the service started a "Relations By Objective" (RBO) program to "introduce union and management leadership to a problem identification and solution process so that both parties will begin thinking and acting more like members of the same team."

Many RBO exercises and techniques share common methods with current QWL programs. Typically, an RBO program begins with a three-day union-management retreat. In a series of highly structured exercises each side airs its criticisms of the other and then acknowledges hearing the position of the other. They then search for "objectives" they might have in com-

mon and determine some "action steps" to achieve these goals.

• In 1976 and 1977 Representative Stanley Lundine attempted to get national funding for cooperation efforts. As mayor of Jamestown, New York, Lundine had organized a citywide QWL-type program that became the model Area Labor-Management Committee. Both times the legislation died. While some unions testified for it, there was significant hostility from the leadership of organized labor. In October 1977 Andrew Biemiller, AFL-CIO legislative director, unofficially circulated a statement:

> This Bill is for well-intended grant seekers and a license for outsiders to muck about in the delicate balance of labor-management relations.
> ...If we in labor want codetermination in a form different than that contained in our agreements or if we want membership on the board of directors of a corporation—we'll bargain for it.[2]

In 1978 the House of Representatives passed a stripped down version of the legislation, attached to the Humphrey-Hawkins bill. It contained a prohibition against grants to plant-level labor-management committees unless there were a union and a contract, as well as a provision that the act was not to "affect the terms and conditions of any collective bargaining agreement." Official labor took a neutral position.

The legislation authorized $10 million for 1979, but no money was actually appropriated until 1981, when the FMCS finally got $1 million. Most of it went to start up area-wide labor-management committees which in turn devoted most of their activities to encouraging QWL plans in local industries.

Reagan and QWL

The Reagan administration has provided a big boost to Quality of Work Life programs. In 1982 the Department of Labor announced that it would begin actively promoting programs that gave workers a voice in shop floor decisions. The Department of Labor's Labor-Management Services Administration established a new division called Cooperative-Management Programs which was elevated to "bureau" status in 1984. Its job was to "encourage and assist employers and unions to undertake joint efforts to improve productivity and enhance the quality of working life." As Secretary of Labor Raymond Donovan put it:

> Central to the Department of Labor's goals in this and other endeavors is the belief that cooperative relations between labor and management, particularly those providing greater opportunities for worker involvement, strengthen the commitment to work together. The result is a decrease in conflict which provides a healthier environment in which competitive enterprise can flourish.[3]

The Department of Labor has sponsored large conferences to publicize and encourage QWL, including one on QWL in the public sector and one on labor-management cooperation. Conferences like these are a tremendous aid to QWL efforts, giving them and the people in them recognition, providing a forum for the ideas, and offering perks (such as trips to Washington) for QWL participants.

The Bureau of Labor-Management Relations and Cooperative Programs is working with the National Association of Broadcasters on an educational campaign to boost worker productivity by using radio, television and print public service ads. The Bureau has also issued a number of publications, several of which contain useful information (see chapter 20).

But perhaps most significantly, the Bureau has tried to help form and consolidate some of the key ideas and directions for QWL. The Bureau is co-sponsoring a "teleconference" with the American Productivity Center of Houston. According to the Bureau:

> It will network for a one-year period approximately 20 top labor, management, and neutral leaders to discuss significant issues affecting the union-management relationship. Participants will also develop findings and recommendations which will be presented at a "face-to-face" meeting with key CEO's [chief executive officers] and international labor leaders.[4]

The Bureau has already sponsored some small, elite conferences to try to work out the next steps for QWL. At these conferences, labor leaders, business leaders and QWL practitioners let their hair down. Free from the pressures of their constituencies, they talk frankly.

— IN CANADA —

The Canadian Department of Labor strongly backs QWL. It publishes a magazine called *Quality of Working Life, The Canadian Scene*, holds periodic conferences and has an annual budget of $1.1 million to provide direct financial aid to companies that want to implement QWL programs. The provincial governments, especially Ontario, also organize QWL activities. The publications and conferences of the Ontario Quality of Working Life Centre are influential throughout Canada and the United States.

In September 1983, the Labor Department invited 25 people to such a conference. Included were top executives from corporations such as Ford, Dana, and AT&T, well-known QWL consultants including D.L. Landen, Michael Maccoby, and Thomas Kochan, and union representatives Sam Camens of the Steelworkers and Ronnie Straw of the CWA.[5] During one discussion conference participants bemoaned the high failure rate of QWL groups.

Another discussion acknowledged that the public stance that QWL must be kept separate from collective bargaining is not possible in reality (see chapter 8). The draft document for the discussion begins:

> The collective bargaining process (including contract negotiations and the administration of the contract) should extensively overlap with a quality of working life (QWL) program. The processes, skills, organization and people of the QWL program should be involved with the collective bargaining process.[6]

The participants discussed ways that the QWL process could be used to handle all issues of the labor contract except "the size of the economic pie."

Another discussion centered around whether QWL could succeed without financial paybacks to workers, or "gainsharing." Participants talked about carrying QWL further, to steps like self-managing work teams and union representation on boards of directors (see chapter 11).

Is it ironic that the same administration which destroyed PATCO, undermined the NLRB, and rendered OSHA useless should be promoting labor-management cooperation through QWL? Or is it logical?   □

Notes

1. *Work In America*, MIT Press, 1973.
2. *The Operation of Area Labor-Management Committees*, Labor-Management Services Administration, U.S. Department of Labor, U.S. Government Printing Office, 1982.
3. Letter in Labor-Management Services Administration information packet, 1984.
4. "Recent Program Highlights and Current Plans," Bureau of Labor-Management Relations and Cooperative Programs, Department of Labor, unpublished, January 4, 1985.
5. "A Conference on Quality of Work Life: Issues Affecting the State-of-the-Art," Office of Labor-Management Relations Services, U.S. Department of Labor, May 1984.
6. "Discussion Draft: What Should Be the Relationship Between the Collective Bargaining Process and Quality of Working Life Programs?", Airlie, Virginia Conference, unpublished, September 9-11, 1983.

PUBLIC EMPLOYEES AND QWL

While public sector unionists can learn many lessons from the QWL experiences of private sector unions, the different conditions faced by public employees make QWL both more attractive and more dangerous. To begin with, government workers are not covered by the National Labor Relations Act. For the most part public employee unions:

Do not have union or agency shops. In effect public employees work under "right-to-work" laws. Employees are not required to join or pay dues to a union even if the union has majority support. In many states, even with majority support public employee unions are not guaranteed exclusive bargaining rights.

Do not have the right to strike. Although many public employees from teachers to postal workers have struck successfully and won important demands, the lack of legal protection and the well known defeats (such as PATCO) make it harder to use the strike as a bargaining tool.

Are expressly prohibited from bargaining over major issues. At the federal level, for example, the law prohibits bargaining over wages, hours of work, insurance, and other conditions of employment. Some state laws are more restrictive, some less restrictive than federal laws.

Federal Workers

While the official policy of the Department of Labor is to promote QWL programs in industry, very few QWL programs exist within the federal government itself. An October 1983 listing of hundreds of participation programs compiled by the Department includes only 19 in government agencies. Most of these were in veterans hospitals or in military operations. (The military has gone in heavily for QWL in operations where it employs civilians.)

Under the Civil Service Reform Act of 1978, federal workers may have a union represent them in the grievance procedure, but bargaining rights are severely restricted. On certain issues, the employer—that is, the government—is supposed to "consult" with the union. But the Reagan Administration has declared virtually all issues to be in the category of "management rights," which by law are not negotiable. Often government unions have to resort to legal action just to get agency managements to talk about minor issues. In some cases the unions have appealed management's failure to consult and have won, but the Administration has flagrantly ignored the appeals decision.

Thus some federal employee unions, looking for any opening, have hoped that QWL programs would provide the opportunity to discuss some questions that

management has previously refused to put on the table. A couple of examples indicate, however, the Reagan Administration's true attitude toward worker participation.

A July 1982 memorandum of understanding between Local 12 of the American Federation of Government Employees (AFGE) and the Labor-Management Services Administration (a division of the Department of Labor) established a "Participation Circles" program. The program limped along. One initial "plus" of many newly-installed QWL programs is that management seems to be listening to its workers for the first time. But the LMSA circle program had less impact in this regard since the white collar professionals there were already consulted about various matters and treated with some respect.

In January 1984, then Secretary of Labor Raymond Donovan announced a reorganization of the LMSA. Local 12 asked for information on the reorganization and for "consultations," and was refused. The union then proposed that the reorganization be discussed in the participation circles. This too was refused since, according to management, all aspects of the reorganization fell under the heading of "management's rights."

Nevertheless, AFGE Local 12 has tried to expand the participation circles to other sections of the Department of Labor besides LMSA. At the same time the local has tried to protect union members and the union from some of the problems typically generated by QWL. Specifically, it proposed to add to the 1982 memorandum four additional points:

1) No innovations which result from participation circles will be implemented if they have any adverse impact on the pay and working conditions of any present employees, whether the employee participates in a circle or not.

2) The union will choose half the facilitators.

3) Increased productivity resulting from recommendations of circles will result in employees being rewarded with increases in grades, quality step increases, credit hours, leave without pay, training opportunities, cash awards or other forms of reward as permitted by regulations.

4) When circles are working on projects that involve matters covered by the collective bargaining agreement, management will make accessible to the union facilities, meeting space, and employee time on an equal basis with the circles.

Management refused to negotiate on these points.

A Local 12 leaflet summed up the general approach of the Department of Labor toward cooperation with its own labor:

At our recent mid-term negotiations, Local 12 submitted a new proposal on participation programs that would have maintained the existing programs. Management refused to negotiate with us on this proposal.

The Department's refusal to negotiate is not limited to this issue. At the recent mid-term negotiations, out of a total of 57 union proposals, 2 were declared non-negotiable, and management refused to negotiate on the other 55! The Department's disdain for cooperation is also evidenced by management's refusal to consult or even share information on issues which affect working conditions, such as changes in the space allocated to employees.

In 1981 the Office of Personnel Management, which oversees employee relations in the federal government, planned a QWL experiment for the Atlanta offices of the Internal Revenue Service. The experiment was cancelled when IRS management was unwilling to agree to two key demands of the National Treasury Employees Union (NTEU): a guarantee that circle members would share in any cost savings and the right to reject volunteers for the circles.[1] The union wanted the latter demand to insure that the circle was not used as an organizing vehicle by anti-union employees. The union also wanted to be sure that a union steward was a member of each circle.

The NTEU subsequently agreed to a quality circle program without getting its key demands. According to NTEU President Robert Tobias, the experiment at least offered a chance to talk about important issues, such as workload distribution, which had been outlawed in formal negotiations as a "management right."[2] Further, the union believed that "the cooperative program helps the Union politically in that it allows the Union to showcase the extent of its influence to its members."[3]

In April 1983, the Federal Labor Relations Authority decided several questions specifically dealing with federal sector labor relations and QWL type-programs. The original case had been brought by the Laborers International Union of North America Local 1276, representing civilian employees at the Tracy, California Defense Depot. An Administrative Law Judge found that the government's unilateral establishment of the circles bypassed the union's right, as exclusive bargaining agent, to solicit grievances and resolve issues. The ALJ ordered the government to stop:

> operating a Quality Circle Program that involves employees for whom the [union] is the exclusive representative, unless and until an agreement is reached with the [union] as to the content, implementation, and impact of such a program....[4]

The Postal Service

Under the Postal Reorganization Act of 1971 the Postal Service became a quasi-private organization. Its management is appointed by and responsible to the government, but operated on a profit making basis. The National Labor Relations Act (which covers the private sector) also covers postal workers. Four unions have exclusive bargaining rights in different jurisdictions in the post office, but under the law they are "open shop" arrangements. Postal workers are explicitly prohibited from striking and the Hatch Act restricts political activity.

Contrary to its public image, the Postal Service is a thriving business. It recorded a $616 million surplus in 1983 and a $117 million surplus in 1984. But under Reagan's appointees the Board of Governors of the Postal Service has carried out a campaign to increase the speed of automation and to cut labor everywhere possible. In 1984 the Postal Service hired a $300,000 union busting consultant to assist in contract negotiations. Postmaster General William Bolger began the talks by declaring that postal workers were overpaid by 18-23% and promising to correct that situation, and at the same time attempted to impose unilaterally a two-tier wage structure.[5]

Post office workers at letter-sorting machines.

Despite the Postal Service's anti-union campaign, the leadership of one of the two major USPS unions, the National Association of Letter Carriers (NALC), and the two smaller unions, the Rural Letter Carriers Association and the Mailhandlers Union (affiliated with the Laborers International) are participating in an Employee Involvement program negotiated in 1982.

Although generally on a budget cutting drive, the

HAS YOUR WORK CLIMATE IMPROVED?

"Have you noticed a perceptive change in your supervisor's attitude toward your well being? Is the work environment safer or more pleasant? Has discipline been reduced? Are your suggestions accepted? Are you told why you are to do certain things?

"Management tells us that this is the very reason for employee involvement—that if we could improve communications we could address these real problems. But no employee has any problems communicating. We communicate when we speak to one another, when we ask our supervisor for leave or to handle some other problem. The problem arises with the supervisor's response. When a supervisor replies 'Because I am the boss' or 'Because those are the rules,' the result is a total halt in communications.

"Perhaps there is a need to train managers on employee involvement. We certainly wouldn't object. But no one has ever asked for our permission before deciding to train supervisors in attendance control, denial of workers' compensation, or how to extract more productivity. The USPS can train its supervisors and managers and workers will continue to attempt to communicate. But we will not be force fed gimmicks that promise improvements while management stands with its foot on our neck.

"Postal employees want a say in their working life and are willing to respond to a receptive managment. But snake oil is snake oil; don't try to convince us that it is perfume." —*The American Postal Worker*, May 1985

Postal Service is committing considerable resources to Employee Involvement, including a separate program for supervisors. As part of the program with the NALC, for example, the Postal Service is putting on the payroll from two to four full-time EI facilitators (half appointed by the unions) at each sectional center (roughly a metropolitan area). In addition, one team of eight to ten letter carriers meets for one hour per week in each station. By the end of 1985 the Postal Service expects to have EI operational in every sectional center.

The motivation given for postal union participation in QWL is the same as that used in private industry. Most common is the need "to beat the socks off the competition," as one union facilitator explained.[6] In some cases sectional EI steering committees have forced higher level postal management to meet with local NALC leaders for the first time.

The other major postal union, the American Postal Workers Union (APWU), opposes QWL. Many of its locals refused to participate in pilot projects and several pulled out later. In April 1984, for example, the Kalamazoo, Michigan local voted to withdraw from participation in "quality improvement teams" because of deteriorating labor relations as well as management's refusal "to address the stress factors at work."[7] The August 1984 APWU Convention issued a strongly worded statement "opposed to union participation or endorsement in any form" and also called for the other postal unions to stop participating. (The convention statement is reprinted in chapter 19.)

State and Local Government Employees

Compared to private industry there are relatively few QWL programs among public employees at the state and local government levels. The primary reason seems to be funding. Few government units have been willing to spend large amounts of money on programs which are unproven and promise no immediate or visible results. Many programs existed only because they got federal grants, and died when the grants ran out. In the last few years, however, a number of state and local governments and school boards have initiated QWL pilot programs. As in the private sector, most unions involved report initial caution and early positive results.

The American Federation of State, County and Municipal Employees (AFSCME) endorses joint labor-management committees and participated in most of the early public sector experiments. The union warns that:

Without proper safeguards, such joint efforts may provide only the illusion of participation. For example, management's goal of boosting productivity becomes a priority issue while the union's goal of job security becomes a secondary issue somehow left behind.[8]

AFSCME believes appropriate safeguards include:

1) [That] initial establishment of the committee should be for a specified period of time...with a built in review process to determine its usefulness;
2) The appointment of people to the committee who are responsible for bargaining and administering the collective bargaining agreement, thus adding knowledge, respect, and power to the process; and
3) An initial agreement that the committee is not a substitute for collective bargaining, and agreements arising out of the committee are advisory for the initial period and cannot automatically supercede collective bargaining agreements.

In 1983 one of the leading consultants for public employee QWL programs, Neal Herrick, edited a book summarizing the state of public employee QWL.[9] Most of the QWL experiments described in the book were failures. The case studies included:

— Springfield, Ohio (AFSCME)—ended 1979
— Columbus, Ohio (AFSCME)—still functioning but found it difficult to expand beyond initial two divisions
— Tennessee Valley Authority (OPEIU and TVA Employees Association)—pilot program did not survive a restructuring in 1978
— Six experiments in Massachusetts (AFSCME plus some other unions)—all six failed
— "Cityville, USA" (AFSCME)—failed after two years
— San Francisco and Berkeley, California (SEIU)—both still functioning although fragile
— New York City and New York State (AFSCME and Civil Service Employees Association)—optimistic report but had just begun to use QWL type groups
— Pima County, Arizona (AFSCME, Pima County Nurses Association, Fraternal Order of Police)—still functioning.

The Pima County program involving AFSCME has existed since 1977, making it one of the longest running in the public sector. It has lasted, however, only because of expensive repair jobs. Due to the difficulty faced by unions under Arizona's "right-to-work" laws, the AFSCME local is weak, representing only about 20% of the employees. For the first two years the QWL program was considered a success. But as the program developed,

> over time a number of items (such as the liberalization of educational reimbursement criteria) were referred from the Meet and Confer [collective bargaining] to the QWL process and were resolved. The nonaffiliated committee members regarded the gains being achieved by [QWL] as clear evidence that no union was needed in Pima County. Their ability to achieve substantial gains in a pleasant cooperative atmosphere without paying union dues represented a striking contrast to AFSCME's history.... At [a September 1982 QWL retreat], the nonaffiliated employees openly raised the question: What do we need the union for now that we have QWL?[10]

AFSCME noted a decline in its membership and that it had lost focus for its organizing efforts. When the union threatened to withdraw the QWL program was restructured, to include increased involvement of third party consultants, unwritten management cooperation in AFSCME organizing, and a new monetary reward system. Whether these features will be continued and whether they are sufficient to maintain interest in the program remains to be seen. Both are doubtful.[11]

A positive feature of the program is that QWL group participants are elected. Neal Herrick, an advisor to the program, is one of the few QWL consultants who supports this procedure. He argues:

> Committee members serve the people who put them in office. Therefore, since a distinguishing feature of QWL—as opposed to such schemes as quality circles—is that it seeks to integrate the interests of the various workplace groups, the groups whose interests are to be integrated must place their own representatives in office. This means open elections by secret ballot.[12]

Implications for Public Employee Unionism

QWL has unmistakable attractions for public employees. For federal workers and many state workers QWL offers the chance to deal with issues that are, by law, not bargainable. But this is not as much of an advantage as it first appears. In the federal sector, for example, many issues are not bargainable because management unilaterally declares them "management rights." If management were truly willing to cooperate and to discuss these issues with the union, it wouldn't need QWL. It would simply stop labeling them management rights.

At the same time the dangers of QWL may outweigh the potential gains. Since public employee unions do not have agency or union shop recognition, the only way they can recruit members is by providing services, handling grievances, and dealing with working conditions. The more that QWL is seen as an alternative and perhaps more effective means of handling these issues, the harder it is for public employee unions to attract members.

For example, EI groups in the Postal Service tend to work initially on issues which could presumably be handled by the union in collective bargaining: parking facilities, bicycle racks, painting work areas, and lighting. EI groups have also worked on such central union issues as getting carriers' routes adjusted. These are often old issues which the union has failed to win in the past. When they are accomplished through QWL the lesson is that the union cannot do much, but QWL can. And since the ideas and operation of QWL undermine the philosophical reasons for unionism, QWL makes it even more difficult to convince public employees of the need for a union.

To combat this problem, the NALC has tried to ensure, through an understanding with the Postal Service, that only union members are allowed to serve on EI teams. Some locals say that membership has grown as employees wanting to volunteer for teams have joined the union.

In a 1985 Advice Memorandum, the NLRB effectively upheld the legality of the arrangement which restricted EI participation to NALC members only. The Memorandum reasoned that even though both union and management explicitly stated that EI was entirely separate from collective bargaining, in practice the EI committees would be engaging in collective bargaining. Therefore the union had the right to choose its representatives.[13] While this backs the union position on team membership, it also clears the way for more collective bargaining issues to be channeled through EI.

The union may collect its dues from these new members, but a person who joins the union in order to be on an EI team can hardly be counted on to look out for union interests. Some NALC locals are trying to strengthen union identity and a sense of responsibility to others by insisting that team members be elected. But the official EI program discourages such elections.

EI also weakens the position of public employee unions when it comes to bargaining. As EI teams handle issues which formerly were handled by the union, the support of the members themselves becomes more fragile and more likely to shatter in a major test such as a strike. When the 1984 contract stalemate occurred in the Postal Service and the anti-union attitudes of postal management were blatant, the leadership of the Minneapolis NALC local gave EI teams the option of suspending meetings until the contract was resolved. But most teams continued to meet.

Most public employee unions are relatively new. They do not have the long traditions of many private sector unions nor a large pool of membership trained in union ideas and methods through years of experience. Thus QWL training, with its built-in management bias, has an even heavier impact in the public sector than in the established unions of the private sector.

Most public sector unions also have a much slimmer structure than private sector unions. Because employees are not required to join and pay dues, dues are generally lower and there are fewer full-time union staffers. There is less employer-paid time off for steward representation. Depending on the union and the point of view, this could make the union either weaker or more democratic. But either way, the impact of QWL on the union is much greater.

In the NALC, for example, stewards are full-time letter carriers and only the larger locals have full-time union officers. But when the EI program is fully established nationwide there will be between 300 and 400 full-time hourly facilitators—about the same as or more than the total number of full-time local and national union representatives.

These facilitators are not elected. They are appointed by the NALC's National Business Agent and are responsible to the joint EI steering committee. Their offices are located near management's. They are given extensive joint EI training but no union training. Postal Service management gloats about how, after training, union and management facilitators become indistinguishable.[14] Even in the short period (since 1982) that the program has been in existence, the facilitator position has often been seen as a steppingstone to postal management. The union-appointed Santa Clara, California EI facilitator, for example, went into management at a considerable increase in pay. Given the advantages of full-time status for politicking in a union with a dispersed membership, facilitators are likely to win election as convention delegates and make up a sizable convention bloc.

In chapter 6 we detailed the critical role facilitators play, either as part of the union or as an alternative power structure. Their importance is magnified in the public sector, where it is harder for the unions to make them part of a union team. □

Notes

1. *Government Employee Relations Report*, Bureau of National Affairs, September 27, 1982.

2. *Federal Times*, October 24, 1983.

3. *Proceedings, Federal Sector Conference on Employee Participation and Cooperative Labor-Management Initiatives*, August 23-25, 1983.

4. Federal Labor Relations Authority, Case No. 9-CA-20241, Decision, December 28, 1982, Order, April 21, 1983.

5. *Labor Notes*, August 1984.

6. Presentation, Federal Sector Conference, August 24, 1983.

7. *The Union Flash*, Greater Southwestern Michigan Postal Workers Union, June 1984.

8. Resolution, American Federation of State, County and Municipal Employees, 25th International Convention, June 1984.

9. Neal Q. Herrick, *Improving Government: Experiments with Quality of Working Life Systems*, Praeger, 1983.

10. Jon Showalter and David Yetman, "Pima County: The Dilemma of Weak Unions and QWL," in Herrick, *Improving Government*.

11. Neal Q. Herrick, "QWL: An Alternative to Traditional Public-Sector Management Systems," *National Productivity Review*, Winter 1983-4.

12. Herrick, *Improving Government*.

13. NLRB Advice Memorandum, U.S. Postal Service, Case No. 19-CA-16909P, January 22, 1985.

14. Eugene Hagburg, U.S. Postal Service Employee Involvement Process, Co-chair, remarks at Federal Sector Conference, August 24, 1983.

THE JAPANESE MODEL— "WE ARE DRIVEN"

by John Junkerman

When the assembly line stops for the morning break at the Datsun plant in the town of Zama, one hour southwest of Tokyo, none of the workers puts down his tools. For a good two or three minutes into the break, the sound of impactors and clanging steel continues throughout the plant. A worker in tennis shoes and a baseball cap finishes attaching a bumper, turns to the next car on the line to fasten a license plate, then squeezes rubber trim around a rear window. Another worker stacks brake fluid reservoirs close to the line and fiddles with a troublesome fastener that has slowed his production during the morning's first stint.

The guide from the plant's public relations office is quick to point out this industrious behavior to the caravans of Western executives who come regularly to the Zama factory in search of the secret of success. The company has become adept at showing visitors what they long to see: an indefatigable work force whose primary goals are to boost productivity and to make the company No. 1.

Nissan Motor Company (the official name of the corporation that manufactures Datsun cars and trucks) conceives of itself as something of an industrial Nirvana. "Quality through harmony...the unsung harmony of man and machine," exults one company film. Mutual trust between labor and management has created a "community full of vitality," declares Nissan's chairman, Katsuji Kawamata. "We don't use the term *worker* anymore," adds a company spokesperson. "Everyone is an employee of the company and a member of the Nissan family."

But there is a dark side to the Japanese industrial miracle, a side that becomes readily apparent after talking with the harried workers on the Nissan shop floor. Over the past five years, Nissan has stepped up its vehicle output by 25% without hiring additional workers. The company has accomplished this astonishing feat by running the assembly line at a frenzied pace. "A few years ago we could talk, even joke around a bit on the line," comments one assembly worker. "Now if the manager sees you talking while you're working, he'll give you more work to do. The other night I saw a television documentary about an American auto plant," he added wistfully, "and the workers were smoking and waving at the camera. Here we don't have the margin to do that—we're driven to the wall." According to another line worker, "If you drop a bolt, you don't have time to pick it up. After all," he muttered, "this is

Nissan; so there is no time to spare."

Nissan would prefer to think that its speedy assembly workers are motivated by a sense of loyalty and gratitude which, in some cases, they undoubtedly are. More to the point, however, is the fact that the company and its union have joined together to create a powerful system of control and intimidation that mass-produces cooperative and efficient workers as reliably as the assembly line churns out subcompacts. Harmony and diligence at Nissan are the product of union and managerial policies that reward conformity, punish even the mildest dissent with wage discrimination and ostracism from the work group, and—in extreme cases—contribute to ruthless persecution and violence. Both the union and management demand total participation and commitment to production from every Nissan employee.

It is this unique and eerie system of joint management-union control that explains why the workers at Nissan's Zama plant don't skip a beat when break time rolls around.

A stone monument stands just inside the main gate to the Nissan assembly plant at Oppama, on the south shore of Tokyo Bay, where the popular Bluebird (Datsun 810) is produced. It is adorned with two sculpted bluebirds and engraved with the words of a former union president, rendered in calligraphy by Nissan's chairman of the board: "It is necessary to insist on one's rights, and it is splendid to fight for that purpose," the labor official's words read. "But the 'bluebird' of happiness does not alight in the swamps of spite where the storms of struggle rage... Mutual trust between labor and management is the wellspring and the pride of Nissan."

For nearly 30 years, the Nissan Labor Union has strived to keep the company's bluebird of happiness from flying away. The current union was established with company support in 1953, during Nissan's successful campaign to smash a more militant auto workers union. The Nissan Labor Union's founding slogan was: "Those who truly love their union, love their company. Wage increases shall derive from increasing productivity."

Ichiro Shioji heads the Nissan labor organization and also serves as president of the Confederation of Japanese Automobile Workers Union (JAW), which represents the industry's 600,000 laborers. Shioji—who earns about $475,000 a year, owns a $200,000 yacht and drives a telephone-equipped Nissan President—is one of Japan's leading champions of cooperative unionism. Says Nissan chairman Kawamata, "Shioji is a man who conceives of things primarily from the perspective of

[A longer version of this article first appeared in Mother Jones, *August 1982. Reprinted by permission of the author. Junkerman is the economics editor of the* Encyclopedia of Japan.]

management." So entwined has Shioji become with Nissan management since he took over the union in 1960 that he has been called "Nissan's other president."

Shioji's union in fact performs many of management's more distasteful tasks, including monitoring workers' performance and attitudes, punishing dissent and boosting workers' output. The union-directed productivity campaign, known as the Three P Movement, aims to raise *productivity* through the *participation* of the workers to bring about the *progress* of the company and society at large. Although the campaign has the specific goal of increasing productivity ten percent and reducing faulty parts 20 percent per year, its actual purpose is much broader: "More than the material results of increased productivity," union documents state, "what is important is whether each individual is productivity-minded, with a high union consciousness and a high social consciousness. It is a movement to improve morals."

The union's emphasis on attitude reflects a basic feature of Nissan worklife: it is not enough just to do one's job; Nissan workers have to believe in their work as well. Since a major portion of their paycheck hinges on their positive evaluation by supervisors, Nissan workers are under constant pressure to prove their commitment.

THE 1953 SHOWDOWN

In 1953, there was a showdown after Nissan imposed paycuts on the union's leadership. Nissan followed this with a lock-out and surrounded its plants with barricades. It also hired bands of strong-arm men to stop the workers from trying to get back in. The dispute lasted four months.

Unlike its workers, Nissan could afford to sit it out. The company was being backed by the Japan Industrial Bank, one of the wealthiest in the land. This enabled Nissan to keep its production lines shut down, while more and more workers called for a return to work. When a break-away union began to form, Nissan seized its chance. Each worker who joined the new union received back pay from Nissan.

The bank's support had proved decisive. On a bitter day the strikers returned to work. Nissan had achieved its aim. It had broken the power of the militant union. . . . Nissan now had a company union it could live with.

—"We Are Driven," WGBH videotape

The primary mechanism for promoting productivity at Nissan is the quality control (QC) circle. These small groups, organized on the shop floor to examine ways of improving product quality and manufacturing efficiency, have become the symbol of Japanese management throughout the world. Ostensibly a voluntary activity on the part of the workers, the groups are said to give each individual a sense of participation in management. Some 4,000 such groups have been organized at Nissan.

Attendance in the QC circles, which meet after work and during lunch, is not officially required; nonetheless, virtually all of Nissan's workers are involved in the groups—not to participate would reflect a lack of "productivity-mindedness."

The ideas that emerge from Nissan's QC circles are of undisputed value to the company: in 1980 alone they helped save the auto firm as much as $60 million. Whether or not the workers themselves benefit from this form of self-management, however, is debatable.

One assembly worker reports that during QC circle meetings employees regularly perform simulated production tasks to devise ways of cutting time. "First we work one machine with the left hand, then another with the right; then we put one machine in front and another behind and work them simultaneously. Sometimes I feel like I'm involved in an experiment to determine how much a human being can stand."

One group decided that instead of knocking off early to clean up the shop and service the machines, they would do this maintenance after work hours. Since the Q.C. circles compete for company recognition and are afraid of being outdone by the others, this idea soon spread throughout the plant, and everyone began working an extra ten minutes a day. "Japanese workers aren't fools," says a square-jawed clutch assembler. "Everyone knows that it's strange to work without pay, but if you complain, you lose—it affects your pay and you won't get promoted."

According to interviews with workers, there has been a rash of accidents at Nissan: workers often try to repair or adjust a machine while it is still in operation to avoid halting production. "They have pushed the spirit of rationalization to the point where workers risk their lives for the sake of production."

"There's a pretense of 'family' at Nissan," Tsutumu Hagashi (not his real name) says, "and workers are forced to put on a good face. The definition of the 'Nissan man' is one who is never late, never takes a day off and never complains. But the workers at Nissan don't depend on the company or on the union—they depend on themselves, their own strength," he says.

"Most workers won't even join the mutual-aid society," Higashi continues. "There's meaning in mutual aid even in a terrible union, and it only costs 100 yen (about 40 cents) a month. But it seems they don't trust people; they depend only on themselves. It really feels like I work in a desert, a shop-floor desert where all the workers are grains of sand—dry, unconnected. There's no sense of warmth, no shared humanity with the other workers."

When he began working for the auto company in 1970, says Higashi, there was a substantial number of young workers who resisted the pressure to become "Nissan men." Many of them had been influenced by the student movements of the late '60's and they brought demands for democracy into the factory. "But most of those with any consciousness quit," he recalls, "because they realized they couldn't stand working for that kind of company until retire-

John Z. Gelsavage

pany—why are we increasing production at the height of summer? Hire more workers!" About the quality of cafeteria food: "Beware the revenge of those who eat!" And about the union: "A regular union—supports a union member who is fired. A good union—supports workers who are fired even if they aren't in the union. A bad union—takes the place of management and fires workers."

This last bitter scrawl is a reference to sanctions taken by the union against a dissident group at the Atsugi Motor Parts Company, a Nissan subsidiary located outside of Tokyo. The "Atsugi Seven" are the most persistent and overt internal opposition Nissan has encountered in recent years. Since the early 1970's, this group of worker-activists has been speaking out on a wide range of issues—from the intense heat in the plant in the summer to the lack of democracy within the union. After suffering years of discrimination in wages and job assignments, five of the workers decided to sue the company and the union. In 1979, the company reached a settlement with the workers, giving them $100,000 in back pay. But the union wasn't satisfied; it pushed through a resolution at its annual convention to have the seven expelled from membership in the union shop—and thus from Nissan.

"We don't like to do things like that, but the other members at Atsugi threatened to circulate a petition if we didn't act," said a union spokesperson. "Those people take their orders from the Japan Communist Party, and we have plenty of evidence to prove it." A Nissan official said: "For those people there is no consensus like we talk about here in Japan, so of course things are uncomfortable for them."

Things got more uncomfortable for them. In 1979, all of the Atsugi Seven were fired from their jobs. In January 1980, more than 200 union members were mobilized to attack them while they were distributing leaflets at a train station near the plant. Five of the dissidents were hospitalized with injuries. The unionists who attacked them called them "termites" who were attempting to undermine the company.

"I like Nissan," says Masaharu Tsukamoto, one of the seven, as we sit in the group's small, cluttered storefront office. "I am proud of the cars we make, and I have confidence in them. That's a natural feeling for a worker to have...but I think it's strange for the union to demand to put the company in our hearts. I won't sell my soul to the company."

Indeed there is much that is peculiar about the Nissan union. It has assumed primary responsibility for disciplining the work force, ferreting out dissidents and squashing opposition. "If there would happen to be someone who seeks to destroy the Nissan culture that we have forged together over the years, we must battle them without restraint," union president Shioji has said.

On the shop floor, members of the union's organizing committee watch vigilantly for signs of dissent. In the tenement-like dormitories attached to each of the factories, where young workers usually live for the first ten

ment. Those who remain say, 'If I'm going to stay, I'll keep quiet and try to get promoted.' " Until about 1975, some 40 percent of Nissan's newly hired workers quit during their first year of employment, but in recent years this figure has fallen to ten percent because of the scarcity of other jobs.

A brief inspection of one Nissan plant's bathroom stalls—not a designated stop on the official factory tour—would reveal a host of complaints. About assembly line speed-up: "This isn't a beer com-

years of their work lives, members of the union's youth committee listen for complaints and report them back to the union office. When workers leave the dorms to enter company housing or to rent an apartment in town, there is a Nissan community organization—primarily a vehicle to mobilize support for the conservative, union-sponsored Democratic Socialist party—to monitor "Nissan culture" on the streets.

It does not take much to be labeled an enemy of the company, and it doesn't take long for Nissan workers to learn the consequences. Masao Kayama, an employee of

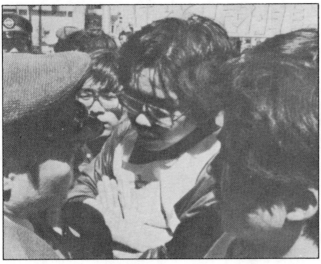

Masao Kayama (center) negotiating with guard to enter Nissan Motors' head office, April 21, 1981.

Nissan Diesel, had the temerity to criticize the union's wage demands at a shop-floor meeting in 1974, at a time when Nissan was pushing for higher productivity and wage restraint in response to the first oil crisis. Kayama says he was promptly tagged a troublemaker and was cold-shouldered by his workmates. Workers in his shop refused to return his greetings and shunned him during breaks. Friends were warned that if they associated with him it would affect their wages and chances for promotion, just as it has affected Kayama: his pay is currently about $2,000 a year less than that of workers with equal seniority.

Exercising leverage over wages—a powerful weapon against dissent—is just one of the ways the Nissan union involves itself in what would be considered a management area in most industrialized countries. Another is promotions: the union reserves veto power over supervisory appointments, and virtually all production supervisors first serve as officers in the union before they are advanced. This type of clout is unusual even by Japanese standards. Most Japanese unions—such as the one that represents Toyota workers—play a much more passive role.

Last year union leader Shioji traveled to Mexico, where Nissan was building a new engine plant, to discuss "cooperative unionism" with a moderate union that is organizing the plant. Nissan has had a long-term dispute with a more militant union at its Mexican assembly plant, and Shioji's job was to prevent a similar situation from developing at the new factory. "It's our job," said the Nissan union president, "to cover for management and do the things they can't do themselves."

Clearly many U.S. business leaders feel the country's economic future lies in adopting some version of the Japanese labor model. Hundreds of speeches at corporate luncheons and articles in the business press all sing the praises of Japan's "productivity-minded" workers.

Ichiro Saga has a markedly different view. Saga, a sociologist at Tokyo University, has been studying Nissan labor relations for the past five years. He is acutely aware of the coercion and regimentation that underlie the Japanese industrial miracle. "The mere thought of Japanese labor relations being copied in other countries," Saga tells me, shaking his head, "is enough to fill us all with horror." □

Resources

John Junkerman, "Blue Sky Management," *Working Papers*, Summer 1983. Describes the postwar history of labor and management at Japan's second largest steelmaker, Nippon Kokan, and its subsidiaries, including the role of QWL in the company's strategy.

Satoshi Kamata, *Japan in the Passing Lane*, Pantheon, 1982. A translation of a Toyota worker's diary.

Terutomo Ozawa, "Japanese Chic," *Across the Board*, published by The Conference Board, Inc., New York, October 1982. An answer to those who think that Japanese industrial advances are a result of excellent Japanese management techniques. It is of special interest because The Conference Board is a well respected business research organization and because General Motors' Organizational Development department was distributing the article as part of its QWL packet in 1984. According to Ozawa, Western managers could do as well as the Japanese if they had the "underlying cultural and social system that has been so instrumental in inducing workers to be loyal, hardworking—and complacent about the quality of work life in Japan." Much of the miracle, according to Ozawa, depends on the 70% of the Japanese who are underpaid "second class citizens" and a system which forces workers to be company players or else.

"We Are Driven," videotape by WGBH Educational Foundation, 1984. (Available from WGBH Distribution, 125 Western Ave., Boston MA 02134. 617/492-2777.) Originally broadcast on the Public Broadcasting System (PBS) on January 23, 1984. Its look at labor at Nissan Motor Co. includes some of the material in the *Mother Jones* article reprinted here, and discusses the attempt to apply Japanese management techniques at the new Nissan factory in Smyrna, Tennessee.

RESEARCH ON QWL

Most QWL programs start by training key participants in a series of guidelines, procedures, and organizational forms as though they were proven methods. Consultants wrap themselves in an aura of objective science. The logic becomes inescapable: The methods have been tried and proven elsewhere. If your program fails, then you must have done something wrong.

But a look at the theoretical literature and research material on QWL reveals that little is actually known about its results. Experts cite psychological theories and experiments with small group behavior, but have little to demonstrate that these experiments apply to relationships between corporate management and labor unions. Certainly, there are no "proven methods" or demonstrated results which justify unionists giving up unionism and embracing QWL.

Limitations of the Research

Despite all the interest in QWL there are very few studies available to the public which even approach standards of scientific investigation. Research is limited because:

1) Serious studies take time to design and execute. Most require measurements over a period of time long enough to isolate transient or one-time causes. Since joint union-management QWL programs in the U.S. are only a few years old, long term studies have not been possible.

2) Researchers are unable to obtain vital information. Most corporations are unwilling to open their books or divulge "proprietary" material about production methods or costs. One researcher, Michael Schuster, wanted to study firms that did not have QWL programs to establish a control group for comparison. He approached 60 firms but found only one that was willing to participate.[1]

3) The philosophy of many QWL programs discourages measuring increased productivity or program costs. Practitioners argue that doing so would undercut the programs' participative and friendly feel. For example, a study of QWL at AT&T said this about measuring "organizational efficiency":

> The researchers did not report much in the way of "hard" measures—in part because many managers avoided the "measurement" of QWL for fear of stifling its early development.[2]

Management, of course, does keep track of the "hard" measures. At Ford, for example, supervisors pay employees for time at EI meetings from a separate account. Most EI suggestions are handled through special project accounts. But the "no measurement"

stance makes objective research by anyone other than the employer difficult.

4) Much of the "research" is self-serving. Companies have claimed great results from QWL on the basis of "studies" done by their own personnel departments or by the consultants who administer the programs.

For example, the UAW-Ford National Joint Committee on Employe Involvement sponsored a survey to determine EI's impact on Ford.[3] The study was designed, analyzed, and written by the Ford personnel department. It surveyed seven plants which had had an EI project under way for at least a year. At the time of the 1982 study, Ford had many other plants which also had EI projects more than a year old. From the list it appears that only projects that the company already viewed as successful were chosen. When questioned about this, Ford spokesperson Gary Blevins told one researcher, "We wanted our best plants to stand out."[4] Not surprisingly, then, the report concludes:

> The survey also revealed that EI is functioning well as a process....Clearly EI "works."

One recent survey of QWL programs in the *Harvard Business Review* sums up the difficulties well:

> ...many reporters, commentators, and consultants have a vested interest in finding that quality circles work, for the opposite conclusion leaves them without a story, a chance to pontificate, or a contract. Because of these biases, few question the success stories about labor-management cooperation.[5]

William Passmore, a consultant on socio-technical systems, and his associates reviewed published accounts of QWL experiments and found "overwhelmingly

positive" results using a variety of methods and measures. They point out, however, that almost all of the "evaluations were conducted by the same parties who were responsible for conducting the interventions," and that this was an inherent conflict of interest: few consultants are motivated to publish reports of their failures and will likely exaggerate the positive results of experiments they do report.[6]

Passmore and his associates note that a study com-

OBJECTIVE CASE STUDIES

Given the difficulties of gleaning hard information from QWL research, in this book we have had to rely mainly on "anecdotal material" or case studies to find how QWL works and what it accomplishes. The few case studies not written by those with a vested interest in the success of a particular program provide valuable information. One description can often tell us more about QWL than reams of "attitude surveys"—the two circles at the phone company which kept functioning although each had a member who crossed the picket line during the 1983 strike come to mind.

In particular, the few case studies by investigators not committed to QWL are valuable, because they do not cover up the day to day problems unionists face in implementing a QWL program. For example, labor educator Don Wells reports on two Canadian plants. Although the identity of each plant is disguised, members of UAW Local 707 identify one of them as Ford's Oakville, Ontario plant. Wells investigated during the period when many QWL practitioners were holding Oakville up as a QWL success story. But Wells found a number of problems developing, and later the local pulled out of QWL.[9]

James Rinehart's paper on the QWL program at General Motors' Diesel plant in London, Ontario draws attention to the specific ways that the program transmits management norms to employees.[10] And Robert Thomas's report on two auto parts plants shows clearly the frustration that results when QWL fails to live up to its promises.[11]

missioned by the New York Stock Exchange, which relies not on consultant reports but on the views of management, reports a significantly lower "success" rate for "interventions"—around 50 percent.[7] The techniques judged most successful by management standards were those usually used independently of QWL, such as job training, flexible working hours, and financial incentive systems.

Passmore and associates also describe an analysis by D. Roitman based on only those consultant reports which had minimum standards of scientific rigor (such as before and after comparisons or comparison groups). Roitman found a much lower success rate than in the full field of published reports and found outcomes inconclusive on several dimensions.[8] Among other results, Roitman found that experiments which involved unions had a lower success rate than those in nonunion situations.

For all of these reasons—the difficulties of designing and executing serious research and the considerable bias shown by those conducting, permitting and reporting the research—very few studies of QWL have any scientific credibility. And those which are sound frequently fail to provide support for QWL claims, even where the

authors have a pro-QWL bias. Keeping in mind the severe limitations of these studies, we will now look at some of their findings on key QWL questions.

Do QWL Programs Last?

A common conclusion of studies of the early QWL programs in the 1970's is that after an initial burst of enthusiasm they do not last. Paul S. Goodman of Carnegie-Mellon University reported that most QWL projects claimed a modest success during the first few years but that after five years:

> the general finding was at least 75 percent of the projects are *no longer* functioning; none of the programs in unionized settings was still in operation. These findings seem similar to other research in this area.[12]

Similarly, James O'Toole characterized the results of experiments in more than 100 plants as "one of a brief leap forward followed by prolonged backsliding."[13] More recently, consultant D.L. Landen estimated that from two-thirds to three-fourths of QWL programs fail.[14]

Academic teams under a federal grant studied in depth eight QWL projects started between 1973 and 1977. The workplaces included government agencies, privately owned manufacturing facilities, a hospital, and a mining operation. All the programs had ended by 1981.[15] Most of the public employee QWL programs described in a 1982 study were also discontinued (see chapter 16).[16]

As more QWL programs are assigned full-time coordinators and facilitators in attempts to keep them alive, it becomes more difficult to evaluate how real they are. In some places the program itself collapses, never takes off, or muddles along without any noticeable results, but the trappings remain.

This is especially true in multi-plant corporations where corporate management has mandated QWL for every plant. A late 1983 study of 13 plants sponsored by the General Motors-UAW Joint National QWL Committee found some plants where "the structure exists but it is not being used." In one plant there was no QWL activity at all and in another the only activity was offsite training. The authors found only two programs they considered successful.[17]

In 1983 the U.S. Department of Labor's Division of Labor-Management Cooperation funded a study of the AT&T-Communications Workers QWL program. The researchers examined 10 of the program's 1,200 teams using attitude surveys, personal interviews and observation. The 10 teams were selected by local QWL coordinators, who were asked to choose neither their best nor their worst. But since teams which had already dissolved or were no longer meeting were not considered, the selection of teams was naturally skewed toward "successful" examples. Further, almost all the researchers were committed to the QWL process; many served as consultants. The research was coordinated by personnel from the CWA and AT&T and by the QWL consultant. These facts all probably resulted in considerable positive bias.

Yet even so, the report indicated very minimal results. Most of the teams could not get going or were unable to get beyond "local" issues (e.g., break area facilities, air conditioning). For this reason, according to the researchers, "many of the groups soon reached a 'plateau,' losing their initial momentum and enthusiasm" and "showed signs of frustration and pessimism about the future." Only two of the ten were successfully dealing with "work-related policy" (that is, issues beyond the "environmental" or "cosmetic" ones).

QWL advocates have become urgently concerned with the inability of QWL to survive and grow. Two practitioners summarize the situation:

> QWL systems usually survive the politics, newness, and uncertainty of the first year or two, but the long-term institutionalization of QWL is often in doubt, and only infrequently achieved.[18]

Why do most groups "plateau" or fail after a short period of time? QWL practitioners offer a series of convenient answers. They argue that the concept is new and will require time for management, unions, and practitioners to learn from mistakes. Most evaluations sound like the answers of political candidates when asked to frankly state a weakness: "My biggest weakness is my failure to get the public to understand that I am the best candidate." The evaluations start with the assumption that the program is essentially sound but that its virtues are not being properly communicated—somebody is doing it wrong or is not really gung-ho in the first place. Middle management and union stewards usually get most of the blame.

Thus QWL researchers rarely ask questions or look at evidence which would challenge the assumption that QWL *should* work. Instead they try to figure out why these "good" programs fail.

It might be more fruitful to start off with a different assumption: that QWL programs have built-in problems which lead them to collapse eventually. We would then need to ask why they appear to succeed in their beginning stages. We can suggest four reasons:

First, the large amounts of money and other resources allocated to the program initially create the impression of change and results. In most cases these resources cannot continue to be increased at the same rate as the program continues, and the sensation of change declines.

Second, workers would like to believe in QWL because they want respectful treatment, real influence, to make a contribution, and to take pride in their work. It takes a while before the realities of management policy demonstrate that these promises will not be fulfilled and that the business will continue to operate as usual.

Third, there is enthusiasm at the beginning because the employees genuinely feel good about contributing their ideas. But after the first stock of ideas is used, the next round is harder to come by, and participants are more likely to come up with suggestions at the expense of fellow workers. The suggestions begin to create bad feelings. At the same time these new ideas tend to be less productive and thus management begins to lose interest.

Fourth, the "Hawthorne effect" (see box) is probably responsible for many initial success stories.

The evidence seems to be that a small group following the QWL model can sustain worker interest for a year or two at most. Where QWL programs continue longer than this and are judged successes, as in the Tarrytown case described at the end of this chapter, it is because the union and management maintain the structure despite worker loss of interest, or because new groups are regularly started to replace the groups which wither after the initial enthusiasm.

THE HAWTHORNE EFFECT

The "Hawthorne effect" takes its name from a series of experiments conducted from 1924 to 1932 at Western Electric's Hawthorne plant in Illinois. Researchers were attempting to identify factors that could increase productivity.

In the most famous experiment they tried shorter hours, longer hours, shorter breaks, longer breaks—and discovered that no matter what they did, productivity improved. Their conclusion: more important than the various physical factors was the fact that the workers were getting attention. They appreciated the concern and were eager to cooperate.

There were, in fact, serious flaws in the original Hawthorne experiment.[19] Nonetheless, the ability of attention *per se* to create changes in worker performance is widely acknowledged, at least in the initial period before the experimental conditions come to be taken for granted.

__Does QWL Improve the Quality of Work Life?___

There is no shortage of statistics which are used to show that QWL has increased employee influence and job satisfaction. However, virtually all of these statistics come from in-house surveys like the one by Ford Motor Company described above, and are therefore suspect. More objective studies of job satisfaction and the feeling of influence cast serious doubt.

AFL-CIO STUDY

One of the few attempts to examine the effects of QWL with some measure of scientific objectivity is reported in a book by Thomas Kochan, Harry Katz, and Nancy Mower of the Massachusetts Institute of Technology.[20] As the first available hard data study of QWL programs across several industries, it is worth examining in some detail.

The study was initiated by the AFL-CIO Industrial Union Department, which was skeptical of QWL. It combines survey data with case study descriptions so that it is easier to understand and interpret the data. Most of the cases include the real company and union names, making it possible to check, compare and add information from other sources. Although the researchers themselves clearly favor participation programs and frequently give their findings a pro-QWL interpretation, the study provides insights into the limitations of the particular programs which do not come through in the reports published by those directly involved.

Surveys of both QWL participants and nonparticipants were conducted at five workplaces which had QWL programs. Since the surveys required permission from both labor and management, the sample of locations was likely biased toward more positive QWL experiences. (A Canadian grocery chain and a meatpacking plant included in the case studies were not included in the survey because the programs there had collapsed.) The five were: Xerox Corporation and Amalgamated Clothing and Textile Workers Union Local 14b; a small auto parts manufacturing company (disguised); a large communications services firm (disguised); Packard Electric Division of General Motors and International Union of Electronic Workers (IUE) Local 717; and Minneapolis and St. Paul Newspapers and Twin Cities Newspaper Guild.

The first four cases involved blue collar workers. The last involved professionals and the participation program was closer to an expanded collective bargaining arrangement than to the usual QWL structure. The researchers looked at the following attitudes, among others:

Desire for Influence. By large majorities participants and, to a slightly lesser extent, nonparticipants indicated a desire for more say over a range of issues including methods and procedures of work, quality, work pace, use of new technology, and pay scale. Only a minority said they wanted more say on such issues as hiring, discipline, and upper management promotions.

Sense of Influence. Workers were asked how much say they had in each of the above areas. On every question less than a majority of workers in the four blue collar programs responded that they had even "some say." The responses were only slightly more positive from the Guild members. But most significant, there were virtually no differences between QWL participants and nonparticipants in their sense of influence.

Positive Views Toward the Job. With the exception of the Packard Electric plant, the survey revealed no general significant difference between participants and nonparticipants in agreement with such statements as: "My job requires that I keep learning new things." "The work I do is meaningful to me." "My job lets me use my skills and abilities."

Views Toward Union Leaders. In the two most elaborate programs (Packard Electric and the Newspaper Guild), QWL participants had significantly more positive responses toward the union leaders than did nonparticipants. Kochan, Katz and Mower thus conclude that:

> . . . there is no evidence in these data to support the critics' argument that the presence of a QWL program will undermine workers' support of their union.
> Indeed. . . the local union is rated [by participants] as significantly more effective in the case of the union with the highest degree of involvement and the most advanced form of participation.

This should not be surprising: we could expect the members who choose to participate in QWL to be more favorable to a union leadership which supports QWL than the members who choose not to participate. But in any case, the test the researchers use to calm union fears (comparison of participant and nonparticipant attitudes) is inappropriate in this case. The issue is not the effect of QWL on individuals' attitudes, but its net effect on the functioning of the union. If QWL undermines the union, it is undermined for everyone, participants and nonparticipants alike. The authors' comparison tells us nothing about whether the union is in fact being undermined. For that we would need information that showed changes over time.

The survey results did show, however, some areas of union weakness which could explain why workers might look to QWL. Less than half the blue collar workers surveyed thought the union was "doing a good job" on issues such as "getting workers a say in how they do their jobs," "helping make jobs more interesting," "representing worker interests in management decision making," and "giving members a say in how the union is run."

AT&T-CWA STUDY

The 1983 AT&T-CWA study cited earlier gave questionnaires to QWL participants and to nonparticipants from surrounding work groups. They were asked to rate such dimensions as job satisfaction, relation to supervisors, and sense of participation. The results were compared with answers to similar questions on a national Bell survey taken several months earlier.

On most of the dimensions the researchers found that both the team members and the nonparticipants were significantly higher than the Bell survey averages. The authors draw most of their positive conclusions about QWL from these comparisons to the overall company averages.

It is hard to evaluate these conclusions, since the Bell survey figures which establish the baseline are kept confidential and results are reported only in relative terms.

But in any case it is doubtful that the comparison says anything at all about the effects of QWL. (See the box on "What Causes What.") For one thing, since QWL is voluntary, it is likely that the locations with QWL teams would be among the more cooperative portion of the overall Bell system to begin with.

Further, instead of randomly selecting the QWL sites themselves, the researchers asked local QWL coordinators "to pick locations which were not due to be disrupted in a major way by divestiture during the research period." This additional factor used to select the sample makes meaningless any attempt to ascribe the departure from Bell System averages to QWL, as the researchers do.[21]

The findings which might tell us something about the effect of QWL on individuals' quality of work life are the comparisons between the attitudes of participants and nonparticipants. But on two important measures, job satisfaction and sense of participation, the differences between the two groups appear not to be

statistically significant. In fact, the only significant difference between participants and nonparticipants appears to be on questions relating to QWL itself (for example, "Goals of QWL process are advantageous to us.").

The only way the researchers could find any other significant differences was to rate the QWL teams and then analyze their data according to the ratings. They classified two teams as "advanced," four as "plateau," and three as "unsettled." Differences among teams were then found in the researchers' expected direction. Participants in what the researchers considered "advanced" teams indicated more job satisfaction and sense of influence than those in the other teams or nonparticipants.

Given the methodology and the small numbers involved here (the two advanced teams together totaled 13 members), attributing causality to QWL would be particularly questionable.

__Does QWL Increase Productivity?

Most of QWL's claims to produce long term gains in efficiency and productivity have not been substantiated. While enthusiasts cite many examples of huge savings resulting from the work of particular circles, it has not been demonstrated that this form of organization is any more productive than other systems, such as employee suggestion programs, or than simply treating employees well and providing adequate benefits.

Further, productivity gains must be considered against the costs of the programs themselves. QWL programs are extremely expensive. Costs include consultant fees (in 1982 Ford Motor Company considered $15,000 a typical fee to establish five groups); coordinator and facilitator wages (some auto plants have more than a dozen such full-time positions); and lost time and other expenses for training programs (participant training often takes two days to a week). The biggest expense is the time lost from production work for the circle meetings and activities themselves. In large plants with a high participation rate this figure exceeds millions of dollars per year. Perhaps as common as the glowing success stories are the comments like that of Chris Hamilton, a plant chairman at a very small Ford local:

> They budgeted $225,000 per year for EI activities. The only thing to show for it is an "employe of the month" award.

A few studies have attempted to go beyond impressions and anecdotes to compare programs over time and over a number of locations with hard figures. None of these studies provides firm evidence for the claim that, when balanced against the costs, the suggestions that come from QWL programs produce a significant net increase in productivity.

Michael Schuster found that the relationship between participation and increased productivity was largely "inconclusive."

Of the 17 sites with some form of employee involvement in which productivity data were available, 8 had [increased], 7 had no change, and 2 were down.[22]

A study by Katz, Kochan, and Gobeille sought to demonstrate the effects of QWL on economic performance (product quality and productivity) by examining data from 18 plants within a division of General Motors. The authors claim that their figures show a strong correlation between economic performance and "good industrial relations." They claim only limited support, however, for the hypothesis that *QWL* improves both economic performance and industrial relations. In fact, the authors' multiple regression analysis shows a slight negative (although not statistically significant) relationship between "QWL rating" and "direct labor efficiency."[23]

Does QWL Affect Union-Management Relations?

Virtually every case study reports that QWL results in better relations between union and management. Here the number of grievances or the grievance rate serves as a readily available objective measure. Robert Guest, for example, includes the following as one of the "measurable results of quality of work life at Tarrytown":

In December 1978, at the end of the training sessions, there were only 32 grievances on the docket. Seven years earlier there had been upward of 2,000 grievances filed. Such substantial changes can hardly be explained by chance.[24]

A careful examination of the Tarrytown case, however, strongly suggests that QWL is not the reason for the decrease (see the last section of this chapter).

Although there are many reports of a decline in grievances associated with QWL, even here research does not always confirm the relationship. The Katz, Kochan, and Gobeille study shows weak if any correlation between QWL activity and grievances.

A study by two members of General Motors' Organizational Research and Development Department ranks five manufacturing plants according to the number of joint QWL activities in each plant. (From the descriptions they appear to be GM plants, although the identities are not revealed.) The authors compare the number of unresolved grievances following the 1976 national negotiations to the number following 1979 negotiations. They found that the plants with the fewest QWL activities had a significant increase in the monthly average number of open grievances, while the plants with many QWL activities had a marked decrease.[25] Yet, as the authors correctly point out:

The nature of the data do not, of course, permit the argument that the QWL activities caused the grievance reduction. Perhaps both parties were ready for changing their relationship and the grievance reduction might be associated with the readiness to change.

An in-depth consideration of the significance of grievances and their different uses by workers and by union leaders is beyond the scope of this discussion.[26] All of QWL literature, however, takes it for granted that grievances are bad. The assumption is that "no grievances" means "no problems." But there are other possibilities:

1) That workers are using alternative non-union channels to deal with problems.

2) That workers feel defeated and see no use in filing grievances.

3) That workers believe (correctly or incorrectly) that the union leadership has essentially closed off the grievance procedure by refusing to pursue grievances filed.

Unionists cannot consider the last three as positive developments. There are no grievances filed in a non-union shop or under a dictatorship, but unionists don't consider that as evidence of happy labor relations.

WHAT CAUSES WHAT?

Showing that A actually *causes* B is one of the most difficult problems in any research. It is particularly difficult in areas involving human relations because many different factors are at work at the same time and it is hard to set up pure experimental conditions.

The most common approach starts by showing an *association* or a *correlation*—that when A changes, B also changes in a consistent way. For example, if we take a sample of people and measure how much each eats (A) and how much each weighs (B), we would probably find a correlation: as A increases so does B—people who eat more tend to be heavier.

If there is no correlation there is probably no causal relationship. But correlation by itself does not imply cause. While it is likely that eating more causes increased weight, it is also possible that being heavy causes an individual to eat more. There also may be other variables at work. For example, a greater proportion of people who go to a hospital die than of people who don't. We wouldn't conclude, however, that going to a hospital will kill you.

This brief discussion of causality should be elementary and self-evident. Yet the literature on QWL regularly makes the leap from correlation to causation.

__What Makes a Success?_____

The case studies of what are deemed QWL success stories reveal certain common themes. First, most involve plants under threat of imminent closing. They may be geographically marginal and suffer from shipping cost disadvantages, such as Ford's Edison, New Jersey plant[27] or GM's Tarrytown plant. Or they may be parts plants where the parent corporation has readily available cheap labor alternatives and is actually moving or preparing to move work out of the plant. Examples would be the Rochester Xerox plant,[28] the Warren, Ohio GM Packard Electric Plant,[29] and the Ford Rawsonville plant.[30] The QWL programs at these plants were developed when the unions were in exceptionally weak positions.

Secondly, most of the apparent success of QWL in these plants does not appear to result from the QWL program itself. By the researchers' criteria, QWL "success" equals a cooperative relationship between the union and management. Frequently cited as evidence of such success are union cooperation in changing work rules to grant management more flexibility, joint activities to reduce absenteeism, or other joint union-management activities. But it seems more likely that these joint activities result from an overall decision by the union to be more cooperative, rather than from the QWL structure itself. In fact, the existence of a QWL program in these plants can often be seen more correctly as a *result* of the cooperative relationship than as the cause of it.

This is illustrated by an examination of the QWL program at GM's Tarrytown, New York assembly plant. As one of the few programs that has survived several years, it is widely publicized.

In fact, the Tarrytown plant has had several QWL programs over the last ten years. The programs themselves have shown about the same results as others. The pilot program begun in 1974 produced a number of suggestions. But in 1975, when management laid off one shift, GM dropped the consultant and the program virtually collapsed.

In 1977 QWL was started up again. Every worker in the plant, 50 at a time, was offered the opportunity for a three-day training program in problem solving skills and plant procedure. More than 3,000 workers had taken the training when this phase ended in December 1978. Departments then held paid voluntary meetings for half an hour after work. A later program established one team of full-time quality monitors in each department, with one member of the team appointed by the union.

In 1982 the author interviewed 35 workers from the plant. All had high seniority, since the plant had just eliminated its second shift. Most were concerned about saving the plant and wanted to produce a quality car. Most also thought that the half-hour meetings were "a waste of time except for the money." Typically, a meeting consisted of a supervisor reporting on production problems, absenteeism or the quality index. If workers brought up anything at the meetings it was

complaints about inadequate protective clothing. The union-appointed quality monitors were not highly regarded; some were described as "spies" or "finks." The only positive comments made about QWL had to do with sports activities and that supervisors seemed to be more polite.

But several writers have ascribed outstanding results to QWL at Tarrytown: a dramatic drop in grievances, a decline in absenteeism, and an increase in quality to the top of the General Motors Assembly Division.[31] If QWL didn't produce these miracles, what did?

The answer seems to be simple: the workers were afraid the plant would shut down. If Tarrytown went down there were no other plants in the area to which they could transfer. And Tarrytown was particularly vulnerable. The old plant was four stories tall, while current management thinking is that single story operations are more flexible and cheaper. Its East Coast location added to the shipping cost of component parts, mostly produced in the midwest. According to UAW

Local 664 Vice-President Fred Rossi, the railroad bridges in the area were too low to permit use of tri-level railroad cars—automobiles had to be transported by truck to New Jersey and transferred there to rail. Rossi also says that the plant has the highest utility rates of any GM assembly plant.

And Tarrytown was in competiton with other GM plants. In 1982, for example, Willow Run, Michigan and Oklahoma City produced the same model cars. There was not the slightest doubt in any worker's mind that the Tarrytown plant was in the weakest position. Several of the workers surveyed analyzed the situation almost identically. One explained:

> We can't beat them on shipping costs, energy costs or taxes. The only way we have a chance is to beat them on quality and good labor relations.

The switch to "good labor relations" began before QWL. Tarrytown workers had felt early in the 1970's what other auto workers were not to feel until 1980—the cold winds of competition. In 1971 the plant lost a truck operation and rumors spread about the imminent closing of the whole plant. Management decided to use the opportunity to try a different approach. According to knowledgeable sources, management directly approached the union leaders and told them that their only chance for saving the plant was to turn around its reputation for poor labor relations and in particular to reduce the grievance rate.

As the graph indicates, the big reduction in grievances took place before QWL was introduced and well before it was spread throughout the plant. Clearly management, the union and perhaps the workers simply decided to change the relationship. Militants in the plant charged that the union was discouraging and in some cases refusing grievances. They cite as an example that no grievances were filed during a mid-1970's heat wave which produced a heat walkout and disciplinary action for 56 workers.[32]

Tarrytown's record on product quality is harder to check, as GM keeps quality figures confidential. Informed observers claim that there was a sharp increase in product quality in the 1970's but that, as with the grievances, significant change took place before the QWL program.

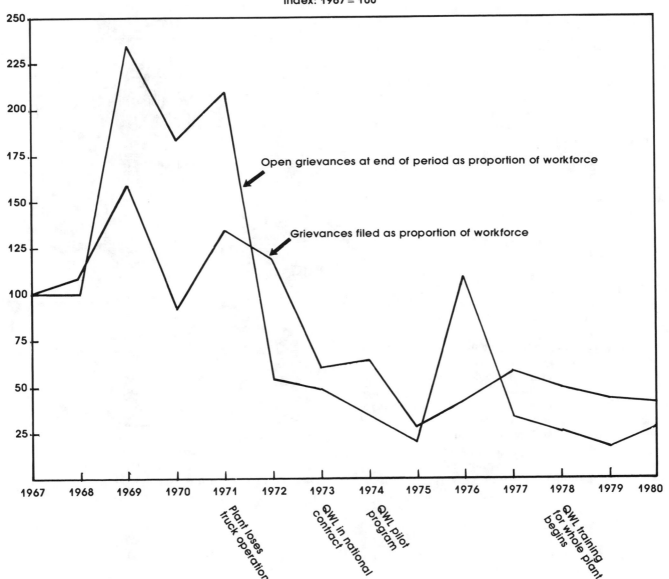

GRIEVANCES & QWL AT G.M. ASSEMBLY PLANT, TARRYTOWN, N.Y.

Index: 1967 = 100

Tarrytown's corporate Quality Index rose to the top in the 1970's but by the early 1980's had plummeted again (see chart). One explanation blames the plant manager, who has since been replaced. Another explanation blames outdated equipment in the paint shop which could not be replaced until corporate headquarters allocated substantial funds. Supposedly the quality index is rising again. But either of these explanations underscores the reality that it is management who has the final say over product quality.

In 1978 the Tarrytown plant was remodeled to produce the X-body car. Some observers have claimed the new investment as a victory for QWL. But the corporation must have decided where to assign the X-car during 1977 or early 1978, before most of the workers had gone through training, let alone produced any results through QWL.

Thus the "success story" at Tarrytown appears to have little to do with QWL after all. It is a story of cooperation between union leadership and management, not of worker involvement or power. The cooperation continues to be extensive, from quality monitoring and reducing absenteeism to union lobbying for reduced utility bills and lower taxes for the plant. For those who define such cooperation as good in and of itself, Tarrytown is a success. But it says little about the success of QWL programs by practitioners' definitions, much less from a union point of view.

__Whose Success?

Most scientific research proceeds by putting forward a hypothesis and then examining the facts to see whether they support the hypothesis. As we have seen, the research fails to support most of the hypotheses or claims made about QWL. The research doesn't necessarily refute the claims—"proving a negative" is extremely difficult—but neither does it confirm them.

QWL proponents argue that while QWL success stories may be few in number, these successes show what is possible when QWL is done well. But they use circular reasoning: properly done QWL produces improvements in worker satisfaction. How do we know which programs were properly done? They are the ones which produce improvements in worker satisfaction. The argument reduces to the tautology that successful programs are successful programs.

One problem here is the definition of "success." We have seen that most QWL programs are not "successful" according to the criteria of their proponents—increases in productivity or worker satisfaction. But it is possible that some day QWL practitioners will indeed design the programs which improve productivity or short term job satisfaction. They may even find ways to institutionalize them so they survive more than a year or two. *It is possible for QWL to be "successful" by these criteria and still undermine unions.* Unionists need a different standard of success.

This is not to say that QWL produces no results. Cor-

QUALITY INDEX
ASSEMBLY PLANT PASSENGER AUDIT

WEEK ENDING: 6-17-83

PLANT	MONT. Q.I.	RAMP Q.I.	% OVER 128 Q.I.	RANGE	PREV. MONT. Q.I.	Y.T.D. MONT. Q.I.
LORDSTOWN (J)	*133	---	100	141/125	130	130
NORWOOD (F)	130	---	93	139/111	123	124
LINDEN (E)	129	---	93	138/117	122	123
LEEDS (J)	128	128	96	135/116	131	127
JANESVILLE (J)	128	---	93	138/116	129	123
BOWLING GREEN (Y)	128	---	80	138/116	126	124
WILMINGTON (T)	128	---	80	140/110	130	128
STE. THERESE (G)	128	---	100	138/120	124	118
OLDSMOBILE (G)	127	---	80	140/104	121	124
BALTIMORE (G)	127	---	73	140/114	123	123
LINDEN (K)	127	---	87	134/117	125	122
OSHAWA (A)	127	---	93	138/111	124	122
OLDSMOBILE (B, C)	126	---	80	136/115	120	124
OSHAWA (B)	126	---	73	136/111	128	125
FRAMINGHAM (A)	125	---	80	139/115	124	121
VAN NUYS (F)	125	---	73	143/109	125	124
TARRYTOWN (X)	124	---	73	135/116	114	117
CADILLAC (C)	*124	---	60	145/110	129	125
BUICK (B, C)	*124	---	67	135/113	126	124
BUICK (G)	123	---	67	134/110	120	121
OKLAHOMA (A)	122	---	60	138/110	126	122
WILLOW RUN (X)	121	---	73	130/108	128	125
DORAVILLE (A)	121	---	67	129/110	122	121
FAIRFAX (B)	120	---	67	133/107	118	123
ARLINGTON (G)	116	120	48	136/101	125	121

† Facility Not Conforming
* AUDIT DURING THE WEEK OF: 6-13-83 (Not Cumulative)

G.M. RESTRICTED

porations do have their eye on the bottom line, after all, and they would not be spending millions of dollars on QWL if they did not expect to get something out of it. As we argued in the first half of this book, the real results of QWL are usually weakened unions, concessions, and a smooth introduction of new technology.

The kind of research results that sell QWL to management are these conclusions from *Fortune* magazine:

> To date, with few exceptions, work rule changes have been won only in plants with well-developed Quality of Work Life programs that give workers a role in management, or in plants threatened with loss of jobs.[33]

From management's point of view, this kind of result makes QWL well worth the price. ☐

Notes

1. Michael H. Schuster, *Union-Management Cooperation*, W.E. Upjohn Institute for Employment Research, 1984.

2. "The Quality of Work Life Process of AT&T and the Communications Workers of America," draft, January 1984, sponsored by U.S. Dept. of Labor.

3. "UAW-Ford Employe Involvement: A Special Survey Report," UAW-Ford National Development and Training Center, Center Report 1, no date.

4. Susan Kozel, "Employe Involvement: UAW-Ford Style," Rutgers University, unpublished, December 1983.

5. Sar A. Levitan and Clifford M. Johnson, "Labor and Management: The Illusion of Cooperation," *Harvard Business Review,* September-October 1983.

6. William Passmore, Barry Morris, Rafael Estavez, "Quality of Worklife and Productivity: Implications for Improving the Performance of Civilian Personnel in Military Organization," available from William Passmore, Case Western Reserve University, February 1984.

7. *People and Productivity: A Challenge to Corporate America*, New York Stock Exchange, 1982.

8. D. Roitman, "Job Enrichment, Socio-Technical Design and Quality Circles: Effects on Productivity and Quality of Worklife," Report to the National Science Foundation, 1984. Cited in Passmore *et al.*

9. Don Wells, *Soft Sell: QWL and the Productivity Race*, Canadian Centre for Policy Alternatives, 1985.

10. James Rinehart, Department of Sociology, University of Western Ontario, "Appropriating Workers' Knowledge: Quality Control Circles at a General Motors Plant," paper presented to Society for the Study of Social Problems, Detroit, 1983.

11. Robert J. Thomas, "Participation and Control: New Trends in Labor Relations in the Auto Industry," CRSO Working Paper #315, University of Michigan, 1984.

12. Paul S. Goodman, "Realities of Improving the Quality of Work Life," *Labor Law Journal*, August 1980.

13. James O'Toole, "Thank God It's Monday," *The Wilson Quarterly*, August 1980.

14. D.L. Landen, Speech, Ann Arbor, Michigan, January 15, 1985.

15. Courtland Cammann, Edward E. Lawler III, Gerald E. Ledford, and Stanley E. Seashore, *Management-Labor Cooperation in Quality of Worklife Experiments: Comparative Analysis of Eight Cases,* Report to U.S. Dept. of Labor, Survey Research Center, Institute for Social Research, University of Michigan, March 1984.

16. Neal Q. Herrick, *Improving Government: Experiments with Quality of Working Life Systems*, Praeger, 1983.

17. William Horner and Howard Carlson, "GM/UAW National Committee on Quality of Worklife Review," unpublished, February 28, 1984.

18. Terry Mazany and Michael Humphrey, "The Role of Self-Evaluation in QWL System Maintenance," *The Work Life Review*, October 1984.

19. See Berkeley Rice, "The Hawthorne Defect: Persistence of a Flawed Theory," *Psychology Today*, February 1982.

20. Thomas A. Kochan, Harry C. Katz, and Nancy R. Mower, *Worker Participation and American Unions: Threat or Opportunity*, W.E. Upjohn Institute for Employment Research, 1984.

21. AT&T-CWA Study, p. 12 and Appendix C, p. 11.

22. Schuster, *Union-Management Cooperation.*

23. Harry C. Katz, Thomas A. Kochan, and Kenneth R. Gobeille, "Industrial Relations Performance, Economic Performance, and QWL Programs: An Interplant Analysis," *Industrial and Labor Relations Review*, October 1983. The same study is reported in Harry C. Katz, *Shifting Gears: Changing Labor Relations in the U.S. Auto Industry*, MIT Press, 1985.

24. Robert Guest, "Quality of Work Life—Learning from Tarrytown," *Harvard Business Review*, July-August 1979.

25. Robert H. Schappe and Richard D. Boynton, "The Relationship Between Quality of Work Life Activities and Open Grievances in Five Manufacturing Plants," *The Work Life Review*, April 1985.

26. See Craig Zaballa, *Collective Bargaining at UAW Local 645, 1976-1982*, Ph.D. Dissertation, University of California, Los Angeles, 1983.

27. *Business Week*, July 30, 1984.

28. Peter Lazes and Tony Costanza, "Xerox Cuts Costs without Layoffs through Union-Management Collaboration," *Labor-Management Cooperation Brief*, U.S. Dept. of Labor, July 1984. See also Kochan, Katz and Mower.

29. *Labor Notes*, September 1983 and January 1985. See also Kochan, Katz and Mower.

30. *Business Week*, July 30, 1984.

31. William T. Horner, "Tarrytown: A Union Perspective," *National Productivity Review*, Winter 1981-82.

32. "Sweat and Blood—Ours!!", leaflet issued by Rank and File Committee, no date.

33. Michael Brody, *Fortune*, April 16, 1984.

__UNION STATEMENTS__

Following are some union position papers and resolutions about Quality of Work Life programs. All except the last are critical of QWL. Other union statements can be obtained by writing to the union in question.

British Columbia Federation of Labour Policy Paper on Quality of Working Life

[In 1983, after considerable study, the British Columbia Federation of Labour Quality of Work Life Committee issued its report, including this policy paper and a twenty-page companion background paper. The Policy Paper was adopted overwhelmingly at the BCFL Convention in November 1983.]

Unions in British Columbia are being asked by employers to embark on a new labour relations scheme called "Quality of Working Life" (QWL). Quality of Working Life is primarily an initiative of management and its consultants, along with academics and government bureaucrats. QWL provides employers with one method of permanently reducing the workforce, introducing automated technologies while still maintaining control of the workplace.

The QWL philosophy proposes a socio-technical view which matches worker and technology. Workers are social, psychological and physiological beings, not just automatons, and the technical aspect of work must be compatible with these functions. Workers must be involved in analyzing their work and environment so that the social and technical aspects can be optimized.

Proponents claim that QWL is a "humanization of work" which will improve the life of workers on the job. Workers will become involved in decisions about operations normally the responsibility of management. These include: production planning, product quality and quantity, machine maintenance, work scheduling and discipline.

There are a variety of ways in which QWL can be applied. One method is *semi-autonomous work groups*—self-managing teams of workers who plan, organize and evaluate their work with little direct supervision. Other proposals include decentralized work planning, the redesign of work roles and careers, new training systems with corresponding upgrading of jobs, job rotation, and most notably quality circles. *Quality circles* are small groups of workers who meet regularly with their supervisors to solve work-related problems. Quality circles do not attempt to alter the structure of work; instead management encourages workers to find ways of making their working conditions more endurable.

Workers originally organized themselves into unions to fight exploitation. The collective bargaining process which emerged from those early struggles remains today the best method for protecting workers' rights and of determining compensation. QWL questions the usefulness of the collective bargaining process which continues to be the only method for protecting workers

against the abuses of industrialization.

Workers have attempted to influence their working conditions by focussing on power and control. Operating on a *collective* level, workers strive for solidarity and trade union action. Workers have organized into unions so that rules, regulations, conditions and wages would apply to all members equally. Under a collective agreement, management is unable to apply different standards of pay to various workers. Exerting whatever power they have, unions struggle for higher wages, equal wages, safer working conditions, etc., and in the long run strive for achievement of economic democracy and social justice.

Quality of Working Life initiatives aim at the *individual* level, where the possibility to influence one's own work situation is created by management relating directly to the individual worker or small group of workers. The way that work is performed may be altered with a QWL program; the conditions under which work is performed, to a large extent, remain unchanged.

The labour movement has improved the working life of workers by organizing them into unions. A larger proportion of the workforce does not have the basic democratic right to bargain collectively with employers. If Quality of Working Life is a government policy aimed at society at large, then removal of the impediments to union organizations and certification should be reflected in amendments to labour law. Organizing the unorganized continues to be one of labour's major priorities.

Collective bargaining is the most important process in establishing economic democracy. It provides a mechanism to resolve conflict arising from the divergent interests of management and labour. Collective bargaining can provide the framework for structuring joint committees and for defining their scope and function. Through collective bargaining some mutually accepted and mutually beneficial solutions can be arrived at—with each side maintaining its independence and reserving prerogatives.

The rights and benefits of unionized workers must be protected in the face of QWL initiatives. The Quality of Working Life Committee recommends:

Affiliates shall not participate in Quality of Working Life Programs. This term includes: work improvement programs, quality circles, team work, semi-autonomous work groups, employee core groups, employee involvement in job progression, or other titles formulated by consultants.

INTERNATIONAL ASSOCIATION OF MACHINISTS AND AEROSPACE WORKERS

MACHINISTS BUILDING, WASHINGTON, D.C. 20036

Volume X, No. 1 & 2
WINTER-SPRING, 1982

QUALITY OF WORK LIFE PROGRAMS

In the past few years, a small but increasing number of IAM Local Lodges have been approached by management to participate in some form of Quality of Work Life program. A recent survey of all IAM Local Lodges indicates that, so far, IAM leadership has been able to resist these efforts. Still, there is every reason to expect that many more will be approached in the future.

Quality of Work Life (QWL) is a catch-all term for a variety of programs supposedly designed to improve communications and involve workers in shop floor decisions that will hopefully do three things: (1) improve worker job satisfaction, (2) improve product quality, and (3) reduce unit costs by increasing productivity. In instituting these programs, management seems to be seeking to utilize a resource it has chosen to overlook in the past, *i.e.* the average worker's ability to help solve shop floor problems.

QWL programs began to make an impact in labor-management relations during the early 1970's. The UAW signed the first national QWL agreement in the United States in 1973 with General Motors. That agreement has become the model for most of the others undertaken since.

A recent article in Fortune magazine indicated that unions representing twenty percent of the nation's organized workers have signed national agreements committing themselves to QWL programs of one type or another. The Work In America Institute has estimated that one-fourth of the U.S. labor force is presently involved in some type of QWL program and the movement is growing.

Overview

The term Quality of Work Life encompasses a wide range of assorted titles: Quality Control Circles, Industrial Democracy, Organizational Development, Workplace Participation, Humanization of Work, Work Improvement Program, Co-determination, Suggestion Systems, Flexitime, Job Redesign, Socio-Technical System, Relations by Objectives. All of these programs involve a wide variety of objectives with the hoped-for end results being about the same. There can be no argument that all workers have the right to dignity on the job, a decent environment in which to work and reasonable compensation for his or her efforts. A QWL program is a vehicle that is supposed to give the worker a right to some determination about these conditions of employment. So, too, is a trade union and, therein, lies the seeds of inevitable conflict.

If, in the unionized plant, there is a vehicle to address worker concerns, why create a new one? Responsible trade union leadership will always be ready to meet with management on equal terms to discuss and deal with legitimate concerns over quality, productivity, etc. Further, experience already shows that, because QWL programs seek to deal with many of the same issues that trade unions do, management often attempts to use these programs as a substitute for trade unions and/or as a means of bypassing the union leadership and appealing to the workers.

In April of this year, International President Winpisinger sent a letter to all IAM Local Lodges which clearly outlines the IAM's position on QWL/QCCs. IAM locals should, in general, oppose these programs as both unnecessary duplication and an effort to undermine the duly elected bargaining agent for the workers. This opposition is especially encouraged when it is able to put an end to management's efforts to establish such programs.

There will, however, be situations where a company will decide to introduce a QWL program with or without union approval. Further, as the IAM's organizing efforts continue, organizers may encounter plants where such programs are already in place and which, for one reason or another, have worker support. The union *might* be wise to participate if only to insure that it is in a position to monitor the program. Under these circumstances, labor's role in a QWL program may be to take the lead in supporting initiatives that reorganize work in such a way that members benefit without undermining its own functions as the collective bargaining agent and worker representative. Such a decision of course, must be carefully thought out and have overall rank and file support.

Risks of QWL Programs

There are a whole series of potentially negative problems which surround the issue of whether or not a union should participate in QWL programs:

(1) **Role Definition**—The union must maintain its clear identity as the representative of the workers. If this is not clear, the problems are compounded. If the union becomes an apologist for management decisions or simply a prod for increased productivity (unfortunately, this has happened in some cases even without QWL), then it loses its authority as the workers' representative. This diminishes its effectiveness as a union and paradoxically makes it less useful to management. If the union

allows communication to go directly to the membership without the union's involvement and acknowledgement of their role, then there is a danger of weakening union allegiance within the workforce.

A perfect example of this is the UAW's recent experience with General Motors. Last December, General Motors used the in-plant union-management QWL Committees to hold captive audience meetings of employees in an effort to "spoonfeed" management's views on the need for substantial wage and benefit concessions in the forthcoming auto negotiations.

(2) **Liability for Decisions**—Another difficult question surrounds the potential liability of the union for the decisions it jointly entered into with management. Worker and/or union participation in decisions which were formerly the sole domain of management spreads responsibility for the outcome to more people. Business failure is often blamed on "bad management." Increased participation by employees in workplace decision-making can put the union in a position where it finds itself sharing blame which more properly should be placed upon management.

(3) **Loss of Jobs**—QWL programs generally result in higher productivity and, while increased productivity can be a benefit for both management *and* workers, management often tries to take advantage of higher productivity (in terms of output per worker) to eliminate jobs through layoff or redefinition of job specifications. It is crucial for the union to protect the jobs of everyone involved in a QWL program. Job protection can be achieved through specific provisions in the collective bargaining agreement, in a separate Quality of Work Life Agreement, and through scrupulous administration of the negotiated agreements.

(4) **Maintenance of Contract Standards**—Negotiations for increased worker participation can possibly affect agreements on job classifications, hiring, scheduling and assignments. Other pitfalls to watch out for include possible speedups, arbitrary changes in job classifications and responsibilities without proper pay adjustments and loss of comparability in an industry. Great care must be taken to protect hard-won gains.

(5) **Union-Busting**—Some corporate managers have used Quality of Work Life and similar programs to pacify employees and keep unions out. A union needs to determine, before going into a QWL program, whether the company is doing it for the legitimate purpose of improving the operation and morale at the worksite or for union busting. In a few cases, companies have instituted programs in their unionized plants and then transported their ideas to their non-union facilities as a way to contain union growth. However, more often than not, in developing QWL programs, companies which have many unionized sections have ignored the unionized parts in favor of non-union facilities or new plants.

Union Considerations

Before involving themselves in a QWL program, there are a number of issues a union should consider:

(1) Such programs require mutual cooperative effort on the part of management and the union. Putting together a workable QWL involves a lot of hard work by both sides. This is why the first stage in the development of any QWL program must be devoted to creating a solid climate of mutual respect and trust between the parties. It is also important to understand that collective bargaining between the parties must not be compromised while the QWL program is in effect. QWL programs are not meant to be used to substitute for portions of the collective bargaining agreement.

(2) For a QWL program to work properly, it must be perceived as being of benefit to both sides—labor and management. A QWL needs to be structured to meet all the goals of such a program and not just the desire of the company to increase productivity and reduce costs. Both sides must be sincere. Otherwise the program will rightfully be regarded as just another management gimmick. To guard against company misuse of the program, the union must insist that they be integrally involved in every aspect of such systems from the moment when they are suggested through all phases of their implementation. This co-equal status is a necessary element to insure that neither side can take advantage of the other.

(3) The union should make sure that the new program has top-management support. This may mean demanding a meeting with top management to be sure of the ground rules.

(4) To protect its membership, the union should seek assurances, in writing, that there will be no layoffs as a result of the program. This can be difficult because it may be hard to separate the causes of layoffs.

(5) The union must insure that the QWL program does not enter into any area of the collective bargaining agreement. The union should obtain solid language to prevent this possibility. This is another good reason why union stewards should be involved in the program.

Involvement in QWL activities ought to be no preamble to softness in negotiations over traditional collective bargaining matters such as wages and benefits. Though an impact of QWL may be to increase the size of the pie available for negotiation, it should not be the forum for the hard fights over who is to get what from whom.

(6) Another concern involves "speed-up." It should be made clear to management that the adoption of a QWL program is not intended to lead to a "speed-up" in the work pace.

(7) Both the union leadership and membership must understand the aims of the program. The company, naturally, wants such management goals as improved quality and cost reduction, whereas the union is interested in improving the quality of its member's work life. Both aims of the program are justifiable and both are required to be part of the program if it is to be effective.

(8) The program should be voluntary and the union should be involved from the beginning. Imposing a program on the union without mutual agree-

ment most likely means the company is really only interested in the benefits it can reap without true regard for the effects on the worker. Entering the program should be voluntary for each employee.

(9) The workers should enjoy some form of reward (monetary or otherwise) as the QWL program progresses.

(10) Either party should have the right to cancel the QWL program if the original intentions of the program are violated.

The union side is often not alone in its skepticism of QWL programs. Some management representatives have expressed opposition to the QWL concept because successful programs might tend to erode managerial authority. Line foremen, particularly, worry about the impact on their duties and responsibilities to "give orders" and "run the show" at the workshop level. If a QWL program is to work, supervision must understand that cracking the whip over workers and acting as constant overseers need not be the essential ingredients of supervisory work.

Conclusion

Management in America often points to quality of work life programs in Japan, Scandanavia and elsewhere to demonstrate how productivity can be improved by labor-management cooperation. They fail to note, however, that in such countries both management and government recognize and accept the need for unions in a just society. Corporate America can hardly expect the IAM to trust their quality of work life proposals while they simultaneously fund and support a so-called union-free environment movement dedicated to our destruction.

The answer to the question of whether or not a particular IAM local lodge should participate in a unilaterally instituted QWL program is difficult. Each local needs to weigh for itself its own situation. It needs to determine whether cooperation is consistent with the needs and goals of the membership and the values of the union. The answer to the question is dependent upon the answer to other questions such as by whom and at what cost.

American Postal Workers Union Resolution on Quality of Worklife Programs

[Adopted at the 1984 National Convention.]

WHEREAS, USPS management is committed to establish so-called "Quality Of Worklife/Employee Involvement" programs to be embraced by bargaining unit employees, and

WHEREAS, Certain employee craft unions have already "embraced" the QWL/EI concept with USPS management while the APWU stands alone in passive opposition to such programs, and

WHEREAS, USPS management has adopted a "Damn the torpedos, full speed ahead" attitude in an attempt to forcefeed APWU bargaining unit employees the QWL/EI concepts, and

WHEREAS, Quality of Worklife/Employee Involvement programs are a sophisticated approach to the old "Company Union" concepts with an appealing name, designed to make an end run-around negotiated contract provisions, Labor-Management relations and the very essence of unionism itself by pitting worker vs. worker and employing carrot-on-a-stick competition among employees, and

WHEREAS, QWL/EI programs, regardless of what innocent sounding titles they are given (such as the term: "Right to Work"), are the products of a modern employer's tactics to create a "union free" environment in the USPS, and

WHEREAS, The APWU is committed to improving the quality of working conditions and dignity of workers through established contractual and labor relations practices as the exclusive bargaining agent for our APWU crafts, therefore be it

RESOLVED, That this convention in Las Vegas, Nevada, August 20, 21, 22, 23, and 24, 1984 goes on record as being unalterably opposed to union participation or endorsement in any form of any and all Quality of Worklife/Employee Incentive programs at all levels of this union with the United States Postal Service, and the 1984 APWU Convention calls upon its sister unions to abandon their support of Quality of Worklife.

United Electrical, Radio and Machine Workers of America

ELEVEN EAST FIFTY-FIRST STREET · **UE** · NEW YORK, N.Y. 10022 • 753-1960

JAMES M. KANE
General President

BORIS H. BLOCK
General Secretary-Treasurer

HUGH HARLEY
Director of Organization

QUALITY CIRCLES

Resolution Adopted by the
46th Convention of the United
Electrical, Radio and Machine
Workers of America (UE)

When the UE was formed in the mid-1930's, the use of company unions was a common tactic among electrical manufacturing companies. Various names were used -- Employee Representation Plans, Works Councils -- but the content was the same. The purpose of these tactics was to convince workers that the interests of management were those of the workers; that any problems the workers had could be solved through company channels; and that therefore, there was no need for the workers to have their own organization capable of conducting a fight against the company.

Behind this smokescreen of "one big happy family," the companies trampled on the workers' rights. Electrical workers rejected company unionism and formed the genuine rank and file unions of the CIO.

Today, the companies are singing the song of company unionism again, to a 1980's beat. Under the names of "Quality Circles," "Quality of Work Life," and "Participation," they are trying to peddle the old line that workers and bosses both benefit from a "cooperative" relationship. In fact, "Quality Circles" are better called "Quantity Circles." Management is not interested in increasing your wages, in how safe your workplace is, or in anything that would improve working conditions. In their circles, they will not listen to solutions that cost them an extra person or another tool to work with. They are just looking for more production at less cost to them.

But management's approach today is more sophisticated than 50 years ago, because it uses group manipulation techniques devised by industrial psychologists and sociologists. The goal is to break down workers' natural mistrust of bosses, and then get workers to begin telling the company how jobs can be speeded up and made more "productive" -- in other words, how to get the work out with fewer people. The companies want to break down the "communications barrier" between boss and worker so they can turn worker against worker, getting people to tell them who's not being "productive" enough.

In sum, Quality Circles are an attempt to create a shop floor structure controlled by management and pushing management's point of view, aimed at undermining the union steward system and bypassing the union. The ultimate goal is to get rid of the union altogether, or transform it into a totally company union.

THEREFORE BE IT RESOLVED:

1. That UE continue to oppose "Quality Circles" and other phony "participation schemes devised by management.

2. That we continue to educate our members on the difference of goals and outlook of working people, as opposed to the corporations.

3. That we strive to educate our members and the rest of the labor movement to the fact that real workers' participation and democracy on the job can only be won through militant rank and file unionism -- in other words, by workers sticking together and fighting for greater dignity and rights.

[The Canadian Air Line Employees Association represents 3,000 white collar passenger agents, 60% of whom are women.]

Union Policy

QWL no panacea for workplace problems

Quality of Work Life (QWL) is an appealing phrase. At its base is a fundamental guideline – decisions about the workplace should be made using "consensus" style decision-making in forums composed of managers and employees called quality circles, semi-autonomous work groups or teams. Proponents claim QWL can replace our adversarial relationship with a co-operative one, make our jobs more satisfying, and provide employers with lower costs and higher quality products through reduced turnover and absenteeism rates and greater equipment utilization.

The rhetoric of QWL sounds great – co-operation, job enrichment, job rotation, consensus decision-making. We all know, however, that management doesn't suddenly offer to make improvements in the workplace with no strings attached. What price do unions and the employees they represent have to pay for this increased input role? Does this role provide real (guaranteed) and long-lasting improvements? Does QWL affect the gains made by the Union through collective bargaining?

To answer these questions CALEA'S Board of Directors established a five-member committee to examine the concept of QWL and review the experiences of both CALEA and other unions in Canada. The committee's findings formed the basis of the policy on QWL recently adopted by the Board of Directors.

Suspicion Warranted

In recent years, unions across Canada have come under increasing pressure to collaborate on QWL programs. The federal government has established a special Quality of Work Life unit at Labour Canada and has committed a total 5.5 million dollars to QWL for the next five years. Yet, the same government that is backing QWL as a method of resolving differences, is using its legislative power to impose wage controls on workers and remove the right to free collective bargaining. The same government also refuses to bring in legislation to provide job security in the event of technological change, to provide strong regulations for safe and healthy workplaces and to provide retraining and adequate severance in the event of layoffs. While actively promoting QWL, the federal government has neglected the concrete improvement of working conditions.

Organized labour has always sought to improve working conditions through negotiations. Paid vacations, seniority rights, paid overtime, hours of work and wages are guaranteed through detailed clauses in collective agreements. QWL is viewed by management as a means to get unions to give up existing rights by offering to share decision-making. In the words of Norm Halpern, manager of Shell Canada:

> "...managers must surrender some control and share decision-making with employees and unions. And, in return, unions must be prepared to give up detailed contract specifications in such areas as job classification, pay systems, jurisdictional boundaries and grievance procedures." (Globe & Mail, Sept. 2, 1981)

It is no coincidence that QWL initiatives are coming during the current economic recession. Historically, managements have promoted QWL and its predecessors in times of crisis in order to extract greater productivity from their employees. QWL's consensus model provides a means to establish direct employer-employee relations and circumvent the union and the collective agreement. The goal is to make unions sacrifice gains by having employees identify solely with management's interests.

QWL does not change the basic unequal power relationship between labour and management. The major decisions that affect our working lives are simply not up for discussion in QWL. Greater input into decision-making does **not** mean that workers have a veto over the implementation of any program that increases workload or causes layoffs.

The Canadian Experience

The experience of other Canadian unions with QWL reinforces suspicion. At first, management appears to be ready to implement many small changes and to listen attentively to employees' concerns. However, through the establishment of quality circles or discussion groups, management problems such as increasing productivity, improving efficiency and reducing absenteeism often take precedence over improving conditions. Workers begin to take over the supervisor's job by monitoring other workers and establishing discipline committees.

Denis Lamothe, of the Energy and Chemical Workers' Union, Johnson & Johnson, noted: "At Johnson's, they pushed the (QWL) program up to the point where the workers calculate their profitability themselves ... This is what I call the velvet whip; maybe it does not hurt as much as a leather whip but in the long run it is more effective."

QWL can also undermine the collective agreement by getting employees to bring their grievances directly to the employer. If the grievance is settled outside of the collective agreement, there is no precedent. Roland Lamoureux, of the United Food and Commercial Workers (UFCW) at Steinberg's commented on the inability to grieve QWL program decisions. "Now that there are problems with [job] rotation, the guys don't even have the right to grieve and the union can't do anything." Richard Mercier, former president of the Quebec Council of the UFCW and now an executive

CALEA News

vice-president of the Canadian Labour Congress, stated: "As far as I am concerned, QWL is the icing on a poisoned cake." Mercier recounted that the workers at Steinberg's in Montreal filed no grievances for a five-year period.

Job rotation and job enrichment, two components of QWL can make job classification clauses meaningless and render seniority provisions for transfers and layoffs useless. Retraining opportunities are always needed, but any changes to the job must be carefully monitored to ensure that job security is not undermined.

The Experience of CALEA

Air Canada has unilaterally launched QWL without agreement from CALEA. In Infomanagement, an Air Canada publication, under the heading 'Job Enrichment' the Company wrote:

"In addition to all the above project types, there are numerous quality of work life projects being established. The objective is to improve the work environment and at the same time ensure effective productivity.

An example has been the enrichment of the Cargo Agent's job to provide greater interest and variety while making a fuller contribution to the cargo business. Another involves the Reservations Agent aggressively

selling our passenger products and servicing our customers."
(Infomanagement, v.13, n.5, May 14, 1982)

In other words, Passenger Sales Effectiveness (PSE) is the forum for the introduction of QWL. Already there appear to be instances where PSE is being used as a 'velvet whip' — workers are monitoring other workers. In one location the suggestion was made to scrap the first level of the grievance procedure and replace it with an employee (not union) — management committee.

Other QWL approaches have been tried in the past by other Companies whose employees CALEA represents but a combination of objections by CALEA and lack of interest by the Companies involved halted those initiatives.

CALEA's Position on QWL

CALEA members have demonstrated that a whole range of issues are of critical concern. These include physical working conditions, job stress caused by electronic monitoring, lack of on-the-job training, and the impact of technological change. We need to negotiate **guarantees** addressing these issues through the collective bargaining process.

QWL approaches provide no

guarantees. They are designed to promote management interests and to undermine the legitimate interests of working people. Past experience both within the airline industry and elsewhere suggests that QWL programs fail to provide employees with significant and continued improvements in their working lives.

For these reasons, the CALEA Board of Directors has voted **not** to adopt QWL as a panacea to solve workplace problems. In rejecting QWL, the Board recognizes the need to address the concerns of CALEA members through the development of union policies and strategies which culminate in the collective bargaining process. Failure to take such action will undermine the strength of the union and open up the doors for employers to propose QWL programs with the support of union members.

Remember W. "H".I. P.

Shortly after wage and price controls were introduced during the last economic crisis in 1976, a pilot project was launched in one CALEA district. It was, ironically, called W.I.P. – Work Improvement Program. The employer promised employees input into decision-making and job enrichment. The Union, conscious of the monotonous nature of the work and hoping for much needed improvements, became involved and even agreed to waive certain provisions of the collective agreement.

A year after the program was initiated, management issued a memo revealing that the Company's productivity goals were not being met. To

meet their long-term goals, electronic monitoring would be introduced to control the agents' productivity.

To the passenger agents these systems became known as putting the "H" back into W."H".I.P. They were brought in by management under the guise of QWL as a so-called "objective" performance measurement. The W.I.P. Program was cancelled in May, 1978 but the electronic measuring systems remain one legacy of QWL. (The adverse health effects of electronic monitoring and machine pacing have been well documented).

We are now much wiser to the QWL delusion.

Reprinted from SKYWAYS, Canadian Air Line Employees Association, March/April 1983.

*Information from the Brotherhood's Industrial Department to assist UBC
Organizers and Negotiators in organizing and securing better contracts.*

JANUARY, 1983

ORGANIZING-INDUSTRIAL

UBC BULLETIN

United Brotherhood of Carpenters and Joiners of America ●●●●● "Workers helping workers to better their lives."

Quality Circles:

How Should Unions Respond?

In the past year, the Industrial Department has received a growing number of inquiries from Councils and Locals about Quality Circles. Most commonly, an employer, with the assistance of an outside consultant, has proposed to institute a Quality Circle program and the Union is uncertain how to respond. A survey of UBC Councils and Locals conducted by the Industrial Department this past September and October revealed that Quality Circles do exist in some UBC shops, and there are indications that more employers will want to introduce them in the future.

There is much disagreement among unions about whether Quality Circles are just a subtle form of union busting or whether they represent a genuine employer effort to deal with difficult economic challenges while at the same time improving workers' lives on the job. The truth is that they can be used for either purpose depending on an employer's underlying attitude toward the union, his intention in introducing Quality Circles, the unity and awareness of the union and its members, and the type of outside consultant used.

This article offers guidance to Councils and Locals that are facing the introduction of Quality Circles in their shops. We recommend a cautious attitude because of the many risks involved in these programs. Many employers are using and have used Quality Circles as a means to undermine and even decertify the union. However, we feel there is a better course for most unions to take than ignoring a Quality Circle program or simply rejecting its introduction. In many situations we believe unions can negotiate safeguards, educate their members, and adapt these programs to serve the needs of their members.

Quality Circles programs often appeal to workers because they offer workers the opportunity to discuss workplace problems of concern to them. If the union is seen as blocking an attractive program without offering an alternative, management can

often drive a wedge between the "negative" union leaders and the "needs" of the rank and file. We therefore urge unions to educate their members about Quality Circles and to make counterproposals such as for labor-management committees, a Scanlon Plan, or a Quality Circle program adapted to the needs of the union and its members.

Quality Circles are also used in unorganized shops to prevent unionization. In a future article we will discuss ways organizers can counter Quality Circles in organizing campaigns.

WHAT TO DO WHEN QUALITY CIRCLES ARE PROPOSED

1. **Start With a Labor-Management Committee:** Because of the many risks posed by Quality Circles (discussed below), particularly where an employer is out to undermine the union, we recommend that unions propose the establishment of a labor-management committee instead of Quality Circles. Composed of union and management representatives, a labor-management committee is a good means to solve problems of mutual concern and to discover if the employer is genuinely interested in working cooperatively with the union. (Contact the Industrial Department for guidelines for setting up a labor-management committee.)

Once an employer participates in good faith in solving problems through a labor-management committee over a period of months, then the union and management can discuss other programs if they so choose.

A union should be very suspicious when an employer, who in the past has not dealt with the union in good faith or has ignored the existing labor-management committee, suddenly proposes a new era in labor relations through introduction of Quality Circles.

2. **Define the Union's Position Toward Quality Circles:** Because of the risks Quality Circles present to unions, it is crucial that the business representative, together with the Local Union, define the

Quality Circles

union's basic position **before** any part of a Quality Circle program is actually introduced or agreed upon. We suggest the following position:

— The union is the elected representative of workers in the shop and it, not the employer or an outside consultant, speaks for workers. Collective bargaining is the process in which decisions affecting employees in the workplace should be made. If collective bargaining or the collective bargaining agreement is undermined, workers lose their ability to be represented and heard. Quality Circles (if the union, in fact, decides to accept them) cannot be viewed as an alternative to collective bargaining, but as a process sanctioned by and always subject to collective bargaining. Therefore, everything about Quality Circles must be established and agreed to through negotiations—who participates, what subjects may and may not be discussed, what consultant is used, what union representative sits in on the Quality Circles, and other groundrules.

There will always be a basic conflict between employer goals (cutting production costs, increasing productivity, generating greater profits, etc.) and union goals (higher wages, shorter hours, better safety and health conditions, a more pleasant work environment, etc.) The union must make it clear to the employer that Quality Circles must address both types of issues if the union and its members are to participate. Management, and particularly outside consultants, too often want Quality to mean **product** quality only, but it must mean both that and quality of worklife as well.

3. **A Union-Management Steering Committee:** If a union decides to participate in a Quality Circle program, do **not** agree to a pre-packaged program. Agree, instead, to a union-management steering committee—with an equal number of representatives chosen by the union and by management—to negotiate everything about the program. The committee (which could be the regular labor-management committee) should continue to meet regularly for the life of the Quality Circle program to discuss its progress as well as any violations of the agreed-upon groundrules and to make necessary changes.

4. **Sharing the Wealth:** We recommend that if a Quality Circle program is accepted, it be combined with some form of gain-sharing plan for employees. The savings resulting from Quality Circles must be shared with employees for two reasons. First, it is only fair that savings achieved as a result of employee suggestions and participation in the Circles directly benefit employees. Otherwise the program becomes a means of manipulating workers for the benefit of the company. Second, employees rapidly lose interest if there is no incentive involved for them. A recent Oregon State University survey found that 75% of Quality Circle programs in the U.S. failed within a few years. There have to be incentives for employees to maintain interest.

The Risks of Quality Circles

We describe some of the common risks of Quality Circles together with recommendations to counter these risks **should the union choose to allow the introduction of a program.**

Problem: Quality Circles can be used to divide workers. For example, a Quality Circle may single out 50-year-old Phil, who can't keep up with a fast pace anymore, as a cause of a department's low productivity. Or the union's insistence that seniority be followed in filling vacancies or assigning overtime may be identified as a problem in a Quality Circle. Or a Quality Circle may propose a questionnaire to see how workers feel about a particular work practice won in negotiations.

Recommendation: A union officer or steward must be present at all Quality Circle meetings both to see that agreed-upon guidelines are followed (e. g., that items in the contract are not revised) and to see that union principles are adhered to (e. g., individual workers are not singled out for blame). The officer or steward should also have the right to call a caucus of employee members of the Quality Circle at any time. This can serve as a safeguard should the Circle move in a negative direction.

If the Circle appears headed toward an agreement on an issue which may be detrimental to the union's interests, the steward or union officer should ask for a recess or for the Circle to move on to another subject until he can meet with the union business representative.

Also, questionnaires of employees **should not be allowed.** The results may be used against the union's negotiators at a later date.

Problem: Quality Circles may lead to greater productivity or speedup which, in turn, will lead to layoffs.

Recommendation: Get a written agreement from the employer at the outset that there will be no layoffs or speedups as a result of suggestions made by

---

SPECIAL NOTE TO BUSINESS REPRESENTATIVES

Employers can most easily use Quality Circles to undermine a local union's authority and the collective bargaining process when the local has newly elected or inexperienced leadership.

In these situations, we recommend that Quality Circles **not** be introduced. If, at a later date, a Quality Circle program is agreed to, the business representative should keep close tabs on it and attend as many Quality Circle meetings as possible.

Quality Circles ▬▬▬▬▬▬▬▬▬▬▬▬▬▬▬

Problem: Management may bypass negotiations, the grievance procedure, and an existing labor-management committee and deal with all serious problems through Quality Circles. Workers begin to view the union as powerless as they see all important issues resolved in the Quality Circles.

Recommendation: Get an agreement that the union can at any time terminate or suspend the program. The union should not lock itself into a program which is undermining its authority in the shop, and it should reevaluate its participation periodically.

Problem: Quality Circles may weaken the union's position at the bargaining table by revealing to management divisions in the bargaining unit. In negotiations, the union can state that its members are united on a particular issue and management may have no way of determining if that it is true or not. If, however, that issue has been discussed in the Quality Circles, management will have a much better reading on the extent of agreement among union members on the issues.

Recommendation: There is no way to completely avoid this problem. In some cases the union officer or steward participating in the Circle can steer the discussion away from certain issues. At the very least, by insisting on participation of a Union representative in each meeting, the Union will know what information the Employer has obtained and will not be surprised in negotiations.

Problem: A foreman or supervisor chairing the Quality Circle may try to always set the agenda and dominate the discussion.

Recommendation: Either have the meetings co-chaired by the union steward or local officer and the foreman or supervisor, or alternate the chair.

The Advantages

The Union is Associated With a Successful Program: In most workplaces workers are rarely asked to contribute their ideas about how work is performed and how to solve workplace problems. To the extent that Quality Circles give workers the opportunity to discuss and solve problems of concern and make them feel their opinion is valued, the program is very appealing to many workers. If the union is seen as being a part of a successful program, it can contribute to employee solidarity and improve in-plant identification with the Union. The many members who don't come to union meetings or file grievances, will now have greater contact with the union, particularly if the local union officer or steward serves as co-chair of a Quality Circle and meets with employees of the Circle on occasion without the presence of management. This may very well lead to a more interested and active union membership. Finally, in the case of some marginal firms, some jobs may eventually be saved due to improvements suggested by Quality Circles. This likely will be viewed to the union's credit.

Union Access to Information: Unions are always handicapped in negotiations and grievance-handling because of their lack of detailed knowledge about company finances, decision-making processes, and future plans. The information revealed in Quality Circle sessions often can be very helpful to the union.

The Consultant

Quality Circles usually involve an outside consultant who sets up the program and conducts problem solving training for members of the Circles. In negotiating everything about a Quality Circle program, the union should insist on the right to evaluate and, if need be, reject the employer's choice of consultant.

We recommend the following in evaluating a consultant:

— Ask the consultant for union references who can provide first-hand testimony about other programs with which the consultant was involved. Be sure to talk with the references about their view of the consultant and his programs.

— Some quality of work life centers have both union and management representation on their boards. Is the consultant associated with such a center? If so, contact the union board members.

— If a local college or university labor education center conducts training programs for your union, ask a sympathetic instructor there what he knows about the consultant.

— Have the union's executive board interview the consultant. While most consultants will tell you what you want to hear, see if the consultant really understands the concerns of the union and your members. How does the consultant describe the Quality Circle program? Does he only talk about better productivity and product quality, or does he also mention quality of worklife issues? Does his main concern seem to be selling the program and making money or does he seem genuinely interested in improving the workplace for all concerned?

— Contact the Industrial Department. In some cases we can provide background on a consultant. Also, send us any information you receive on a consultant so we can add it to our files and use it to help other Councils and Locals.

INTERNATIONAL UNION OF ELECTRONIC, ELECTRICAL, TECHNICAL, SALARIED AND MACHINE WORKERS, AFL-CIO

WILLIAM H. BYWATER *President*
EDWARD FIRE *Secretary-Treasurer*

IUE
RESOLUTION
ON
QUALITY CIRCLES

Members of IUE have much to offer to the production process besides their muscle and specific skills. They can contribute not only their creativity, but also their views on improving the production process where they work.

In recent years, a number of companies have come to recognize the potential of worker participation in management decision-making and have instituted programs to enlist worker support and contribution.

IUE recognizes the need for workers to participate and the benefits derived from work participation -- benefits to the worker, as well as benefits to the company.

In 1974, delegates to IUE's 16th Constitutional Convention adopted a Resolution on Worker Alienation, which called for formation of joint labor-management committees not only to investigate the causes and solutions of worker alienation, but also to develop programs "involving job enrichment, organization changes giving workers input and a feeling of pride in the final product, self-determination in the work. . . ."

These efforts adopted in that Resolution in 1974 are typical of a new trend in industrial relations taking place in our nation, known as Quality of Working Life.

The psychology underlying this process suggests that the majority of workers want to be productive, and given the proper incentives and work environment, will become deeply involved in their assigned jobs and tasks.

Over the past few years, we have witnessed a tremendous increase in one of the techniques of Quality of Working Life, known as Quality Circles; where small groups of workers meet, and led by a facilitator, select and attempt to resolve problems that fall within their work.

Because of our special interest in and concern about this specific technique, this resolution will address itself solely to Quality Circles.

While some Quality Circles appear to work successfully, others have not. Our experience, and that of other unions, has shown that for Quality Circles to accomplish their goals, there are several suggestions that local unions should follow:

1. Go slowly. Make sure the Quality Circle idea is not just a gimmick of management to improve its own positions. Make sure, too, that union membership knows what Quality Circles are designed to accomplish.

2. Be sure the union is an equal partner in the Quality Circle program. In this way, the union can insure that its interests and the interests of its members are protected and respected.

3. Be sure that any management initiation of Quality Circles can deliver top management support -- and that means demanding meetings with top management.

4. Get assurance that the circle will not be involved with conditions of employment and work which is provided for in the terms of the collective bargaining agreement. One way of insuring this is to make certain that Quality Circle facilitators and leaders are adequately and properly trained.

5. To protect its membership, locals must get some written guarantee that the implementation of Quality Circles does not eliminate jobs.

6. Locals must be assured that the adoption of Quality Circles does not turn into a speed-up.

7. Locals must insist that management maintains a balance between the two aims of the program: management benefits and worker benefits.

8. Unions must insist that savings resulting from the circles must be

shared with the employees.

Once the Quality Circle is set in motion, the union must:

° Insist workers who take time off for Quality Circles be paid for that time.

° Keep workers fully informed on all activities beginning with the first meeting with management.

° Insist on union representation at every Circle.

° Make certain there is an organized evaluation system to see if the program is serving its agreed-upon purpose.

° Establish extensive communication with its membership in regard to what is taking place.

> ° One suggestion has been that the union start with a survey of membership to determine their needs and interests.
>
> ° Another is to get an agreement with management for periods of discussion on the proposed program.
>
> ° A third is to propose that bulletin boards be placed throughout the plant to post what is developing within Quality Circles.

And, finally, local unions should keep the International informed of the establishment of Quality Circles so that the Union can keep track of, as well as develop an analysis of, the impact of these on its members.

THEREFORE, BE IT RESOLVED THAT:

(1) IUE go on record in support of the concept of Quality Circles and encourage union participation where the union feels such participation is in the best interest of its membership and where it is determined and assured that management has made an equal commitment to the mutual goal of such a program.

(2) Where Quality Circles are considered, that the Union insist that it be a part of the planning, development, implementation and evaluation process.

(3) Local unions should make certain that Quality Circles do not in any way infringe on the collective bargaining process or on matters and conditions covered by the collective bargaining agreement.

(4) The union be guaranteed that the innovations resulting from Quality Circle programs will not result in speed-ups on the job or in layoff of workers, or negatively affect the pay or status of any employee of the bargaining unit.

(5) Educational programs on Quality Circles should be made a part of the planning process before Quality Circles are introduced.

These programs and materials will be developed by the Education Department of the International Union for distribution to IUE membership. In addition, classes will be conducted at the local level for officers and stewards on this issue.

(6) Local unions should apprise the International where management plans or suggests introducing Quality Circles, and

BE IT FURTHER RESOLVED THAT:

The final determination of whether or not the Quality Circles technique is introduced will be made by the local union and management as equal partners.

Adopted
IUE International Executive Board
January 1982

Adopted
IUE 20th Constitutional Convention
September 1982

__Inside the Circle: A UNION GUIDE TO QWL____
Labor Education and Research Project, P.O. Box 20001, Detroit, MI 48220. (313) 883-5580.

RESOURCES

Following are some resources for unionists who are trying to get a handle on Quality of Work Life programs. A longer list of general resources for union activists is contained in *Concessions and How To Beat Them* by Jane Slaughter (Labor Education and Research Project, 1983, P.O. Box 20001, Detroit, Michigan 48220, $4.50).

Those who wish to look at QWL in more depth should check the notes at the end of each chapter in this book. Those for chapter 18 include a number of important academic studies. Chapter 12 lists extensive legal references. In addition, three chapters have brief resource sections: chapter 14 on union organizing, chapter 17 on Japanese labor relations, and chapter 10 on practical information to aid in doing pro-worker QWL projects. Chapter 10 also contains a model questionnaire for evaluating a QWL program and an outline for a union QWL educational conference, as well as lists of suggestions for dealing with QWL.

PRO-QWL MATERIALS

• *Perspectives on Labor-Management Cooperation.* A compilation of reprints of some of the important pro-QWL articles. If you are unfamiliar with that side of the story, here is a convenient and cheap way to get them all together. It includes the 1981 *Business Week* article on "New Industrial Relations," several major articles from the *Harvard Business Review*, and some brief pro-QWL articles from union sources. Available by writing for the "Information Packet," the Division of Cooperative Labor-Management Programs, Labor-Management Services Administration, U.S. Department of Labor, Washington, DC 20210.

• *Resource Guide to Labor-Management Cooperation.* Lists more than 200 in-plant programs with descriptions of each. The listings rely on public relations handouts and many have died or were never more than the paper on which the publicity was printed. The most valuable part is the cross-indexing, and the addresses and phone numbers for company and union contacts. Order from the Superintendent of Documents, Washington, DC 20402, Publication 1983 0-381-608/6924. Your congressperson will probably send you one free if he or she thinks you are someone important.

• *QWL Focus.* Published quarterly by the Ontario Ministry of Labour, it includes occasional articles that go into more depth than the usual PR handouts. Available from the Ontario QWL Centre, Ontario Ministry of Labour, 400 University Ave., 15th Floor, Toronto, Ontario M7A 1T7.

• "Participative Decision-Making at Work: A Guide to Bibliographic and Program Resources," by William Parsons. A fairly complete pro-QWL bibliography. *Labor Studies Journal*, Winter 1984, Transactional Periodicals Consortium, Department 8010, Rutgers University, New Brunswick, New Jersey 08903. $10 for single copies.

CASE STUDIES

• *Worker Participation and American Unions*, by Thomas Kochan, Harry Katz and Nancy Mower. 1984. 202 pages. Report of study initiated by AFL-CIO Industrial Union Department. Contains material on Xerox-ACTWU, GM Packard Electic-IUE, and Minneapolis/St. Paul Newspapers-Newspaper Guild (see chapter 18 for description). W.E. Upjohn Institute for Employment Research, 300 Westnedge Ave., Kalamazoo, Michigan 49007. $12.95.

• *Workplace Democracy: A Guide to Workplace Ownership, Participation, and Self-Management Experiments in the United States and Europe*, by Daniel Zwerdling. 1980. 195 pages. Harper and Row. A collection of case studies of a wide range of experiments in the 1970's. Of particular relevance are the chapters on General Foods, Rushton Mining Company, and Harmon International Industries. $5.95.

• *Soft Sell: QWL and the Productivity Race*, by Don Wells. 1985. A detailed report on two Canadian plants. Canadian Centre for Policy Alternatives, 251 Laurier Ave. W., Ottawa, Ontario. $5.

• "Appropriating Workers' Knowledge: Quality Control Circles at a General Motors Plant," by James Rinehart. Presented to the Society for the Study of Social Problems, Detroit, 1983. A study of the QWL program at General Motors' Diesel plant in London, Ontario. Available from James Rinehart, Department of Sociology, University of Western Ontario, London, Ontario.

• "Participation and Control: New Trends in Labor Relations in the Auto Industry," by Robert J. Thomas. CRSO Working Paper #315, University of Michigan, 1984. $1.25.

ARTICLES

• " 'Quality of Work' Experiments: Progress or Union Busting?" *American Labor* #14. Describes the operation and failure of a QWL experiment at Rushton Coal Mine in Pennsylvania. 11835 Kilbourne Pl. NW, Washington, DC 20010. 202/387-6780 or 462-8925. $1 plus 65¢ postage.

• "What's Creating an 'Industrial Miracle' at Ford?" *Business Week*, July 30, 1984. Describes the implementation of EI programs at several Ford plants, as well as the cooperative relationship which was developed between Ford management and the UAW leadership to sell contract changes to Ford workers.

• "The Circle Game," by Mike Parker and Dwight Hansen. *The Progressive*, January 1983. Discusses problems QWL programs create for unions and workers and suggests possible responses. 409 E. Main St., Madison, WI 53703. $.50.

VIDEOTAPES

• "QWL: Nothing to Lose But Your Job," 30 minutes, 1985. The tape looks at QWL in the context of recent trends in labor-management relations. Using footage of QWL circle meetings and interviews with QWL supporters and critics, it examines the ideas and attractions of QWL as well as its implications for the adversary relationship. It raises many of the questions unions must deal with in QWL programs. Order from Labor Media Group, P.O. Box 7266, Ann Arbor, Michigan. Rental $20. Sale $50. 313/668-0011.

• "We Are Driven," 60 minutes, 1984. Originally broadcast on the Public Broadcasting System (PBS) on January 23, 1984. Its look at labor at Nissan Motor Co. includes some of the material in the *Mother Jones* article reprinted as chapter 17, and discusses the attempt to apply Japanese management techniques in the new Nissan factory in Smyrna, Tennessee. Available from WGBH Distribution, 125 Western Ave., Boston MA 02134. 617/492-2777.

DEVELOPING LABOR'S STRATEGY— GENERAL PUBLICATIONS

• *Labor Notes*. Monthly 16-page newsletter which reports on and analyzes labor events from a progressive viewpoint. Aids in communication among activists, includes debates on topics of interest to the labor movement, and contains information often not available elsewhere. P.O. Box 20001, Detroit, MI 48220. 313/883-5580. $10/year, $20 institutions. $14.00 Canadian funds.

• *American Labor*. Bi-monthly publication of the American Labor Education Center. Articles on effective strategies unions can use in a wide variety of areas; each issue concentrates on one subject. ALEC, 1835 Kilbourne Pl. NW, Washington, DC 20010. 202/387-6780 or 462-8925. $9.95 for six issues.

• *Labor Research Review*. Twice-yearly journal which provides in-depth coverage of labor struggles and controversial issues in the labor movement. Midwest Center for Labor Research, 3411 Diversey Ave., Chicago, IL 60647. $10 for three issues.

• *Unions Today: New Tactics to Tackle Tough Times*. Published by the Bureau of National Affairs. 1985. 140 pages. Begins with an overview of the present challenge to union power and influence. Contains 30 case studies of how unions are trying to reverse their slide. Includes examples of innovative bargaining, employee ownership, corporate campaigns, community involvement and more. Bureau of Nationnal Affairs, RSPD, 1231 25th St., NW, Washington, DC 20037. 800/452-7773. $30.

• *Union Democracy Review*. Bi-monthly newsletter of the Association for Union Democracy. Follows developments in union demoncracy cases, mostly from a legal standpoint. Association for Union Democracy, YWCA Bldg., Room 619, 30 Third Ave., Brooklyn, NY 11217. $7/year, $10/year for organizations.

• *The Labor Page*. Bi-monthly news and analysis on Boston area union activity. 670 Centre St., Jamaica Plain, MA 02130.

GETTING HELP

Besides international union sources, there are other organizations which can provide help on QWL and other issues:

The Labor Notes QWL Task Force conducts QWL workshops for local unions which reflect the analysis found in this book. They range from half-day sessions to three-day conferences. Contact Labor Notes, P.O. Box 20001, Detroit, MI 48220. 313/883-5580. Fees are negotiable.

Labor Studies programs at colleges and universities are often excellent sources of information. These programs vary greatly. Develop a clear idea of what kind of assistance you need and ask around.

There are projects in a few locations specifically designed to help local unions with tough problems:

Midwest Center for Labor Research. Does research for negotiations, corporate analyses, marketing studies, and feasibility studies for employee buyouts. 3411 W. Diversey, Chicago, IL 60647. 312/278-5418.

Labor Institute. Does education, research and audiovisual materials on economic issues, including bargaining and concessions. Trains locals to do their own teaching and research. 853 Broadway, Room 2014, New York, NY 10003. 212/674-3322.

Corporate Campaign, Inc. Runs campaigns against corporations to aid in union struggles. Targets top officials and interlocking institutions. Headed by Ray Rogers, architect of ACTWU's campaign against J.P. Stevens. 80 Eighth Ave., 16th Floor, New York, NY 10011. 212/741-1766.

Wisconsin Union Resource Center. Holds roundtable discussions and teaches financial analysis. 4530 W. Lloyd, Milwaukee, WI 53208. 414/444-4419.

Massachusetts Labor Support Project. Provides support for strikes and boycotts, advice on strike preparation and resisting concessions, research on employers, and legal referrals. C/O HERE Local 26, 58 Berkeley St., Boston, MA 02116. 617/623-8113 or 524-6050.

TO ORDER

To order more copies of **Inside the Circle: A Union Guide to QWL**, please send $10.00 each (plus $1.00 postage each) to:

Labor Education & Research Project
P.O. Box 20001
Detroit, Michigan 48220
Phone 313/883-5580.

Inquire about bulk rates.